MW00616445

B
Plus

B
Plus

Dancing for Mikhail Baryshnikov
at American Ballet Theatre

A Memoir

MICHAEL LANGLOIS

Epigraph Books
Rhinebeck, New York

B Plus: Dancing for Mikhail Baryshnikov at American Ballet Theatre: A Memoir Copyright © 2018 by Michael Langlois

All rights reserved. No part of this book may be used or reproduced in any manner except in critical articles or reviews. Contact the author for information.

Paperback ISBN: 978-1-948796-13-2
Hardcover ISBN: 978-1-948796-14-9
eBook ISBN: 978-1-948796-15-6

Library of Congress Control Number: 2018943347

Cover photo by Nick Norwood
Book design by Colin Rolfe

Epigraph Books
22 East Market Street, Suite 304
Rhinebeck, NY 12572
(845) 876-4861
www.epigraphPS.com

A Note From the Author:

This memoir has been assembled from letters, photographs, souvenir programs, interviews I've done for Ballet Review, and memory. Memories, of course, are fickle, and if I have gone astray here and there from actual events, I apologize. My intent was to tell as honest a story as I could about a time in my life that is now more than twenty years behind me. Whatever criticisms or observations I have made here are made from the perspective of the person I was at that time. I do not necessarily share those opinions today. If you have any comments, questions, or concerns, you may contact me at: langloism50@gmail.com.

Michael Langlois

Table of Contents

Act I

1977. Age 16. New York City.   3

In the Beginning   9

1977. Age 17. New York City.   11

1970. Age 10. Winston-Salem, North Carolina.   14

1977. Age 17. School of American Ballet.   20

Stanley   23

1971. Age 11. Andover, Massachusetts.   27

1977–1978. Age 17. School of American Ballet.   34

1972. Age 12. Andover, Massachusetts.   36

1977–1978. Age 17. School of American Ballet.   39

1972. Age 12. Andover, Massachusetts.   44

1978. Age 17. New York City.   46

1972. Age 12. Boston, Massachusetts.   49

1978. Age 17. School of American Ballet.   52

1973. Age 13. Andover, Massachusetts.   54

1978. Age 18. School of American Ballet.   57

The Dance Belt   60

1978. Age 18. School of American Ballet.   65

1973. Age 13. Boston, Massachusetts.   70

1978. Age 18. School of American Ballet.   74

1974. Age 14. Greensboro, North Carolina.   76

Fall 1978. Age 18. School of American Ballet.   78

1976. Age 16. Winston-Salem, North Carolina.   82

1979. Age 18. New York City.   86

1976. Age 16. Winston-Salem, North Carolina.   90

1979. Age 18. New York City.   93

1979. Age 19. Europe.   96

January 1980. Age 19. Italy.   102

1980. Age 19. New York City.   108

August. 1980.   114

Act II

Fall 1980. Age 20. New York City.   119

ABT Primer   125

Peter Fonseca   131

David   134

Revelations   137

Opening Night   141

Musical Appreciation   146

First Positions   149

Metropolitan Opera House. Spring Season. 1981.   157

On Fire   161

Romeo and Julie   166

Fall. 1981. Age 21.   172

Tour of Duty   179

Spoleto   186

1982   191

Charles the First   198

1982. Locked Out.   202

Woytek   208

Solitary Confinement   217

Spring. 1983. New York.   226

Gelsey   235

Balanchine's Memorial   241

1984   244

Rotten to the Corps   249

Man's Best Friend   259

The Fall of Fernando   265

I Think I'm Speaking Japenese. I Really Think So...   268

And the Beat Goes On   272

A Grecian Holiday   277

Misha   280

Home Stretch   289

Finale   296

Act II

1986. Ex-Pats.   307

Alfonso and Ballet du Nord   311

The Socialist Agenda   316

1987. Repatriation.   322

Eliot   330

Lost   335

And Found   340

Valediction   343

Act I

1977. Age 16. New York City.

IT WAS THE SECOND WEEK OF MARCH, and at 9:30 in the morning I was walking along West 61st Street in Manhattan. It was sunny and clear, but there was a chill in the air. A steady stream of businessmen and women coursed through canyons of light and shadow, their faces grim and determined as they leaned into the wind that whipped along the sidewalks. My mind was preoccupied with what lay ahead of me that day, but I couldn't help thinking, as I looked at all of those nine-to-fivers, that theirs were lives I had happily not chosen.

As this thought drifted through the back of my mind, I cast my gaze up at the Gulf+Western building to my right. At the base of this fifty-story tower was the Paramount Movie Theater, its white, circular marquee adorned with one word: *Wizards*. Up ahead, clouds of steam spewed from somewhere beneath the street. Beyond the clouds, across Central Park West, stood a line of massive oaks, their barren branches dancing in the breeze.

In the middle of the short block between Broadway and Central Park West, I ducked into a nondescript brick building. Several teenage girls were chatting away in the small vestibule, bunheads darting back and forth as they looked alternately toward the door to see if anybody famous might be coming in and up at the old elevator dial on the wall.

When the elevator finally arrived, the outer door slid back and an accordion gate was thrown open. An elderly black gentleman stood in the near corner, his hand resting on an old lever whose wooden handle had been rubbed smooth from years of ascents and descents. He stared down at the gap as the girls and I piled in. When enough bodies were squeezed inside, he pulled the gate closed, then rotated the lever. There was an upward tug, followed by a slight compression in my legs and the straining sounds of weights and cables, and the uncomfortable silence of young men and women unfamiliar with one another come suddenly face-to-face.

At the top floor, the elevator bounced to a halt. The outer door slid back, the metal gate was again thrown open, and I was thrust out into a two-story reception area where I saw, emblazoned across an enormous wall in front of me:

AMERICAN BALLET THEATRE

Like many of my high school friends from the North Carolina School of the Arts who'd come up to New York during spring break, I was essentially on my own. My de facto chaperon was my best friend Eddie, a college-aged ballet dancer who, like me, was at American Ballet Theatre to audition for their upcoming summer dance program.

Over the course of the ensuing days, we took men's class every morning with Leon Danielian and, on at least one occasion, Patricia Wilde. Danielian was fifty-six at the time. He had studied with some of the legends of the ballet world—Mikhail Fokine and Antony Tudor, to name just two—and had danced with American Ballet Theatre and the Ballet Russes de Monte Carlo.

Fokine, for those of you who aren't dance historians, was one of the most influential choreographers and dancers of the twentieth century.

A graduate of the famous Imperial Ballet School in St. Petersburg, Russia, he worked with Marius Petipa and created, most notably, *The Dying Swan* for Anna Pavlova, herself one of the most famous ballerinas of the late nineteenth and early twentieth centuries. Tudor was a British dancer and choreographer whose "psychological" ballets such as *Jardin Aux Lilas* and *Pillar of Fire* were cornerstones of the American Ballet Theatre repertoire.

Danielian's connection with Mikhail Fokine arose as a result of the Russian Revolution, an event that forced many of the finest Russian dancers, teachers, and choreographers to emigrate to the West. Fokine landed in New York in 1919, where he started a ballet school and taught throughout the 1920s and 30s. Danielian studied with Fokine and made his professional debut with the Mordkin Ballet in 1937 at age seventeen. The Mordkin Ballet was the precursor of American Ballet Theatre, which was founded in 1940 with Danielian as one of its original members.

I mention all this to highlight the fact that classical ballet is an art form that is handed down from individual to individual, from choreographer or teacher to young dancers, and it is these dancers who become the next generation of teachers and choreographers. This passing down of information via direct personal contact has survived for centuries because for most of its existence ballet had no formal method of codifying steps. Ballet existed and, to a great extent, still exists, in the memories of the dancers who dance a particular ballet or study from a particular teacher; and the springboard to this memory lies within the music itself.

So at age sixteen I wasn't merely walking into the home of American Ballet Theatre—entirely ignorant of the company's history as well as who Leon Danielian might be—I was walking into a world that connected me to the most influential man in all of classical ballet, Marius Petipa, the Frenchman who settled in St. Petersburg in 1847 and created, alongside the composer, Tchaikovsky, *The Sleeping Beauty, The Nutcracker,* and *Swan Lake.*

Leon Danielian turned out to be the perfect blend of discipline and humor in the classroom, and after four days he offered me a scholarship to ABT's summer program. I was thrilled, of course, but there was still one other school in New York I wanted to consider—the school founded by Lincoln Kirstein and George Balanchine in 1934 as a training ground for the New York City Ballet: The School of American Ballet.

———————————

When I walked into the Juilliard building the morning after receiving Danielian's offer, I entered through a bank of modern glass doors on 66th Street between Broadway and Amsterdam. Walking up a gently sloping, glistening granite floor, I arrived in a massive, dimly lit lobby. A couple of aging, black, uniformed guards sat behind a desk chatting with one another. I was about to tell them where I was going, but they waved me through, pointing to a bank of elevators to my right. These were the kinds of elevators that needed no operators. They were enormous, silent creations with heat-sensitive numbers that turned orange when you touched them. I stepped in and pressed '3'.

After exiting the elevator, I meandered along the perfectly polished corridors of the Juilliard School until I arrived at a simple, frosted glass door. Printed on the door in very elegant, discreet lettering were five of the most influential words in the history of ballet in this country:

THE SCHOOL OF AMERICAN BALLET

I opened the door. A long, empty corridor stretched out before me. Vintage lithographs and photographs of ballet dancers throughout history, nearly all of them from New York City Ballet, were scrupulously hung along the walls. A handful of black doors were spaced far apart along the left side of the corridor. Behind these doors were gigantic ballet studios with perfectly sprung, gray Marley floors; wooden barres set at three different heights; shiny black grand pianos; and a wall of spotless mirrors. Each of SAB's four ballet studios had big windows that stood a good fifteen feet off the ground, affording the students some much needed daylight, but little else that might distract them from their studies.

The School of American Ballet, unlike its American Ballet Theatre counterpart, did not allow just any Tom, Dick, or Harry to waltz in off the streets of New York and take classes. Only students at the school or professional dancers from New York City Ballet or other well-known companies were allowed in. Soon enough, I became one of those select few.

Antonina Tumkovsky, a.k.a. Tumey, was the woman in charge of my "audition" that day. She would have been about seventy-two at the time, but still, she was not to be underestimated. She had been a soloist at the Kiev State Theater before World War II and had been teaching at the school since 1949. She didn't really have much to do with the boys, but suddenly there she was in front of me in the studio in her black heels and black ensemble, blinking oddly and looking me over like a questionable veal chop. I hadn't a clue who she was. To me she was just some aging Russian babushka who needed an ophthalmologist and an English teacher.

She made me stand at the barre and do a few simple steps and then, in the center, it was much the same. The whole thing was over in five or ten minutes, and I didn't even break a sweat. Tumey thanked me. "Vee vill send you letter," she said, squeezing her eyes shut and looking me over again.

As it turned out, I needn't have auditioned for SAB in New York, because about a month later Peter Martins and Suzanne Farrell came down to the North Carolina School of the Arts to look for dancers for SAB's summer program. I didn't know much about Suzanne or Peter, save that they were big stars in New York City Ballet and were friends with my teacher, Mimi Paul, who'd only recently retired from the company. After class, I shook Peter's hand. He was a giant of a man. A handsome Danish god with blonde hair and a deep Scandinavian voice. "It would be nice to have you at SAB this summer," he said.

In The Beginning

I SOMETIMES THINK THAT HAD MY CHILDHOOD been more tragic I might have had more success as a dancer. A good beating, an untimely death, adoption, being left by the side of the road—any of those might have pushed me to go the extra mile. Sadly, my parents were simply too nice, too alive, and too well adjusted for that.

Solidly middle-class, we lived in suburbia and basked in all that that entailed in 1960s America. We were white, active, physical people surrounded by other white, active, physical people. As a family, we swam and played tennis in the summer and skied or ice-skated in the winter. And while my parents appreciated the arts (my mother played the piano and could draw beautifully) I don't recall this being much of a focus in our household. My parents, like many who came of age in the 1950s, were good social dancers, and they often danced around the living room to Perry Como or Frank Sinatra. The only theater we ever attended, however, came with speakers to hang inside the car window.

On an emotional level, again, my parents were rather stereotypical. My mother was loving and completely engrossed in my life, while my father played the distant family provider. As a child I can't recall my dad ever telling me he loved me, and never in a million years would he try to prod me into divulging any deep dark secrets about myself. He kept his own secrets locked away and never spoke about his innermost feelings or his childhood. Working in the yard after a long day at the office or looking at new cars with my older brother and me on weekends was his idea of intimacy.

Given my father's personality, it seemed logical that one of the only ways I could figure out if he loved me was to do something so extraordinary he would have little choice but to express that love. So I became the exemplary son. I became the son who won the swimming and diving awards and the football championships. I became the son who made the honor roll, won the science fair, and was put into the advanced placement classes. I became the son who garnered the attention of my schoolteachers and ballet teachers and had articles written about him in the local newspaper. The only downside to this exemplary plan of mine was that the time and effort required to be so exemplary prevented me from spending much time with the man I so desperately wanted to get close to: my father.

My parents, Howard and Mandy.

1977. Age 17. New York City.

IN SPITE OF MY FONDNESS for the American Ballet Theatre school and Leon Danielian, I chose to go to the School of American Ballet for two reasons: money and my father. The making and careful handling of money was something I knew my father appreciated. He had, after all, spent his entire adult life working for one company, Western Electric, and he was nothing if not careful with the fruits of his labor. Cheap, my mother called him. Well, if there was one thing SAB exuded that its competitor, American Ballet Theatre, did not, it was money.

Because of the money and connections provided by one of its founders, Lincoln Kirstein, and a seven-million-dollar grant from the Ford Foundation in 1963, the School of American Ballet could afford to build state-of-the-art ballet studios in the Juilliard Building and offer living stipends to certain students who attended SAB during the regular year. I wanted one of those living stipends because I wanted to make things easier for my father. I never told him money was the reason I chose SAB, just as he never told me that his main concern with ballet wasn't whether or not it meant his son was gay, but whether or not I could make a living at it.

At the conclusion of that first SAB summer session in New York, I was invited back for the fall, but nothing was mentioned about a living stipend. My dad, as was his style, didn't say anything about whether or not this was a deal-breaker, so I accepted SAB's offer, piled all of my worldly possessions into the back of our shiny red pickup truck, and drove with my parents up to New York at the end of August. I had just turned seventeen.

———————————

I was never given any indication by anyone at SAB which class I should attend when the fall term began: the intermediate or advanced men's class. I was terrified of being relegated to the single class a day the intermediate men were offered in the afternoon and thought if that were to happen my career would be over before it had even begun. You can't get anywhere as a ballet dancer taking one class a day—everybody knows that. To make matters worse, I had injured my foot on a diving board over the summer and was hobbling around in quite a bit of pain. I didn't bother telling anyone at SAB about this because, again, I was terrified of the consequences.

It never occurred to me that I might supplement my classes at SAB by studying elsewhere or that, in fact, it might have been a wise thing to do regardless of what class I was in at SAB. Sadly, my parents knew nothing about the dance world in New York and, after one summer at SAB, I knew only slightly more.

With a massive amount of trepidation, I showed up at the first advanced men's class in early September and tried to act as if I belonged there. When class was about to get underway, Ms. Finn, SAB's secretary, came in with a big black book to take attendance. Walking along the barre, she asked each boy his name, then wrote something down in her book. A white-hot fear shot through my body. When she arrived next to me, she asked my name, looked down in her book, scribbled away, and moved on. Class began without incident. I kept looking at the door, wondering when Ms. Finn was going to return to toss me out, but she never did.

The next day came, and with it came Ms. Finn, her reading glasses, and her attendance book. When Friday rolled around, I was still there, hobbling around in the back of class on my injured foot, hoping no one would notice how little dancing I was actually doing. I may not have convinced the world, but somehow I had managed to convince the most important person at the School of American Ballet, Ms. Finn, that I belonged in the advanced men's class.

School of American Ballet.
Photo: Reed Jenkins.

1970. Age 10. Winston-Salem, North Carolina.

A S A CHILD, I DISPLAYED a certain talent. I could watch someone throw a football, shoot a basketball, or ski down a ski slope and translate that vision into my body. I was the great ape. I was also an extremely rigid, overachieving, competitive little monster who desperately wanted to please his parents and be the best at everything he did. There was no time to dilly-dally.

By the time I was ten years old, the ribbons I'd won as a swimmer and diver were draped across the ceiling of my bedroom like a mass of blue stalactites. These accomplishments aside, after four years of jumping into pools and swimming mile after mile with someone's foot in my mouth, I was really coming to despise the monotony of swimming. I was having great fun playing football with my neighborhood friends, however, so I decided to join our local Pop Warner football league.

Accustomed as I'd become to winning just about every aquatic event I entered, I assumed this move to the gridiron was going to be a mere stepping-stone to an illustrious career in the NFL followed by my induction into the Hall of Fame in Canton, Ohio. My mother was apprehensive. Her mood brightened, though, when I came to her prior to the start of football season and told her I'd seen some professional football players on the news who were taking ballet classes to enhance their coordination and balance. I thought this was something I should try so as to get leg up on the competition.

"Okay," she said, and off she went to find me a teacher, scouring the nether reaches of Winston-Salem, North Carolina for a school that did not have a sign over its door advertising "Ballet, Tap, Jazz, and Acrobatics." Despite her ignorance of the ballet world, my mother was savvy enough to know that ballet was not an art form to be sullied by the likes of tap, jazz or, God forbid, acrobatics (whatever the hell that was).

———————————

Perhaps the first inkling I had that my new hobby was not going to be accepted with open arms by the world at large (nor by my very own family) took place after my first private lesson.

"Michael," my mother said to me on the drive home, "I think it would be best if you didn't tell your brother you're taking ballet classes. Tell him you're taking...acrobatics."

"Acrobatics? Are you nuts? What about my ballet shoes?"

"Acrobats wear shoes, don't they?"

"How should I know?"

"Well, don't worry about that. He won't know what they're really for."

And I believed her because, as she often reminded me, she was always right.

When we got home, my brother took one look at my ballet shoes and screamed, "You're taking ballet class!"

"Am not."

"Are too!" he snarled, holding up the evidence. "What are these, then?"

"They're for...er...acrobatics."

"Are not."

"Are too!"

"Are not!"

"Ow!"

My first ballet teacher was a dark-haired, barrel-chested, unfiltered-Camel-smoking war veteran I addressed as Mr. Wallace. Paul Wallace fell in love with ballet as an adult and decided that while it was too late for him to become a professional dancer, he could still learn enough about ballet to teach, and that's what he did.

Mr. Wallace was incredibly kind and thoughtful, and his studio, stuck into a dark corner of the Oldtown Shopping Center in Winston-Salem, was a rare sanctuary unknown to most. There was no sign with a tutu, ballerina, or pair of pink pointe shoes advertising its existence. Mr. Wallace did no advertising. You had to know the right people to find him—the people in the dance department at the North Carolina School of the Arts, for example, who recommended him to their students when NCSA was closed.

My mother didn't know anyone at NCSA, but she knew quality when she saw it. After meeting Mr. Wallace, she realized that he was a man who did not suffer fools gladly. There were no children's classes per se at his Atelier Ballet School, and no annual recitals or Nutcrackers. *Atelier* means "workshop" in French, and, as the name suggests, it was a studio for those looking for what Mr. Wallace had to offer: a serious investigation of the art form. If you weren't interested in that, he wasn't interested in you.

What made my introduction to ballet unique was that, for me, it was an entirely male affair. Two other boys, brothers, who were more or less my own age and football players as well, were students at Mr. Wallace's school, and the three of us joined forces. One afternoon a week, under Mr. Wallace's guidance, we began learning about pliés and tendus and glissades and jetés. And while we were learning these things, we were also learning that our interest in ballet was something that inspired a great deal of hatred in our peers, many of whom could be counted on to pull open the door to the studio at some point during our weekly class and yell, "Faggots!" before scampering off. Mr. Wallace invariably ran for the door as they ran away, advising us to ignore them when he returned. But there was no ignoring them, and there was no ignoring that word.

In spite of these incidents, I persevered because I was fiercely competitive and willing to do whatever it took to succeed. And while I was a long way from having any serious interest in pursing ballet as a career, I continued going to class because, quite frankly, ballet was the hardest physical endeavor I'd ever done in my life and I was determined to figure out how to do it. I wasn't going to let a sissy thing like ballet get the better of me, by gum!

An example of the difficulty I'm speaking about takes place during the first and most basic exercise at the barre: pliés. To the untrained eye, pliés look like a simple series of knee bends with the feet placed in four strange-looking, outwardly rotated positions. What accompanies those seemingly simple knee bends, though, is a very specific, highly coordinated movement of the working arm (the one not holding onto the barre)—a movement that bears absolutely no relationship in terms of patterning to what the legs are doing. At first, it is like rubbing your belly and patting yourself on the head at the same time.

What I could see from the outset was that a ballet dancer's brain must learn to distinguish the soft, lyrical fluidity of an arm movement from the linear bending of the legs in a plié exercise. It must further coordinate the correct points in space where the arm is supposed to be relative to the leg movement, making sure that each movement—one simple and one rather more complex—arrives at the intermediate and finished positions as dictated by the overall technique, a particular exercise, or a specific school. The finished and intermediate positions are determined by the music, which you must pay great attention to while your arms and legs are trying to coordinate their respective actions. To further complicate matters, the head is also involved and, depending on the school, the placement of the head and gaze will be as choreographed and as important as the movement of the limbs. In one case the gaze might actually be into the palm of the hand as it moves through space; in another it will be out toward a particular corner of the room. Add to this the fact that, for every ballet dancer, the first exercise at the barre is the beginning of the quest to find one's center—"to get on top of your legs" as we say—and you have an enchantingly simple exercise that is far more difficult than meets the eye.

In those early classes with Mr. Wallace, I struggled to coordinate my arm and leg movements. Putting my feet into first position at the barre was initially so strange I found myself turning out my wrists as I tried to turn out my feet. I was accustomed to things like football, an activity where my body generally had one objective: to elude a tackler. Sports were not that complicated as far as I was concerned. Ballet, on the other hand, necessitated a brain that could multitask to a high degree, and in the midst of this multi-tasking, everything had to look a certain way. It wasn't good enough to simply accomplish a step. It had to adhere to some mysteriously accepted notion of what constituted classical beauty.

The dream. Imperial Ballet School. St. Petersburg, Russia.
The World of Ballet and Dance. 1972. Hamlyn Edition.

1977. Age 17.
School of American Ballet.

WHEN I ARRIVED IN NEW YORK, I settled into an illegal sublet at 64th Street and Central Park West, a few blocks from SAB. My roommate, Peter, was an awkward English boy I'd befriended at SAB during the summer. In spite of our age similarities, Peter proved far more capable of taking care of himself than I and far kinder than I ultimately deserved. He offered me the choicer of our two rooms to sleep in, often invited me up to his parent's home in New Paltz for the weekend, and was always willing to let me partake in the bounteous meals he habitually cooked up on Sunday evening to see him through the remainder of the week.

I was secretly envious of Peter, but would never have admitted that to anyone, least of all myself. I had, after all, spent the better part of my year at NCSA working part-time in a professional kitchen, an experience that taught me a great deal about washing dishes, chopping vegetables and drinking beer—skills that didn't exactly translate to the practicalities of everyday life in New York.

As those first few months in New York flew by and my foot injury healed, I became slightly more comfortable at SAB. I came to understand that the boys at the school, the vast majority of whom were straight, were not so different from the boys I left behind in public school. Try as they might to avoid it, they simply could not resist their Darwinian roots. They were not violent towards the weaker, peculiar, or more effeminate boys—as their public-school brethren were apt to be—but, surprisingly, they weren't far from it. One of the boys they singled out in this manner, sadly, was my very own roommate, Peter.

Peter, who'd been put into the intermediate men's class, began distinguishing himself as a bit of a klutz as the school year wore on. On more than one occasion he ended up on the studio floor, grabbing his nose or his nuts, an indication that he'd been waylaid by the elbow or knee of a girl he was partnering too closely. On other occasions he would simply trip over his own feet and fall. These incidents, along with his bright red hair, English accent, and somewhat nerdy persona, made Peter the butt of many a joke. Peter was not alone, however.

Pale, thin, and strangely effeminate, Blair was a boy whose street clothes consisted of a rotating supply of polyester dress shirts with big collars, jeans, and what looked like bedroom slippers. Thus attired, he arrived at SAB every afternoon at 5:15 p.m., waddling down the hall like a duck, his small dance bag clutched under his arm like a purse.

In class, Blair wore white leotards with short sleeves and a scoop neck rather than the typical T-shirts most of us wore. What truly set Blair apart, however, was his obsession with picking at his skin. Between every combination, he would launch into an attack on some aspect of his arm or upper back. And the more he picked, the worse the rashes and red marks became, standing like sentinels along his pale, bony frame.

Blair was openly mocked by the boys who presumed themselves to be cooler than everyone else at SAB. This coolness factor was a bit of a gray area, but its more salient points seemed to involve the ability to hold one's liquor, work the carburetor on a bong, and lure an assortment of SAB ballerinas into bed. Given my history with bullies in public school, I could not willingly participate in any of this behavior toward Blair or

Peter. Thankfully, most of it was done behind their backs, so I managed to convince myself it was not as awful as it sometimes appeared. I knew—or maybe time has since revealed—that however innocuous I wanted it to appear, it was a terrible thing for those boys to endure, doubly so because of where it occurred—namely, in a school filled with boys who were looked upon as queers by most of American society.

Stanley

FOUR DAYS OUT OF EVERY WEEK at the School of American Ballet, Stanley Williams—a trim, handsome, salt-and-pepper-haired former principal dancer from the Royal Danish Ballet—sauntered into my classroom between 12:35 and 12:40. His teaching attire consisted of a pair of impeccable slacks, a dress-shirt (the cuffs always rolled halfway up his forearms), and spotless character shoes.

Upon arrival, Stanley would walk to the piano, pull out a tobacco pouch, fill and light his pipe, and mosey over to the most famous dancer in the room. More often than not this was Peter Martins from New York City Ballet, but it also might have been Rudolf Nureyev or Mikhail Baryshnikov or a host of others from the ranks of New York City Ballet or the ballet world at large. Occasionally, a woman would appear in class. More often than not, this woman was Suzanne Farrell, the most famous ballerina at New York City Ballet and George Balanchine's muse and unrequited love interest. Suzanne rarely stayed for more than the barre. She hid herself in the corner behind one of the gigantic pillars, her thighs concealed beneath a pair of plastic pants, her midsection covered with a colorful red and black shawl. She seemed to want to make herself invisible.

My reaction to seeing these world-famous dancers in class was a strange mix of awe and indifference, although indifference doesn't quite describe what I felt. What I felt was that this was how my exemplary life and exemplary career were meant to be. I expected to be granted access to a school as renowned as SAB. I expected to study with the most famous teacher in the world. I expected to eventually rub elbows with the likes of Nureyev and Baryshnikov, because, for as long as I could remember, everyone had always told me how special I was, and I had come to believe it.

For the first few years of my training, I was, as is often the case in America, the only boy in ballet class. Later, when I went to the North Carolina School of the Arts, I could look around the classroom at the handful of boys my own age and convince myself that I was the most talented dancer in the room. After three or four months at SAB, however, I was beginning to wonder just how special I was.

━━━━━━━━━━━━━━

Stanley Williams's class typically began with all sorts of odd little tendu combinations at the barre, most of which were focused on differing accents. A tendu, by the way, is a simple movement of the foot along the floor. It starts from a flat position with the feet touching and moves to a pointed position with one foot extended away from the standing leg but still touching the floor. With Stanley, tendus had accents that were either *in in in* or *out out out* or *out out in*.

After about forty-five minutes, Stanley's peculiar barre was finished, and we moved to the center, where there was a break in the action before we started mucking about with tempos and accents again, doing lots of pirouette combinations and odd little Bournonville-inspired small jumps, the bulk of which were made infinitely more interesting by Stanley's brilliant pianist.

Lynn Stanford may have been an effeminate, skinny, longhaired country boy from Ector, Texas who looked like Jesus, but he understood

Stanley Williams and, more importantly, he understood what would motivate and support a dancer in one of Stanley's exercises. A vast repertoire at his fingertips, Lynn played everything from Scott Joplin to Stevie Wonder, Cole Porter to Prokofiev. He was our cheat sheet, providing us with the clues to Stanley's balletic haikus.

Without Lynn, Stanley's class would have been a pale facsimile of what it typically was, and I say this because on the one evening a week when Stanley taught the intermediate men, his pianist was the inimitable Frieda, an overweight Russian woman with matted hair, oddly incongruous blue eye shadow and fake eyelashes, whose piano playing seemed inspired by the Great Siberian Ice March. Every nuance in phrasing was pulverized into 4/4 hamburger by Frieda's playing, and Stanley generally seemed to be wishing he were somewhere else, like sitting at home with a cute boy and a gin and tonic.

———

Whatever Stanley was and however lofty his world-famous reputation, he was not the kind of teacher who ever gave you a straight answer about anything. In Stanley's world, ballet was explained via Danish Deconstructionism. You turned by not turning. You jumped by not jumping. When it came to the teaching of pirouettes, for example—something Stanley spent an inordinate amount of time on—he would occasionally demonstrate what he wanted by merely indicating a turn with his body and jerking his head quickly from side to side as if he were spotting and doing five or six pirouettes. Upon completing this confusing display, he would look at us and say, "You see boys? I turn, but I don't turn." If this didn't get the desired result he might say, "Don't turn boys, just go *fwont*."

One of Stanley's continual leitmotifs was phrasing. What he seemed most intent on cultivating was a sense of anticipation, of moving slightly ahead of the beat and giving nothing away in terms of your preparation. Suddenly you were just *there*. How you got *there* was never explained. If you tried to pin Stanley down on any technical matter (which I did on numerous occasions), he would just giggle and say, "Oh, boysss...I don't know...just watch Peter." At which point Peter Martins would dutifully demonstrate his seamless Scandinavian technique with his perfect line while Stanley stood there looking on, a Cheshire Cat grin on his face, the wise Dr. Frankenstein showing off his masterful creation. Invariably, when Peter finished, Stanley would say in his Danish-inflected English, "You see boysss? You see how Peter just goes *ovah*? He doesn't jump. He just goes *ovah*."

1971. Age 11.
Andover, Massachusetts.

I HAD NO IDEA WHETHER STUDYING BALLET was having a positive affect on my football playing, and I was not going to be finding that out in North Carolina, because my father accepted a job transfer to Massachusetts, and we moved to Andover halfway through my sixth-grade year. Not long after our arrival, my mother found me another ballet teacher.

Rail thin and dressed perpetually in black, Aina Jansons wore what amounted to stage make-up day and night. Her nonexistent eyebrows were mere painted lines across a translucent forehead. Her hair, which had never been cut in her life, was braided and wrapped about her head like a tiara. Between long, delicate fingers she cradled a silver and black cigarette holder from which she smoked Dunhill's and only Dunhill's, pulled one after another from a stack of shiny red and gold boxes sitting atop her desk.

Aina ran a small ballet studio on the second floor of a building just off Main Street in the center of Andover. Nearly sixty years old at the time, she taught class seated in a simple wooden chair, demonstrating the combinations with her hands while one of the advanced girls stood and demonstrated the movements in their entirety.

When Aina wasn't teaching and smoking Dunhill's, she spent most of her time in her asbestos-shingle house, drinking, popping pills, and smoking Dunhill's. Her favorite drink, the Nikolashka, was basically a big shot of Hennessey with a sugared-lemon chaser. Aina's favorite place to drink these Nikolashkas was the Ritz Carlton in Boston, and every three or four months—a time span arrived at because John, her music-teaching husband, didn't make enough money to keep her living in the style to which she seemed destined—Aina descended on The Ritz, arriving back in the provinces with the names of waiters and maître d's tripping off her tongue as if they were her long lost family from the old country.

The reality, however, was that Aina Jansons, the great Latvian ballerina, had been forced to abandon her ballet career because of World War II. She ended up scrubbing floors in a London hospital to keep a roof over her head, then married and came to America, as many did, with dreams of a life far grander than the one that awaited her.

━━━━━━━━━━━━━━━━━━━

During my first two years in Andover, I studied with Aina one or two days a week. Each fall, I played for my new football team, the Andover Colts, and between seasons, I joined the track and gymnastics teams at Andover East Junior High. Eventually, someone from the local newspaper got wind of my mutual interests in football and ballet and decided this would make a good human interest story.

Shortly after the article appeared, calls of "Faggot! Hey, faggot!" began accompanying me up and down the hallways of the school, uttered primarily by a snot-nosed, oily-haired, skinny kid named Kevin or one of his equally alluring friends.

Kevin and his crowd were the "bad" kids of Andover East—the worst of the *townies*, as the rich kids from Philips Academy referred to us. These were the kids who rarely washed their hair or jeans or, seemingly, their bodies, judging by the stench that followed them through gym class. They got bad grades and smoked dope after school in the park, and I pitied them when I wasn't wishing the worst hell on them.

══════════════

Not long after I began hearing my new nickname, I met my first real faggot. His name was Fred Alexons, and he flew in from Chicago to assist Aina with her production of Glazunov's *The Seasons*. This would be my first real stage experience, and, as the only boy in the production, Aina assured me I would have something worthwhile to do—a solo of some sort that this mystery man, Fred, would create for me.

Fred was not only the first openly gay man I would meet in life, he was the first legitimate male dancer I'd ever met, and as such, I looked to him for clues as to what sort of person I could expect to become should I make it that far. My future, as I saw it, looked something like this: I would smoke and, as a result, speak with a soft, raspy tone. I would become partial to leather. I would sport a beret and a rotating assortment of colorful scarves.

I was aware that Fred was gay, but I wasn't entirely sure what that meant. I didn't know what gay men did with one another any more than I knew exactly what straight men did with women. Second base was as far as I'd gotten in the sex department.

What struck me about Fred from the moment I met him wasn't his sexuality—it was his walk. He walked like a real ballet dancer, with a sleek, outwardly rotated stride that glided gracefully over the ground. And he spoke with a similar grace, clearly and calmly, his soft voice roughened from the cigarettes he smoked (all ballet dancers smoked in those days). And Fred dressed in ways I'd never seen before and smelled not like the Mennen's Skin Bracer my father wore, but of something wondrous and exotic.

Fred had seen the world as a dancer. He'd done things. And in the middle of my tiny ballet studio in the center of Andover with that beret on his head, he seemed like a magical being, a creature accustomed to being looked at and admired, a man whose very existence evoked a world I desperately wanted to inhabit.

A few days prior to our first performance, a small, handsome, young, blonde gentleman appeared in the studio one night. He arrived with Fred in the midst of our frantic last-minute preparations and was introduced as "Warren, my friend from New York." Warren, I quickly learned, was a dancer with American Ballet Theatre and Fred's boyfriend.

We shook hands, and I could tell, despite his winter clothes, that this fellow Warren was as agile as an alley cat. He moved as gracefully as Fred, but with more power, as if he were aware of every part of his body and where it resided in space from one millisecond to the next.

They took off their coats. Warren sat down off to the side while Fred got busy running rehearsal. Every once in a while, I would look over to see if Warren was watching me. He appeared dispassionate, like a god observing the less-godly masses.

I knew nothing about Warren Conover or American Ballet Theatre, save that it was one of the finest ballet companies in the world, and a photo of Carla Fracci, one of its famous ballerinas, could be found in the only ballet book I possessed, *The World of Ballet and Dance*. To my way of thinking, if Warren was in that ballet company, he must've been a spectacular dancer.

Although Fred was well past his prime, he was practically an adolescent compared to Aina, and as such he was given the task of hoisting her all over the Andover East Junior High School stage as she relived her glory days, emoting to a fare-thee-well in her Norma Desmond makeup and gigantic fake eyelashes.

When our one and only show had come and gone, my first taste of the limelight was not altogether unfamiliar. I had, after all, stood on many a diving board in front of crowds of people. There were a few butterflies before I went onstage, certainly, but once I started moving, I was completely focused on the task at hand.

What was particularly ironic was that our performance had taken place in my junior high school auditorium. The backstage area was the same gymnasium where, one afternoon, I stumbled upon Mr. Maglio, the beefy, dark-haired Italian man who was my gymnastics coach and one of two gym teachers. After school one day, a few members of the gymnastics team were working out on the high bar in the gym, so I stopped to watch. Mr. Maglio saw me in my street clothes and said, "Oh, look who's here, boys. Are you coming to practice or are you on your way to ballerino class?"

I said nothing.

"Show us some ballerino moves," he said. "Come on. Show me how you dance on your toes. Here, how's this?" he said, placing his fingertips on top of his head and twirling around on tiptoe like a ballerina in a music box. The boys broke up laughing.

I waited a few moments, then turned and walked away, thinking about the advice my mother often gave me. Don't lower yourself to their level, Michael. Just ignore them.

"What's the matter?" Mr. Maglio said as I reached the door. "Did I hurt your feelings, you little faggot?"

Downstairs in the locker room, my head resting against a locker, there was no ignoring what had just happened. The tears came, and, try as I might, I couldn't stop them. I simply could not comprehend Mr.

Maglio's behavior. How could any adult say those things to a twelve-year-old boy? What sort of person would do that? I didn't know. All I knew was that I was despised for doing something that seemed completely innocent. What was it about ballet that inspired so much hatred in people?

This incident, along with the constant harassment I would endure at Andover East Junior High School because of my interest in ballet, left an indelible mark on my psyche. Years later, I understood, from an intellectual standpoint, why those boys treated me the way they did and even, to some extent, why someone like Mr. Maglio would say the things he said to me, but at the time I felt as if the only truly safe place for someone like me was in solitude.

After my world premiere as a wood nymph was compared to that of Nijinsky by my mother, a gala party took place at our home. Everyone was in high spirits. Aina was drinking her Nikolashkas and basking in the glory of having awed the locals with her Latvian genius. Whether people were, in fact, awed, I have no idea. It didn't seem to matter. Judging by the crowd stuffed into every square inch of our house, the town had never seen anything like it. Toward the end of the evening, my mother, who was on her third Manhattan, came to me and said, "Michael, Fred would like to speak with you privately before he flies back to Chicago."

When we got to my parents' bedroom, I followed Fred inside. He shut the door. We both sat on the edge of the bed. It was at the foot of this bed that I was sometimes allowed to sit when my mom and dad let me stay up past my bedtime to watch Johnny Carson. My dad was a big *Tonight Show* fan, and he giggled and laughed uproariously throughout the episodes, occasionally letting out one of his patented farts. "Oh,

Howard!" my mother would moan, "*that* is disgusting." A comment that made my dad laugh all the more.

"Michael," Fred began, "I don't know what you're thinking about ballet...how serious you really are about it, but there's a ballet teacher in New York that I think could help you a great deal. His name is David Howard. I've told your mother about him. If you have a chance, I think you should go down and take some classes with him." I nodded my head. "Listen," he added, "I really think if you applied yourself you could become a professional dancer, if that's what you're interested in."

1977–1978. Age 17.
School of American Ballet.

LIKE MOST OF THE BOYS in Stanley Williams's class at the School of American Ballet, I became accustomed to seeing the most famous dancers in the world. Peter Martins, who, like Stanley, came from the Royal Danish Ballet, was in class nearly every day. Mikhail Baryshnikov was a consistent presence; a daily presence after he joined City Ballet in 1978, my second year at the school. Rudolf Nureyev was there as well, albeit less often, owing to his demanding touring schedule.

Misha and Peter appeared to be good friends and had a brotherly affection for one another, which left Rudolf a bit on his own out in left field, a place he seemed quite comfortable in, actually. Though he might have been characterized as Russian, Rudy seemed the complete antithesis of Misha. Where Misha kept his distance from the students and generally only spoke to Peter Martins or Stanley or Lynn, Rudy was talkative and friendly. He clearly loved being the center of attention and enjoyed a good laugh. He could have cared less if you were a student; if you were a boy and reasonably cute he was game for a bit of lascivious flirtation, or possibly more.

Unlike Misha, Rudy never came to class alone. He had a Man Friday, if you will. Luigi was his name, and he was in his thirties, perhaps forty, at the time. A handsome, dark-haired fellow, Luigi spent most of his life carrying Rudy's fur coat around, though I'm sure he did other things as well. He took care of Rudy, basically, though he called himself a *masseur*.

One day I was standing next to Rudy during class, and I said to him, "Don't you ever take a day off or a vacation?"

I asked him this because, for some reason, it struck me that he was continually working. He had that look about him: tired from the inside out. Not that he wasn't full of energy—he was. But there's another look that dancers get, a look that Misha had as well—a darkness around the eyes that never seems to leave. In Rudy's case, I got the sense, just by looking at his body, that it had been used and abused. He would have been about fifty years old at the time, and, despite the fact that he was thicker and stiffer and lacked the elevation of his earlier years, he never stopped trying to dance like the Rudy of old.

"Are you joking?" he said. "I never take day off."

"Really? Never?"

"If I take day off, is finished."

"You do class every day?"

"Yes, every day."

I had no way of knowing whether this was true or not (after reading his biography, I rather doubt it), but I believed Rudy, and in believing him, it struck me that I was going to have to work a hell of a lot harder than I was in Stanley Williams's class if I was going to set the ballet world on fire the way Nureyev had.

1972. Age 12.
Andover, Massachusetts.

RUDOLF NUREYEV ARRIVED IN BOSTON in the winter of 1972 to dance *Swan Lake* with Karen Kain and the National Ballet of Canada at what was then called the Music Hall (later the Wang Theatre). My teacher, Aina, got tickets as soon as they went on sale, and she, along with my mother, accompanied me to the big event.

It was frigid the night we arrived in the city. As we neared the theater, the streets swelled with cars and crowds. Women in furs punctuated a sea of dark winter coats as people moved en masse toward the brightly lit marquee on Tremont Street. Limousines lined the block in front of the Music Hall, tailpipes tossing cloudscapes into the air while the drivers sat comfortably inside reading the newspaper. Just inside the entrance, a man's voice rang out over the throng: "Will call! Windows to your left! This performance is sold out! Those with tickets please proceed up the ramp! Will call..."

I followed Aina and my mother inside, the heels of my shoes making crisp contact with the marble floor. Once in the lobby, I stared up at the crystal chandeliers, breathing in the mixture of perfumes that swirled about my head. As we made our way into the house and toward our seats, I was stunned by the theater's immensity. A football field of people stretched back from a huge curtain that hung down over the stage. Above the orchestra level was a semi-circle of filigreed boxes; above those, balconies ascended high up into the darkness where thousands of patrons were waiting to get their first glimpse of the world-famous Nureyev.

When the curtain opened and Rudy appeared onstage, the audience went berserk. For several very long minutes he was forced to stand center stage doing his level best to stay in character as everyone screamed and applauded. At last, unable to pretend any longer, he gave a slight bow and smiled. This little acknowledgement seemed to be the reaction everyone was hoping for because, as soon as he broke character, the applause died down.

The performance continued in much the same vein. Whenever Rudy did something besides breathe, there was applause—thunderous or more thunderous. At last, when the big suicide scene that ends the ballet was complete and the curtain descended, the applause and the bowing went on and on. After the second or third curtain call, my hands were beginning to ache from all the clapping, so I was quite relieved when Aina suggested we run to the backstage door and get in to meet the man in person. She seemed certain that, because she was from Latvia, she would be welcomed with open arms by the great Russian dancer whose childhood home was a mere 1,300 miles from the Latvian border.

Moments later, we were standing out in the cold, staring at our breath as a crowd of people watched Aina try to convince the guard at the stage door, who understood not a word of Russian, that she was Rudy's long lost friend from the old country. He wasn't buying it.

On the ride home, Aina seemed a bit crestfallen about the backstage incident. My mother, hoping to boost her spirits, told her it wasn't that important. We'd gotten to see the great man dance, and that was what mattered. Turning to me, my mother then asked what I thought of Nureyev.

"He was okay," I said, convinced that one day I would outshine the world-famous Russian.

Aina stared at me, a look of horror on her face.

Ballet Requires Dedication

By Carrie Smotrich

With the coming of Spring, most of Andover's young people are out riding their bicycles or playing baseball.

However, a dedicated group of young devotees of the ballet, are spending their Saturdays and Sundays rehearsing for a presentation of Alexander Glazounov's ballet, "The Seasons." These children are training under the direction of ballet mistress Aina Janson.

At this Sunday's rehearsal of Miss Janson's ballet troupe, I was extremely impressed with the dedication of the young boys' and girls' training in the exacting art of ballet. When we are constantly made aware of the lackadaisical attitude of our youth, this highly disciplined activity must build confidence in some of our young people of Andover.

Speaking with Aina Janson before the four hour rehearsal, she stated that a ballet dancer must have a well built body and lots of will power. Two of her young dancers Lisa Griffin and Michael Langlois, have these qualities.

Lisa Griffin, daughter of Mr. and Mrs. Alan Griffin who will dance the part of a Swallow, is a nine year old attending the Shawsheen School. Lisa is an excellent fourth grade student who would like to teach ballet some day. Lisa also swims, takes piano lessons and makes stuffed animals as a hobby.

Michael Langlois, the son of Mr. and Mrs. Howard Langlois has studied ballet for three years. I asked him how he got started in ballet and he told me he had heard of football players taking ballet for coordination and balance. Michael wrote letters to Joe Namath and many ohther athletes and they all recommended ballet. Starting ballet studies in North Carolina to help his athletics, Michael has become interested enough to consider a career in ballet if he is good enough. Michael is an excellent athlete, he plays football, competes in track, is a gymnast and does competitive diving and swimming. Michael is twelve years old and attends East Junior High School where he is an honor role student. Michael commented that even though his friends have expressed great interest in ballet they have found it difficult to convince their parents to allow them to dance. I asked him how it feels to dance with 48 girls and he said, " you get used to it."

Some of the younger ballerinas who will dance in the June performance of "The Seasons" are: Christina Rubio, Carrie

There's no such thing as bad publicity.
Unless you're a twelve year old boy who takes ballet class.

1977–1978. Age 17.
School of American Ballet.

IN SPITE OF STANLEY WILLIAMS's world-famous reputation, I worked harder and learned more in the intermediate men's class at the School of American Ballet. Both Richard Rapp and Andrei Kramarevsky, who taught nearly all of the intermediate men's classes, were more demanding from a purely physical standpoint, and after that first class of the day my body was loose and warm; as a result, I felt more prepared to really sink my teeth into those evening classes.

Mr. Rapp, a former New York City Ballet dancer, was a thorough, methodical teacher who taught class dressed in Lacoste shirts, black jazz pants, and ballet slippers. He looked as if he might have worked in a bank and organized his class with the meticulousness of a chess champion, all the while sucking on a cough drop. His petit allegros (small jump combinations) in particular were physical, musical, and intellectual brainteasers, and I loved trying to decipher them.

As much as I liked Mr. Rapp, he had one oddity as a teacher that I could never quite fathom. He would occasionally try to get us to hold our free hands at the barre such that our middle fingers and thumbs formed a circle joined at the fingertips only. The effect was not unlike someone holding a little teacup in hand. I never understood the reasoning behind this hand positioning, and every few weeks when he came around and placed my fingers that way, I would look at him, wait for him to move on, then go straight back to positioning my fingers the way most classical dancers do, in a more or less relaxed manner with the pinkie curving slightly under and the thumb contracted slightly into the palm.

The teacher closest to my heart at the School of American Ballet was Andrei Kramarevsky. Krammy, as everyone called him, was a balding, powerful Russian who reminded me of my Swedish grandfather, Björn, an equally powerful character who spent his life working on ships and whose athleticism sparked my interest in all things physical.

Krammy was trained at the Bolshoi Ballet Academy in Moscow and later joined the main company, where he became a principal dancer, working extensively with the famed dancer, choreographer, and coach, Asaf Messerer. In 1975, Krammy defected to Italy, and the very next year Balanchine invited him to teach at the School of American Ballet.

In class, Krammy wore sleek, bell-bottomed jazz pants and a white tank top over a well-muscled chest. Thus attired, he sat in a chair at the front of the room, a small white towel draped around his neck, his face a mixture of boredom and despair as he watched us run through his barre, a rote sequence of exercises that never varied and, basically, had to be memorized.

Unlike any other teacher I'd ever had or would have, Krammy rarely demonstrated barre work, preferring instead to sit and indicate the combinations with a grunt or a small hand gesture. The only time this routine varied was when he noticed a newcomer in the room, but even then, his stab at demonstrating was so casual that the new dancer was usually left looking around for someone to follow.

However routine or brief Krammy's barre may have been, it was surprisingly effective. The time we typically would have spent watching a teacher demonstrate an exercise was instead spent moving from one exercise to another almost without pause, our muscles growing warmer and looser and stronger because there was no downtime. Once we got off the barre, the remainder of class was spent getting quickly past the adagio so we could start turning, jumping, and doing the big bravura steps that were the backbone of every male variation in the classical ballet repertoire. It was at this point that Krammy literally sprang to life, using his towel with increasing frequency as he leapt from his chair to demonstrate multiple double tours en l'air or some other acrobatic trick that, even at age fifty, he performed with remarkable elevation and panache.

Most of the Russian teachers at SAB spoke a very basic brand of English, but in Krammy's case there was virtually no English at all. If you executed a step well, he would look at you and, in his thick Russian accent, say, "Oohhh, expenseeef." If, on the other hand, you did something poorly, he would say, "Cheap, cheap." When that admonishment was forthcoming, however, it was clear that there was no malice. Krammy's "cheap" always conveyed the notion that we were all capable of greatness and that, with enough hard work, greatness would be ours; it was a pat on the back or a friendly kick in the ass, a reminder to just keep doing the steps until you mastered them. That was Andrei Kramarevsky's approach to teaching, and his class was a nightly circus that I absolutely adored.

―――――――――――

When I arrived at the School of American Ballet, I couldn't help but look around at the other boys and begin an assessment of where I stood. The standards by which I made this assessment were based on certain technical benchmarks that seemed implicitly worthwhile and important to both the teachers and the other boys. At the top of this list was the ability to turn, or to do multiple pirouettes, as we call them.

A boy who could execute four pirouettes consistently was seen as a good dancer but hardly an extraordinary dancer. Five, six, seven, or more pirouettes was what most of us were hoping for, and a number of the boys in the advanced men's class were capable of this.

I was a consistent, four-pirouette type of dancer, if only because four pirouettes were something I knew I could master, and I practiced that number over and over again. On good days, I could manage five, six, or occasionally seven pirouettes, but my inability to reach those numbers consistently led me to focus on four—a number that, in retrospect, sums up the type of dancer I would become. Not an A. Not a B. A B-plus kind of dancer.

Having been a springboard diver and a gymnast when I was younger, I was reasonably good at ballet's airborne maneuvers: the double tours, double revoltads, double assemblés, and double saut de basques that advanced male dancers were all expected to do and, at SAB, generally could do. The big rotating jumps in the air that were then becoming ever more alluring to young dancers and audiences as a result of seeing Mikhail Baryshnikov perform those feats in the film *The Turning Point* were something that all the boys at SAB were enamored with and wanted desperately to execute. Unfortunately, we had no one to teach us those steps because none of our teachers knew how to do them.

One of the few teachers at the School of American Ballet who noticed that the boys in the advanced men's class were too focused on pirouettes and acrobatic tricks at the expense of being able to actually dance in a coordinated fashion was Suki Shorer. Suki was a lively, intelligent woman who'd been a member of San Francisco Ballet before joining New York City Ballet, where she danced from 1959 to 1972.

Friday was Suki's only day to teach the men, and it was typically a day of hair pulling for her and bewilderment for us. Every week, she demonstrated a step at the barre, a step she had probably given to her advanced girls hundreds of times, then watched as we butchered it like a bunch of amateurs.

"Why can't you do this?" she would continually ask.

We had no answers. We were used to doing Stanley's barre. Tendus in demi-plié were our perpetual plat du jour, not grand ronde de jambes en l'air or the controlled lyrical movements that were more common in women's dancing.

When we got into the center, things with Suki usually went from bad to worse. Without the barre to hold onto, we struggled to make her combinations look polished. Most of the boys, unfortunately, didn't take her that seriously and weren't troubled by their inability to execute her steps. Everyone was waiting for Stanley to come back on Monday so we could go back to going *ovah* rather than jumping, and turning without turning in the center.

The attitude toward Suki was a pity, really, because she was one of those rare teachers at SAB who could really teach technique—and tried to. She was fighting a losing battle with the boys, however, and her once-a-week stab at trying to influence our dancing was never going to be enough. I think she knew that, but still, she never stopped trying.

1972. Age 12.
Andover, Masachusetts.

S HORTLY AFTER SEEING RUDOLF NUREYEV in Boston, Edward
Villella—then a principal dancer with New York City Ballet and,
arguably, the most famous American male dancer at the time—was invited to give a master class along with a lecture demonstration at Phillips Academy in Andover. In addition, there was going to be a cocktail
reception for a few invited guests. As the only young male dancer in
town and Aina's protégé, I managed to secure an invitation to all of
these events.

I knew little about Edward Villella when he walked into the studio. He would have been about thirty-eight years old at the time. For
the previous seventeen years, he'd been dancing with New York City
Ballet. He was closely associated with ballets such as *Tarantella*, the
"Rubies" section of *Jewels*, and *Prodigal Son*. He was about to appear
on television in *The Odd Couple*, playing himself.

Villella was, at first glance, a bit rough around the edges. Muscular and short, with black hair and a dark complexion, he spoke with a
distinctive New York accent, the result of his upbringing in Bayside,
Queens. Of his class I recall next to nothing, save that he was kind and
patient in spite of the fact that his *master* class was filled with house-
wives, college students, and a few youngsters like myself.

Later that evening, during the lecture-demonstration, he sat on the edge of the auditorium stage at Phillips Academy between bouts of dancing excerpts from *Tarantella* and *Prodigal Son*. Beer in hand, a towel draped around his neck, sweat dripping from his brow, he looked very much like the boxer he'd once been. Over the course of the hour that followed, Villella spoke frankly about his life: the difficulties he had with his father and the wider world because of his interest in ballet.

In order to appease his conservative father, Villella consented to go to college at the New York Maritime Academy. Once that obligation was satisfied, however, he returned to dancing, joining New York City Ballet at age twenty-one, a decision that caused his father to stop speaking to him. More than a year later, after his father saw him dance three major roles in one evening with City Ballet, his dad realized the mistake he'd made and forgave his son for becoming a dancer.

It was a great story and, as Villella recounted it, I realized my troubles might not be so bad. Yes, I was being called a faggot every day at school. Yes, my gym teacher, Mr. Maglio, was an asshole, and I was miserable much of the time, but my father, while certainly not enthusiastic about my interest in ballet, was at least not insisting I go to the Maritime Academy.

1978. Age 17. New York City.

A S A GENERAL RULE, the central plaza at Lincoln Center in New York is abuzz with excitement at around eight o'clock each evening as one, two, or all three of its massive theaters gear up for a performance of dance, opera, or music. The fountain that stands at the center of the three massive theaters (New York State Theater, now the David Koch Theater; Avery Fisher Hall; and the Metropolitan Opera House) is surrounded by people, most of whom have told a friend to meet them there before the show. Taxis and limousines, meanwhile, arrive from all directions (at least they did prior to the renovations of 2012), unloading passengers on the drive that passes along Columbus Avenue.

Crossing the enormous glass threshold of the Metropolitan Opera House for the first time, I looked up at the gigantic Chagall murals that flanked the entrance and realized I was in a completely different world from the one that existed over at the New York State Theater, a venue I was quite familiar with after six months at the School of American Ballet because students at the school were often offered free tickets to see The New York City Ballet.

City Ballet and its home, the New York State Theater, were, to my way of thinking, characterized by absence: the absence of costumes, of plot, of "stars" (the choreography of George Balanchine was supposed to be the star), of opulent décor, and, for that matter, windows. There were no windows in any of the rehearsal rooms or dressing rooms at State Theater and, as a result, the dancers at City Ballet never saw the light of day once they set foot in the place.

The Metropolitan Opera House, on the other hand, was all about grandeur. From the chandeliers that retreated magically upward when the house lights dimmed to the brilliant gold curtain that opened so dramatically at the beginning of each ballet, everything was done on a grand scale. This grandeur aside, there was something much more prosaic about my first experience at American Ballet Theatre that inspired me: the quality of the dancing.

The complete details of that first program now escape me, but there were two ballets that left a lasting impression: Jose Limon's *Moor's Pavane* and Antony Tudor's *The Leaves Are Fading*.

In the former, I saw Erik Bruhn, Carla Fracci, and Sallie Wilson portray the central characters in Limon's interpretation of Shakespeare's *Othello*. This twenty-minute ballet set to the music of Henry Purcell wasn't a ballet as I'd come to know ballet—it was dance theater. Done in heavy costumes with a great deal of psychological symbolism, it was unlike anything I'd ever seen at City Ballet.

I was too young to truly appreciate *Pavane* because at that point in my development as a dancer, I was obsessed with line and technique. (Peter Martins was everything I aspired to be.) I was smart enough to realize, however, that *Pavane* was a brilliant piece of work and a fascinating compliment to Antony Tudor's *The Leaves Are Fading*.

It was in *Leaves* that I saw Gelsey Kirkland for the first time. Gelsey was a dancer unlike any. She didn't seem to have any real bones in her body, so languid and fluid were her arms, so pliant her feet—feet that caressed the stage like a cat, never making a sound. And it wasn't simply her technical skill or her "plastique" that was so impressive, it was the abandon with which she seemed to toss all that technique out the window. Watching Gelsey dance was like watching a sacrifice. It took my breath away.

What American Ballet Theatre epitomized for me was that classical ballet dancing was an overall process. It wasn't about arriving at the apex of a movement or the end of a movement as quickly as possible with the vague hope that no one would notice your preparation or the linking steps that brought you there. The preparation and all of the transitional movements may not have been the primary focus, but they were nevertheless an integral part of the whole picture and deserved respect and consideration. Beyond this, there was a very refined quality to the port de bras at Ballet Theatre, something that, I had to admit, was strikingly absent at City Ballet, a company which had become a repository of hyper-extended elbows, flailing arms, and limp wrists. My attraction to Ballet Theatre was strange, actually, because what I saw as its finest traits were actually my greatest weaknesses as a dancer.

1972. Age 12.
Boston, Massachusetts.

NOT LONG AFTER I MET EDWARD VILLELLA, my ballet training went in a decidedly more serious direction. At the suggestion of a fellow dancer in Andover, I began commuting into Boston to study with a gentleman from the Royal Ballet, David Shields, and his American wife, Terry. Terry was teaching a class for younger dancers, and I understood this was a step up from the kind of training I was getting with Aina in Andover, so, even though I knew it would hurt Aina's feelings, off I went alone, at age twelve, on the Trombley Motor Coach to Boston a couple of times a week after school.

Despite its many supposed dangers, I adored Boston. Between the grimy bus station on the edge of the Combat Zone and the ballet studio near the corner of Arlington and Boylston Streets, there was more human variety than I'd seen in the entire state of Massachusetts. Winos, panhandlers, drug dealers, scam artists, and streetwalkers lurked around every corner. Businessmen went into and out of the Playboy Club looking for a little action while just a hundred yards away in the Boston Common, a Beacon Hill socialite and her young daughter might be enjoying a Swan Boat ride on the pond.

Boston became my sanctuary. It was a place where I felt safe from the teasing and bullying I endured in Andover. It was a place where everyone, it seemed, could be whatever they chose to be, and no one cared if you were a boy who took ballet class.

My trips into Boston continued for about a year, and then one day, shortly before my thirteenth birthday, Terry Shields called me into her office after class. "Michael," she said, "I think it's time you made a decision about whether or not you want to dance professionally. Taking class two times a week or not taking class at all during the football season is fine if you don't think it's something you want to pursue in life, but if it is, then you cannot wait until you are fifteen or sixteen to make up your mind. It will be too late."

When my mother picked me up at the bus stop that evening, I began telling her about my conversation with Terry. By the time I had finished dinner, most of my thoughts were drowned in a wealth of tears as I sat at our kitchen table and tried to come to terms with my life and ballet and what sort of future I envisioned for myself. Why did I have to make this decision? Why couldn't I just go on doing what I was doing? I didn't know whether or not I wanted to be a ballet dancer.

But there was no turning back. I had to decide, so I tried to think things through clearly. As much as I loved sports, and football in particular, I was quite small for my age and suspected I would never be big enough to play in the NFL. I also knew that ballet, though I'd yet to fall in love with it, was something more challenging than any sport I'd ever tried, and as such it was unlikely I'd ever get bored with it.

There were other, less obvious feelings I was having that only years later did I begin to understand. First among those was that I didn't want to disappoint my parents or tarnish their whole "finish what you start" mantra in life. I took this idea seriously because I was a kid with concrete ideas about how things should be done. Had I been able to give my parents some friendly advice, however, I might have suggested they teach me less about perseverance and more about knowing when to quit. My older brother Mark, for example, happily quit the swim team because he hated the drudgery of swimming mile after mile, winter and summer, but I stuck it out for five long years because I didn't want to be labeled a quitter and disappoint my parents. And then one day, years beyond when I should have, I mustered the courage to tell my mother I'd simply had enough of swimming. "Okay," she replied, then went back to fixing dinner.

It was then that I realized I had absolutely no idea what my parents wanted or expected from me. Years of my life had been spent being miserable in swimming pools all over the South, and all because they never bothered to clarify this small detail in their child-rearing protocol. The fact that my brother didn't seem too concerned about quitting the swim team, yet was still treated like one of the family, should have alerted me to the fact that my thinking in this regard was terribly flawed. Somehow, it didn't.

Another factor in my decision to pursue ballet was that I had a mad crush on my ballet teacher, Terry (who resembled a young Mia Farrow), and looked at her husband, David, as a god. Pleasing all of these adults or, at the very least, doing what I *thought* would please them was extremely important to me, and I was almost certain that deciding to dance would please David and Terry and, more importantly, my mother.

1978. Age 17.
School of American Ballet.

T HE SCHOOL OF AMERICAN BALLET was, and still is, a springboard hovering over the deep end of the New York City Ballet.
And while I cannot deny that I would have been happy to receive a job
offer from Balanchine, his first visit to Stanley Williams's class in early
1978 gave me the distinct impression I wasn't going to be signing a contract at New York City Ballet any time soon.

The boys Balanchine was interested in were dancers such as Christopher d'Amboise, the son of Jacques d'Amboise (one of City Ballet's
most recognizable male dancers); Christopher Fleming; Doug Hay; and
Tim Fox. All of these boys were a bit older and had been at the school
longer than I had. They were given starring roles in Jerome Robbins's
Interplay during SAB's spring workshop and went on to dance those
very same roles after joining the company.

My sole interaction with SAB's annual talent show was as an understudy in Stanley Williams's presentation of a Bournonville pas de
deux from *The Guards of Amager*. D'Agoberto Nieves, one of Stanley's
favorites, was the male lead in this excerpt and, presumably, a star in
the making.

From a tough, troubled background and skinny as a stick, D'Ago had
a vertical leap to rival Michael Jordan's. With seemingly little prepa-

ration, he would suddenly rocket into orbit, his body sailing around, revolving, doing entre chat six, huit, douze—who the hell knew? It was startling. D'ago lacked a certain polish at the time, but his partner, Darci Kistler, more than made up for that. She would soon join the rank and file of City Ballet, becoming Balanchine's last ballerina before becoming Peter Martins's wife.

During workshop rehearsals with Stanley, I stood at the back of the room with Stacy Caddell (a future member of City Ballet), and we marked through the movements as best we could with what little room we had. I don't recall ever feeling as if we were actually preparing to perform this ballet, however. Stanley never said a word to us, never let us rehearse, and as time went on I began praying that nothing would happen to the ever-unpredictable D'Agoberto because I wasn't the slightest bit ready to fill the void should the need have arisen.

Fortunately, everything went off without a hitch, and my grand SAB workshop experience consisted of sitting out in the dark, air-conditioned theater at Juilliard, watching D'Ago and Darci and many of my friends perform for Mr. B, *The New York Times*, and Manhattan's ballet cognoscenti.

For this, and myriad other reasons, I felt completely cut-off from the SAB conveyor belt that funneled dancers from the school to the company. This state of affairs didn't trouble me, however. I had always been skeptical of the cult mentality that surrounded City Ballet and extolled Balanchine and SAB as the absolute last word in ballet. I knew there were a multitude of approaches, other schools, and companies that were as good as, if not better than, SAB and City Ballet, and one of those companies had a school and a company I was already familiar with: American Ballet Theatre.

1973. Age 13.
Andover, Massachusetts.

MY DECISION TO BECOME A BALLET DANCER at age thirteen marked the beginning of a separation from family and friends and any sense of normalcy in my life. From the outset, I understood that ballet was considered a sissy thing, but that did me little good, and no one, not even my all-seeing, all-knowing mother, was able to protect me from the outpouring of hatred that came my way as a result of my choosing to dance.

And it truly was hatred. I could see it in boys' eyes and hear it in the tone of their voices. I had betrayed them, and they would make me pay for that betrayal by reminding me every chance they got that I was no longer one of them. I had strayed from the acceptable path, and this was an act that could not go unpunished.

According to the boys at Andover East Junior High, I was now a pussy, a candy-ass, a queer, a dick-sucker, a pansy, a fairy, a homo, a 'mo, a faggot, a fag. I was all of those things, and I was none of those things. I was a boy like most of the boys my age. I loved girls. I loved sports. I was intrigued with ballet. Unfortunately, there was no box in anyone's mind that a boy like me fit into.

As soon as I quit playing football in order to dance, I instantaneously became a pariah. My new friends became the chess champions and the Trekkies, the brainy kids with ridiculous IQs destined for MIT or Harvard, and not for one single solitary second did I feel any sort of kinship with them. Having once been admired for my athletic ability, I was a misfit in the land of misfit toys, bored out of my mind as I listened to discussions of chess moves or the inner motivations of Captain Kirk.

I'd sunk to the bottom of the junior high school fish pond, but at least I knew that, down there in the muck and mire, the teasing and the name-calling would cease. By the time I reached the ninth grade, not only was I never asked to be a captain when teams were selected in gym class, I became one of those kids I once used to agonize over having to pick myself—the ones who were either too skinny or too fat or too uncoordinated or too weak to be desirable.

To make matters worse, most of the boys my age had become much bigger and faster, and I just couldn't keep up. I could no longer count on beating everyone in foot races or outscoring them on the annual President's Physical Fitness Test, something I had always excelled at and took a great deal of pride in.

I became increasingly unhappy in school, and the unhappier I became, the more I came to see the world as a sea of unconscionable brutality. My mother knew some of what I was going through, but she pooh-poohed it. "Just ignore them," she would say. "Don't lower yourself to their level." And because I had always believed she knew better than I how I should lead my life, I followed her advice. The verbal and physical abuse went on and on, however, day after day and year after year. There was the occasional cheap shot in gym class, the occasional rock thrown my way, the occasional unexpected shove into a locker, and the continual presence of a word that came to define my everyday existence: faggot.

I will say this: I was stubborn enough, even at age thirteen, not to care if I fit into some definition of what a boy or man was supposed to be. The notion that something as physically challenging as ballet could be deemed feminine or effeminate made me all the more appreciative of the power of femininity and all the more skeptical of anything that smacked of conventional thinking or machismo.

My involvement in ballet forced me to decide who I was going to be, and the person I was going to be was a defiant young man who mistrusted the world and wanted to exact some revenge on the Mr. Maglios who populated it. My determination to succeed as a dancer was fueled by more than just anger or a desire for retribution, however; it was fueled by parents who instilled in me this supposedly American idea that you can be whatever you want to be in life if you're willing to work hard. What my parents neglected to inform me was that, as with so many things in America, there's a flip side, and the flip side is that the person who's different in America is the one who's often tied to a post and bludgeoned to death for those differences.

1978. Age 18.
School of American Ballet.

A s I saw it, there were two schools of American Ballet. There was the school with the reputation for being one of the finest ballet schools in America, if not the world—a place where young men and women toiled away in ascetic splendor, dreaming of the day when Balanchine would deem them worthy of a place in his company—and there was the school I went to.

The SAB I attended was a gigantic, secret enclosure run by a bunch of old Russian women who barely spoke English and didn't really seem interested in trying. They had no idea what was really going on in the lives of their students. All they were concerned with was whether we were wearing the appropriate outfits in class and whether or not our bodies were developing into something Balanchine considered attractive.

One might forgive the administration at SAB for taking so little interest in our extra-curricular lives, but even within the confines of the school, we were not given much of an education. There were no music classes in those days. No dance history classes. The only other dance forms we were introduced to were the occasional character classes taught by Madame Danilova. The distinct impression this left me with was that Balanchine (or whomever was in charge of the school) wanted the dancers young and dumb. "Just shut up and dance," was the oft-quoted refrain everyone attributed to Mr. B. For this, and myriad other reasons, SAB was a place I was a part of, but never actually felt I belonged in.

The most distinct division at the school was the sexual one, a distinction best exemplified by our own country's battle for independence. The girls of SAB were like the Redcoats of the English army. Highly skilled, impeccably dressed in identical regalia, they arrived for battle each day with their buns firmly in place and followed the strict orders of their commanding officers, nearly all of them former Russian ballerinas.

As the soldiers of Balanchine, these girls were expected to attain a certain proficiency, and when that proficiency was achieved, they moved up into a new regiment marked by a differently colored leotard, where the demands and competition were more intense and the differences between those with superior talent and extraordinary ambition and those who were merely very good dancers became increasingly obvious.

The boys of SAB, on the other hand, were a ragtag bunch of revolutionary guerillas who arrived for battle with whatever weapons they happened to pick up along the roadside. Some had very little experience, some a great deal. Some were short. Some were tall. Some were graceful. Some were clumsy. Some had beautiful feet and legs, others less than ideal. The look, skill, and discipline of the boys at SAB was a far cry from that of their Redcoat female counterparts.

One particularly awkward Russian boy never washed his dance clothes and took his only shower at SAB each evening, drying himself with a raft of paper towels from the lavatory dispenser. Another group of boys smoked pot with abandon, both before and after class. Still others were drinking so much and so frequently that they were borderline alcoholics. Years later, many of these boys and girls from SAB who'd gone on to dance in City Ballet would confess to being actual alcoholics and drug addicts before becoming lifetime members of AA.

There were numerous examples of the discrepancy between the sexes at SAB, but perhaps the strangest was an odd young man who appeared in our advanced men's class periodically. I never knew his name, but it was rumored that he was the object of a bet between Balanchine and someone else, perhaps Lincoln Kirstein. In any event, Balanchine had apparently wagered that he could turn any man into a ballet dancer (which just goes to show you how little regard he had for male dancing). How capable a ballet dancer, I wasn't certain, but I recall being told that this fellow in our class, who was at least twenty years old and not even at an intermediate level of proficiency, was expected to rise to a level commensurate with a City Ballet corps de ballet dancer. This never happened.

Admittedly, the level of the male corps de ballet at City Ballet in the late 70s was hardly impressive. Many of these men had been in the company since the late 60s, a time when technical standards were such that any guy with a reasonable body who could hold up a girl was considered usable materiel.

It was always obvious to me that the boys at SAB had been given a bit of a free pass by virtue of the fact that we were ballet dancers with penises. Decent male dancers were in short supply in America, and as a consequence, the deficiencies that would have kept a girl from SAB or New York City Ballet were overlooked. The men of my generation were certainly much better dancers than the previous one but, then again, so were the girls.

The Dance Belt

WHEN I FIRST SET FOOT in the Atelier Ballet Studio at the Old Town Shopping Center in Winston-Salem, North Carolina in 1970, I had no idea what I was getting into, and that went doubly for my dancing attire.

I'd been involved in competitive swimming and diving since I was six years old and owned a pair of very snug, bright red diving trunks reserved for competitions. Those, along with a white t-shirt, white leather ballet slippers, and white socks became my ballet attire for the entire first year of my ballet-dancing existence.

I wasn't the least bit embarrassed by this outfit. My teacher, Mr. Wallace, made a point of showing me pictures of young ballet students at the Imperial School in St. Petersburg who were all barelegged, the girls in leotards, the boys in trunks that looked strangely similar to my own. I was fascinated by those grainy black-and-white photos of stoic young Russian children with long necks and lithe physiques, and I began thinking that, one day in the not-too-distant future, I might fly over to Russia and live like a monk in that austere, black-and-white world, molding my body into the very essence of balletic purity, before returning triumphantly to America, where I would speak with a Russian accent and be adored by millions.

When my family left the South and moved to Andover, it was too cold most of the time to be barelegged in class, so, at Aina's urging, I bought my first pair of black tights.

"What am I going to wear under those?" I asked my mother as we were perusing the various styles at the Capezio store in Boston.

"What do you wear now?"

"Nothing. I've got my diving trunks on and that's it."

"You could wear those underneath."

"That will look silly."

"I'll find out," she said, running off to find a salesperson.

Moments later, she was back with a young man who seemed to know about such things. "You have two options," he said. "At your age I would recommend this." He held up something that looked like a pair of tan-colored underwear, only they were made entirely of thick elastic material.

"Looks like my diving trunks," I said to my mom.

"Why don't you try them on," the salesman advised.

I went into the dressing room and put on this dance-belt-contraption, just as I would a pair of underwear or my diving trunks, with the larger piece of fabric in the back to cover my butt and the smaller in front. Everything fit in there quite nicely, so we completed our purchases, left the store, and I went about my business much as I had before.

Years passed, and, yes, my balls would periodically slip out the side of my dance belt in class, but I would just reach in and put one or both of them back in place. With no other boys around to consult, I assumed this was something that just came with the territory.

When I was thirteen and the ballet ante was upped to David and Terry Shields's studio in Boston, I found myself in a dressing room with other men for the first time. And not just any men—black men, white men, straight men, gay men. I was a bit self-conscious about changing in front of them, particularly the gay men, who I assumed would be leering at me.

I usually arrived a good forty-five minutes before class, so I was almost always alone in the dressing room then, but afterward I started noticing a lot of ugly, bare asses. One day, Jack, a tall, lanky, curly-haired, very heterosexual Italian cab driver who wore flat caps and moonlighted as a ballet dancer, saw me getting undressed. "Michael," he said, "you're wearing your dance belt backwards. The big part goes in the front."

"It does?"

"Yes. The larger part is to hold your shit in place, which I don't think yours is doing very well, because I always see you sticking your hand down there to arrange yourself."

"You're kidding."

"No. I'm serious. Look." And with that, Jack stood up to display his bare ass and the ample, tan-colored pouch holding up his Italian gifts, everything neatly tucked away.

"So, where does this smaller bit of fabric go that I've got here?" I asked, pointing to what I assumed was the front of my dance belt.

"The smaller piece should slide up into your butt crack." He then pulled this smaller piece from between his butt cheeks and I could distinctly see a dark brown skid mark.

"That's disgusting."

"It's not so bad. You'll get used to it. You'll have to get used to it. You can't wear a dance belt like this any other way," he said, pulling something from his dance bag that had a padded pouch on one side, a thick elastic around the top, and a single narrow strip of material up the back. "You see," he added, putting this second dance belt on and sliding the extremely narrow strip of fabric between his hairy, naked butt cheeks.

"I see," I replied, my heart sinking.

On the bus ride home, I pondered the sudden turn my life was about to take with this dance belt business. Clearly, a milestone was being reached. I was about to make the leap from being one of those young boys who take class in their underwear because they or their parents don't know any better, to a serious dancer—or at least one who dressed the part.

When I got home that night, I went up to my room and put on my old dance belt the correct way. It felt strange and looked even stranger. On the bright side, with the bigger piece of fabric in front, I felt certain my nuts would stay put. The downside loomed equally large though, if not larger, because now my ass would be covered by nothing but those thin ballet tights and, almost too gruesome to contemplate, a piece of material up inside my butt crack.

After a few minutes during which I distinctly felt as if my body and been turned around back to front, I pulled my old dance belt off and, sure enough, there was a little skid mark. It was then that I recalled Jack's shit-stained demonstration in the dressing room earlier that day. How could such a thing be possible? What was my mom going to think when she pulled this out of the clothes hamper?

As with many things in life, I grudgingly accepted the fact that I'd been wrong, but, in this particular case, it seemed inconceivable that some adult could have purposely created this dance belt. It just wasn't right. It wasn't natural. American men didn't parade around in any other aspect of life with their butt cheeks so exposed, a piece of fabric shoved inside their butt cracks, their dicks and nuts all hiked up in the front in some padded, silver-platter presentation. It was just too strange.

As hard as it was for me to face, I was somewhat grateful that my dance belt gaffe had not escaped the trained Italian eye of my cab-driving buddy. Jack hadn't laughed at me. He was a good guy, kind and considerate. Why it had not occurred to the folks at Capezio, the company who created my original dance belt, to put some label inside—'B' for back or 'F' for front or 'NH' for nuts here—who the hell knows? Something, anything would have helped. Did they think it would be so obvious to a boy who was putting one of those things on for the first time that it should be worn exactly opposite to the way its quotidian counterpart, a pair of briefs, would have been?

Strange as it appeared, I came to understand that a dance belt served a very practical purpose; a male dancer simply cannot do batterie—the scissor-like beating of the legs—as it is done in a great many classical ballets, if their balls are hanging down. What is odd about the dance belt is that, in a world where the majority of men are looked upon as flaming queens, it elevates the male genitalia, presenting it as something we are forced to reckon with, something to be whispered about and judged by certain members of the audience as a mark of one's hetero- or homosexual allure.

1978. Age 18.
School of American Ballet.

THE SCHOOL OF AMERICAN BALLET might have been a place where a slew of talented dancers were all being squeezed toward the small end of a very select funnel, but for a straight boy, SAB was a harem filled with scores of beautiful young girls, many of whom could be coerced into bed with varying degrees of effort. Sometimes the only effort required was an evening at an average SAB party, an event defined by loud music, dancing, excessive drinking, occasional vomiting, and casual pot smoking, followed by not-so-casual sex.

Sex was, without a doubt, a big part of my life at SAB. Beyond possibly being selected by Balanchine to join City Ballet or getting into American Ballet Theatre, virtually the only other thing my brain would allow me to think about at the time was sex. My hormones were absolutely raging, and six days out of every single week I was surrounded by the most beautiful teenage girls with the most phenomenal bodies this country has ever produced. Many of these girls, moreover, were parading around in front of me with virtually nothing on.

On days when the older girls had variations class or partnering class, they would all wear white leotards. This was a special day because we could practically see through those leotards, bra or no bra, so that everywhere I looked it was nipples, nipples, nipples, ass, ass, ass, mound of Venus, mound of Venus, mound of Venus. Such a wonderful variety of shapes and sizes, and each more delicious than the next. I'm not sure I can adequately convey how mind-bogglingly lucky I felt, or how horny.

———————

And then one Sunday morning sometime in April, after that first long winter in New York, I was standing in the narrow kitchen of my apartment on 64th Street with Kelly, my first girlfriend at SAB. My roommate, Peter, had gone up to his parents' house in New Paltz for the weekend, leaving me alone for this long-awaited opportunity.

Kelly was a sexy, gum-chewing, blonde ballerina from Los Angeles. She made it clear from the outset that I should think of her virginity as an Everest and myself as the oxygen-deprived Edmund Hilary. As such, I would be allowed to plan and pay for all of our dates, even though I was making minimum wage working part-time at a delicatessen and Kelly's father was a millionaire. I would be allowed to buy her flowers and open every door for her. I would be allowed to treat her like the princess her parents had raised her to be, and, for all this, I would be allowed to kiss her, nothing more.

Nearly every weekend throughout the long New York winter, I outfitted myself for another ascent from base camp in hopes of reaching Kelly's Hilary Step. I made sure I had money in my pocket, flowers at the ready, and dinner reservations well in hand. 1978 was the very height of the disco era, and, Kelly being Kelly, I was expected to show her off while displaying a John-Travolta-like degree of proficiency in that department. And so it came to pass that, nearly every Saturday night, she would pour her perfect ass into a pair of Fiorucci jeans, and we would head out to a disco with our fake IDs, where, without fail, she would find fault with something I was doing on the dance floor and glare at me.

Finally, after months and months of Kelly's special brand of hazing, she decided I'd been sufficiently acclimatized and the time to push for the summit had arrived. Spring was upon us, and the Juilliard School where SAB was housed was having a big party to which the ballet students were invited. Kelly and I attended along with many of our friends. I was quite anxious about what I knew would happen afterwards and, in order to quell this anxiety, had more than a few too many drinks. By the time we got back to my apartment, my head was spinning, and I was feeling a bit sick to my stomach, but we'd both waited so long for this moment, and there seemed no possibility of turning back.

When it was all over and we were waking up for the first time together, it seemed as if Kelly had lost more than her virginity. I couldn't tell if she was happy or relieved or sad. For my part, I awoke feeling awful about the way things had transpired. To take our minds off the obvious, I went to the kitchen to make breakfast. As I was standing next to the stove in nothing but a pair of shorts, Kelly said, "You're starting to get a little chunky, Michael."

I was trying to focus on the omelet I was making while simultaneously deflecting the two-by-four Kelly had slammed into my head. This was the first time in my life someone had mentioned my weight, and until that very moment, it never occurred to me to think about dieting. I'd always eaten what I felt like eating without giving it a second thought.

When the omelet was ready, I prepared two plates. Kelly and I sat on my bed eating—or I should say, *trying* to eat—for I suddenly saw what was in front of me not as something pleasurable or necessary, but as something I needed to be wary of and pay careful attention to. A self-consciousness descended over me that, try as I might, I couldn't shake, and for the first time since we'd been together, I was actually happy when Kelly said she had to leave.

Things between us went downhill after that. Kelly began fooling around both in front of and behind my back, and, after spending the summer in L.A., she came back to SAB and told me her new boyfriend was coming to visit. Would I mind making myself scarce for a week while he was in town? I will give myself credit for one thing: I had just enough self-respect to tell her that when and if her new boyfriend came to New York, I would become her old boyfriend. And that's exactly what happened.

Kelly would leave SAB at the end of the year and move back to L.A. Five years later, I reconnected with her in Beverly Hills. She was married and had kids, but was still as beautiful as ever. She sat across from me playing with a piece of pizza when, suddenly, tears started rolling down her cheeks. "I am so sorry, Michael," she said.

"For what?"

"For how I treated you."

At first I had no idea what she was talking about, but then the images returned: the boy I found her kissing in a dark corner of the disco during one of our "dates," her constant demands and expectations, and, finally, the visit from the boyfriend that ended it all. In spite of those memories, I almost laughed, for I looked back at our time together not as something tragic, though there were many tragic aspects to it, but as something filled with the kind of intensity you only feel when you are young and in love and have that herculean ability to turn water into wine. It made me feel good to be chivalrous, and Kelly's expectation that I should treat her like a princess didn't diminish that feeling in the least. In fact, it was quite the opposite. And so, in spite of everything, I still liked Kelly. We were kids then. What did we know?

"It's okay," I said. "Whatever I did, whatever I thought or felt was my own doing. I don't blame you."

And I didn't blame her, not for what she said in my kitchen, anyway. She may have said the words, but it was up to me to interpret them and, for whatever reason, let them affect me the way they did. From the moment Kelly mentioned my weight, though, I began to see myself differently. It might seem like a small thing, her comment, but it wasn't. It triggered something in me: a fragile alliance with food and an understanding of my body in relation to food that would linger for years.

1973. Age 13.
Boston, Massachusetts.

S HORTLY AFTER MY THIRTEENTH BIRTHDAY, Terry Shields informed me that her children's class was going to be discontinued and I would have to begin taking the adult class with her husband, David.

Dark-haired and handsome with a thin, powerful physique, David Shields had once been a soloist at the Royal Ballet in London. He smoked and stalked around the room during ballet class, pounding out the rhythms to the combinations with a straight wooden cane while his blind, obese pianist, Rosie, pounded equally hard on the keyboard. David was a man I both worshipped and feared. There was no talking or joking around between combinations in his class. And you had best be practicing whenever you weren't dancing.

"Why are you standing there?" he said to me a couple of days into my training with him. "Did you do that last step perfectly?"

Without waiting for me to respond, he said, "Get to work. This isn't play time."

I felt David's eyes on me at all times, so I tried never to do anything I thought he would disapprove of. But what were those things, exactly? Hell if I knew. They were the things David didn't like, that's what they were, and I got the feeling there was a long list of them. Mostly it just seemed important to look like you were serious and working hard at all times.

Occasionally there were those who came to David's class who didn't know his unwritten rules. One afternoon, a dancer from Boston Ballet arrived—a young man. David took an immediate dislike to him. Perhaps the boy was too effeminate? Dressed too flamboyantly? Perhaps he simply gave the impression that he was there to have fun or do his own thing, and that, most definitely, was not on David's agenda that day, or most other days for that matter. At one point during the barre, David said to him, "What are you doing? What do you *think* you are doing?" Moments later I heard David say, "Okay, that's it, that's it. That is it! Now you, *who*ever you are. *What*ever you are. Take your things and get out of here. Go on. Get out! I said, get out!" The poor boy gathered his dance bag and headed for the door. "And I don't care if you are from the Boston Ballet. Don't come back!"

Taking class with David Shields was not for the faint of heart. He could smell vulnerability a mile away, and when he was in the right mood, he would latch onto it and gnaw away at it until one of two things happened: you steeled yourself and showed him you could take it or you caved. If you caved, you might cry, as many of the women did, or you might stare at the floor, silently agreeing with his perception of you, which was that you were weak and would never amount to anything if you couldn't stand up to his criticism. You might think to yourself, "Yes, he's right, I am a worthless piece of shit." This, strangely enough, might appease him, but it would by no means please him.

I wallowed in David's world for a long time, commuting between his many charms and the equally alluring charms of the boys at Andover East Junior High. At one point, I began having almost daily headaches that occasionally became full-blown migraines for which the only cure seemed to be lying motionless in a dark room with ice over my eyes. My mother suspected all was not well where David Shields was concerned, but she also knew I was deeply attached to him and would have rebelled against any plan to remove me from his school, so she left me alone.

As if I needed confirmation of the fact that my thirteenth year on this earth was not going to be a lucky one, I broke my foot in ballet class one afternoon and ended up in a cast for six weeks. And then, a week before Thanksgiving, during a pickup game of street hockey in front of our home, I was hit in the eye with the puck. I spent the next two weeks lying in a hospital bed in a partially upright position so blood could drain from my eye. Afterward, I was told my retina had been severely damaged and I would be virtually blind in my right eye for the rest of my life.

Several months went by after the accident before I was allowed to return to ballet class. When I did, I was told there could be no jumping for at least six months for fear that my retina might become completely detached. Much to my surprise and secret horror, David Shields offered to teach me privately. I didn't consider saying no.

We began working in a small studio with no music, several afternoons a week, David's cane beating out the tempi for an hour or more as I desperately tried to please him. And every day that we worked together, I swallowed another dose of his disapproval until he needn't have been there at all. I could do every bit of disapproving for him. I knew immediately when I'd made a mistake or had failed to execute an exercise the way I knew he wanted it done, and before he could open his mouth, I was silently apologizing or actually apologizing.

On the rare occasion when David had to cancel a private lesson or I had an eye doctor's appointment or the bus was late or some other circumstance intervened, I felt a tremendous sense of relief. I knew I shouldn't have had those feelings. I knew I should be looking forward to class, but I never did. I was becoming accustomed to hardship and unpleasantness, so these feelings hardly seemed consequential.

As young as I was, I knew that becoming a ballet dancer was going to be a long, hard journey, and if I couldn't weather the difficult moments when I might like to quit or was a bit sad or depressed, I knew I would never make it. And no one could really tell me whether to quit or stick it out—not my mother who thought she was always right, not my father who hardly knew me, and certainly not David Shields, the ballet teacher I adored but could seemingly never please.

1978. Age 18.
School of American Ballet.

UNLIKE MOST OF MY PEERS, I was not initially introduced to the dancing of Mikhail Baryshnikov via the film *The Turning Point,* which opened in New York in the fall of 1977. The first time I saw Misha dance was at City Center in March of that year, during my spring break audition trip to New York.

The seven-minute pas de deux he performed with Christine Sarry, *Variations on America,* was a staggering mix of technical wizardry, patriotism, and laugh-out-loud buffoonery, choreographed by Eliot Feld. It was a Greatest Hits of American history that showcased Misha's remarkable abilities to carve a character from the slightest physical expression.

Misha's technique was as astonishing on stage as it was on screen, but what was more astonishing was the fact that he dispensed this technique in service to a character and a ballet. When he leapt into the air, he wasn't Mikhail Baryshnikov, the great Russian dancer—he was the patriotic war hero, the cowboy, the Indian.

When the short piece was over, cries for a reprise were so insistent that Misha and Christine danced the entire duet again, thrilling everyone as much as they had the first time.

After I'd been at the School of American Ballet for about a year, Misha joined New York City Ballet and became virtually an everyday presence in my life. In the classroom, sadly, most of Misha's pyrotechnics were nowhere to be seen for the simple reason that Stanley Williams didn't give those types of exercises. Hell, we were lucky if we ever got to grand allegro (big jumps) after all the schmoozing, pipe smoking, and farting around with petit allegro. As a result, I spent a lot of time watching Misha stand around and look at himself in the mirror, something he seemed quite obsessed with.

He was perpetually preoccupied with his hair, always fussing with it, sculpting it, brushing it back away from his face with one or both hands while simultaneously pressing the tops of his toes into the ground and rolling back over onto demi-pointe, a habit so ingrained in him that Twyla Tharp put it into *Push Comes to Shove*, the ballet she choreographed for him at American Ballet Theatre.

When I first saw Misha dance with the New York City Ballet, I have to admit it was jarring. I had been going to see City Ballet every week for more than a year before Misha came along, and I'd become accustomed to their dancers and their ballets. The City Ballet men I saw in class on a daily basis were the same men I saw performing onstage at New York State Theater, so, in general, I knew what to expect from them. What I expected from Misha was something else entirely.

Watching Misha perform with City Ballet was like watching a Ferrari drive through a school zone. You knew what he was capable of and you were itching like hell to see it, but you also knew you were never going to see it because George Balanchine's life and work was about one thing and one thing only: women.

1974. Age 14.
Greensboro, North Carolina.

WHEN I RESUMED NORMAL BALLET CLASSES after my eye injury, my migraine headaches returned, and it was suggested by my doctor that I take some time off. During this hiatus, my father was asked to move to Greensboro, North Carolina, a forty-minute drive from our former home in Winston-Salem.

Despite my misgivings about what this might mean for me as a dancer, I realized the move to Greensboro would be an opportunity for me to turn over a new leaf. After years of being called a faggot, I made the stunningly astute observation that my mother's advice to turn the other cheek had done absolutely nothing to stem the tide of bullying and name calling, and I was simply going to have to come up with another solution. One afternoon, not long after our arrival in Greensboro, I hit on it.

Classes at Grimsley Senior High School had ended for the day, and I was riding home in a car with my brother, Mark, and some new friends of his. Mark had, for some inexplicable reason, decided that his return to the south would be a good opportunity to befriend a bunch of ignorant, racist, rifle-toting Confederates who enjoyed the finer things that southern living had to offer, such as hunting, crew-cuts, ROTC, and Skoal. I gathered they stopped short of cross burning but have no doubt they didn't object to the practice.

"So yer Mark's brother, huh?" one of them said.

"Yeah."

"You the faggot ballet dancer?"

And then, much to my surprise, I happily lowered myself to the level my mother told me not to and hit this kid as hard as I possibly could in the face.

"What the fuck?!"

"Don't you *ever* call me that again!" I screamed, my rage at being called a faggot rising, at long last, to an appropriately feverish pitch.

"All right! All right! Damn, Mark. This little brother of yours is one strange little motherfucker."

I sat back, shaking, my lip quivering.

And that, strangely enough, was the last time anyone ever called me a faggot.

After deciding I would no longer tolerate being bullied, I decided the best way to avoid the possibility altogether was to tell absolutely no one at my new school that I studied ballet. As a result, my year at Grimsley Senior High School began and ended in more or less complete isolation. I went to school alone. I ate lunch alone. I told no one what I did.

Every day after school and several days a week before school was over, my mother would pick me up in our black Volkswagen Beetle with my requisite snack—a bowl of cereal—and take me to one of two places: UNC Greensboro, where I took ballet class with Joseph Levinoff and a group of undergraduate women, or Winston-Salem, where I reconnected with my first teacher, Paul Wallace. In either case, I would arrive home sometime in the evening, eat dinner, and start in on my homework. On Saturdays, my mother again drove me to Winston-Salem for class, leaving me one day of the week when I might conceivably do something with a friend, if I'd had one.

Fall 1978. Age 18.
School of American Ballet.

A ND THEN ONE DAY, for no apparent reason, I was invited to Lincoln Kirstein's townhouse in Gramercy Park. Lincoln was a frequent visitor to Stanley Williams's class in those days. A tall, imposing figure with big features who always wore a black suit, white shirt, and black tie, he looked like an undertaker and scared me to death.

I was so ignorant of the ballet world, I really had no idea who Lincoln was for a long time. The first time he spoke to me, which just happened to be when I was standing in his living room, all of that changed. He bent over, craned his gigantic pale head even farther forward than it was normally placed, shook my hand, and practically whispered in my ear, "Thank you for coming. Please make yourself at home."

From the outset, I wasn't sure why Alex, Benji, and I had been invited to Lincoln's. Alex, who just happened to be Andrei Kramarevsky's son, mentioned that we were expected for drinks and a bite to eat one night, and that was that; no particular reasons were given. I didn't contemplate saying no.

When I arrived at the townhouse, I was greeted by a small black woman who looked as if she'd just stepped off the set of *Birth of a Nation*. She wore a traditional black-and-white maid's outfit and ushered me into Lincoln's home where, among my many surprises that evening,

I discovered ten or more male dancers from City Ballet, along with Jerry Robbins. We all looked at one another and smiled.

As I nibbled on some hors d'oeuvres, I wandered the ground floor. The walls were covered with oil paintings, drawings, and photographs; the bookshelves full of beautiful tomes; the tables laden with all sorts of Greek and Roman statuary. There was a decidedly homoerotic bent to the art that, as young and naïve as I was, I couldn't help noticing.

"Is Lincoln married?" I asked my friend Benji as I stared at yet another painting or drawing or sculpture of a man in some state of undress.

"Yes. I think her name is Fidelma."

"Where is she?"

"Who knows? Maybe she's upstairs. Maybe she's not in New York."

Lincoln's wife, it turned out, was the artist Paul Cadmus's sister, and upstairs was a place I likened to the Bat Cave, a mysterious lair where Lincoln hid his wife and just about everything else, including himself, much of the time.

A buffet table had been set up in a small dining room off the kitchen, and most of us gravitated there to sample the wonderful food on display, much of it devoted to the dessert end of the spectrum. There seemed to be no particular focus to the evening. Lincoln would appear for a few minutes, then disappear. It was a male mixer, I suppose, and the mixing that was meant to take place was between Lincoln's almost-exclusively male acquaintances and the beautiful male dancers of New York City ballet. For those with younger tastes, there was Benji, Alex, and myself.

During the spring and fall of 1978, Lincoln came frequently to the school to watch Stanley's class. He often arrived with a male companion, but whether accompanied or not, he would stand, never sit, at the front of the room near the door, where a few chairs were always placed for visitors. Dressed in his black suit, his big pale head with close-cropped hair poking out the top, he would generally watch for ten or fifteen minutes, then leave. On one of these occasions, however, he stayed until the end of class, then asked if I would go over to Jack Silver's, a tailor in the same building that housed the American Ballet Theatre School at 61st Street and Broadway.

"I've been thinking about you boys," he said somewhat pensively, his hand on my shoulder. "When I see you at the State Theater, watching performances, well...I thought it would be nice if there were some way to distinguish you. To set you apart so people know you represent the school. I'm going to have some uniforms made, much like the ones from the Imperial Ballet School in Russia. I want you boys to wear them when you come to State Theater. Would you mind going for a fitting?"

And off I toddled, lickety-split, eager to do whatever it was Lincoln asked. He was, after all, Lincoln Kirstein, the man whose father had been the chairman of Filene's; the man who brought Balanchine to America and helped establish the very school I was then standing in. I assumed that whatever this man decided should happen, happened.

As I walked over to Jack Silver's, I began to wonder about this uniform business. On the one hand, I mused, we'd probably be offered tickets to the ballet more often. On the other, we'd probably be stared at like a bunch of monkeys at the zoo (or guests at one of Lincoln's soirées). On a more personal note, I'd always chafed at the notion of uniforms such as the black tights, white t-shirts, and white shoes that the school tried, with varying degrees of success, to get the boys to wear, but because Lincoln had asked me himself, I put all my life-or-death principles aside and went along with the idea.

Some time passed after that initial fitting, and I began wondering when my uniform was going to magically appear. Eventually, I heard through some sources at the school that Balanchine had gotten wind of

Lincoln's little Imperial-Ballet-School-uniform-plan and squashed it. I have no idea if that was what happened, but somebody put a stop to it, and about the only person I could think of who had that power was Balanchine.

This incident with the uniforms was, I later realized, a sign of Lincoln's increasing mental deterioration. I say this because it was around this same time that he showed up at SAB wearing something that looked suspiciously like a Cub Scout's uniform. It consisted of a neckerchief, a khaki shirt adorned with some merit badges or emblems of some kind, khaki shorts, and knee-high socks. When I saw Lincoln appear at the front of the room in this outfit, it was hard not to burst out laughing. Everyone, including Stanley, did a double take.

The last thing in the world I wanted was for any of the boys to laugh at Lincoln, but they couldn't help themselves. In their defense, they didn't know him and had not developed any sort of feelings for or about him. They saw him as I once did, as a big, black-clad beast of a man with a murderous countenance who'd been born into money and had used that money to create a dance dynasty. But to know Lincoln at that time of his life, even as superficially as I did, was to feel some sense of his frailty. Because of that and the beauty to which he'd devoted his life, I couldn't help but feel a great deal of sympathy and respect for the man.

1976. Age 16.
Winston-Salem, North Carolina.

AFTER A YEAR OF COMMUTING back and forth between Greensboro and Winston-Salem three days a week for ballet class, I enrolled in the summer dance program at the North Carolina School of the Arts. For the majority of students, myself included, NCSA was the first school we had ever attended where we could be ourselves. If you were gay, it was place where you could come out, hold hands, kiss, and have boyfriends or girlfriends without worrying about being assaulted verbally or physically. If you were straight, it was a place where you looked around and saw scores of kids who were interested in the same things you were, kids who'd lived through the same abuse you'd lived through in public school and were as thrilled to find you as you were to find them. It was this sense of being in a safe haven surrounded, literally, by a ghetto that wanted nothing to do with you, that made NCSA the remarkable artistic sanctuary it was.

With some regularity, mock Shakespearean fights broke out in the cafeteria among those in the drama department. There were both planned and impromptu performances of all kinds going on all over campus, alongside organized dances, concerts, and costume balls. All types of music could be heard blasting from dorm windows, everything from Vivaldi to The Velvet Underground, and live music could be heard just about anywhere at any time. Parties were frequent, but this did not, as far as I could tell, distract anyone from their artistic pursuits.

At the end of my first summer there, NCSA offered me a scholarship to return in the fall, so, a couple of months after my sixteenth birthday, I packed my bags and moved into a high school dorm at NCSA with Todd, a preternaturally blonde-haired ballet dancer from Cherry Hill, New Jersey who was obsessed with The Beach Boys.

My initial euphoria about finally escaping public school aside, it took me longer to adjust to life at NCSA than I anticipated. I struggled mightily with homesickness and, as a result, went home nearly every weekend. Meanwhile, when I was at school, I was discovering what a rigid, uptight, judgmental little prick I'd become.

There were a multitude of behaviors among my NCSA peers I found shocking, most of them practiced by my very own roommate. I was convinced I didn't want to be like Todd or most of his friends, all of whom I saw as terribly undisciplined. Not the kind of people David Shields would have approved of. I never drank, didn't smoke weed or cigarettes, and was intent on preserving my virginity until marriage. To cap it all off, I went to bed every night at nine o'clock because I was convinced I needed ten hours of sleep in order to be rested up for my 8:30 a.m. ballet class with Mimi Paul.

Mimi arrived in the studio every morning wearing dark cotton sweat pants, a plain leotard, flat pink ballet slippers, and huge glasses that made her look like an owl. Thus attired, she would put her feet into the most perfect first position I had ever seen in my life and say in her somewhat high-pitched voice, "We'll start in first position."

As a young girl, Mimi studied with Mary Day in Washington, D.C. After a brief stint at the School of American Ballet, she joined New York City Ballet in 1960 at age sixteen. Three years later, she was pro-

moted to soloist, and in December 1965, she made her debut as Sugar
Plum in Balanchine's *Nutcracker.* Clive Barnes, then dance critic for
The New York Times, described her as "tall, svelte, and elegant. One of
those thoroughbred dancers who take to ballerina roles like young heir-
esses boldly come into their rightful and expected inheritance."

Two months after her debut as Sugar Plum, Balanchine promoted
Mimi to principal dancer, and in 1967 she created one of her signature
roles opposite Violette Verdy in Balanchine's *Emeralds.* Two years later, Mimi abruptly left City Ballet and joined American Ballet Theatre,
where she stayed for about three years. By age thirty-two, she had retired and was teaching at NCSA.

Mimi taught the advanced high school ballet class every morning at
NCSA in what had once been a high school gymnasium, later rechris-
tened *Studio A.* As if watching Mimi's flawless positioning every day
weren't enough to influence how I worked, I managed to get hold of a
book on ballet technique, and it was those photographs and drawings
that truly cemented my neurosis for the foreseeable future.

I pored over those pages like they held the secrets to the universe,
committing each perfect position to memory and vowing to make those
positions an integral part of my class work. In order to increase my turnout, I would lie on the floor with my butt against the base of a wall
and splay my legs open above me so that gravity would bring my ankles
down to the ground, at which point I would have achieved my goal of
perfectly flat, 180-degree turnout. I did this before class every day for
fifteen to twenty minutes, and after a year or so my ankles were on the
ground.

I began a more comprehensive effort at perfection by trying to hold
my legs in those perfect, 180-degree-turned-out positions while I was
doing my barre work. It was a strange game I played. I knew what I was

doing wasn't making me stronger, but I considered "turning-in" ugly, a sign that I was less than capable of looking like an accomplished dancer. Process and common sense be damned. For a brief moment, I would see something in the mirror that fit my definition of balletic perfection, and once I fit into that little box, even if I fell over the next instant, I was off the hook. I was okay.

To Mimi's credit, she tried on numerous occasions to get me to work in a more realistic manner that would help me build strength at the barre, but as soon as I could I would move my feet back to where I liked to see them, at 180 degrees of perfection.

Somewhere inside that thick skull of mine, though, I knew Mimi was right. I knew my working habits were doing nothing but making me look good temporarily, and I knew I had weaknesses that my turnout-at-all-costs approach was doing nothing to remedy, particularly with respect to adagio movements that required sustained control of my legs in the air, but I was incapable of changing. I just couldn't do it. I couldn't take a step back. Couldn't turn in. I couldn't appreciate or accept the fact that I needed to walk before I could run. It seemed to me that I could already run. Why bother walking?

1979. Age 18. New York City.

I'D BEEN AT SAB FOR NEARLY TWO YEARS when, at seven o'clock on a cold Saturday night in February, I arrived at the Minskoff Rehearsal Studios on Forty-Fifth Street. The room where my first professional audition was to take place was an enormous space with high ceilings and a bank of windows that looked down onto the street below.

About thirty boys had been invited to audition for the role of Tadzio in San Francisco Opera's upcoming production of *Death in Venice*, and when I arrived, they were all going through the motions of limbering up at one of many portable barres that had been placed around the room. Seated at the front were the director, Bob Brewer, and the choreographer, Margo Sappington, both of whom I met during their visit to SAB weeks earlier.

Written by Thomas Mann in 1912, the story of *Death in Venice* revolves around the infatuation of an older man, Aschenbach, with a beautiful young Polish boy, Tadzio. Throughout the story, the two never actually meet; rather, there are series of observations and fantasies that become ever more intense as Aschenbach succumbs to the cholera epidemic that was then sweeping Venice. In the final scene, Aschenbach dies sitting in a beach chair, staring at his unrequited love, Tadzio.

Margo Sappington's back story was that she'd joined the Joffrey Ballet in 1965 and four years later choreographed the all-nude review

Oh! Calcutta! Obviously no slave to convention, she gave our audition sporting a low-cut leotard, jazz shoes, and loose pants that exposed a bit of flesh around her hips. During the many hours that followed her warm-up class, we learned some of her choreography and danced those sequences in various groupings. At around eleven o'clock in the evening, three boys remained. "Would you mind taking off your shirts?" Margo asked. "We want you to just walk around the room, keeping your distance from one another."

For several long minutes, there was no sound at all save that of the occasional car horn, or siren, and in that stillness, with the cool air wafting down over my sweaty skin, I could hear my heart beating in my chest and feel my bare feet making soft contact with the black Marley flooring. What I am going for here? Confident and alluring. Do I look confident and alluring? What a night. It must be after midnight. I wonder if they're going to pick me for this part? Isn't this Tadzio character a blonde, Polish boy? I'm not blonde. And I doubt I look Polish. Oh well, not much I can do about that now.

"That's fine boys," Margo said quietly. "You can get dressed now."

When I emerged from the dressing room, Margo pulled me aside. "Would you object to having your hair dyed blonde?" she asked.

My portrayal of Tadzio in *Death in Venice* marked the beginning of many things for me as a professional dancer and as a person. Some of those things I was aware of, but most I was not. The notion that I might be perceived as gay seemed inconceivable, yet *After Dark*, a popular gay magazine at the time, ran a topless photo of me in their March issue while I was performing in San Francisco. The caption read: "New Boy in Town." I cut out the whole of it and showed it to my mother when she arrived for my big debut.

"Oh, Michael," she said, bursting with pride, "that's wonderful."

During the six weeks I spent in San Francisco preparing the role with Margo and, finally, performing on the slippery, raked stage of the Curran Theater, I felt as if I'd landed on a strange and unfamiliar planet. I was anxious about the responsibility that had been placed on my shoulders but didn't feel the role was beyond me, because Margo tailored the choreography to suit my particular talents and weaknesses. What truly shocked me was just how fragile and one-dimensional my technical foundation had become at SAB.

All ballet dancers take class on a daily basis, but once I arrived in San Francisco, I was left to figure out for myself where and when this was going to happen, and because I'd never had a professional job before and knew nothing about the ballet scene in San Francisco, I was just hoping someone would take me by the hand and guide me through it all. But no one did. Margo hardly mentioned a daily class, so initially I just warmed up on my own before we began rehearsing together. When I finally did meet some of the other dancers in the production and ventured out to take class, I felt so out of my element and so embarrassed by what I was incapable of doing that I stopped taking class almost entirely. I had become so accustomed to the teachers and classes at SAB and so good at glossing over my weaknesses it was nearly impossible for me to cope with a different situation. Fortunately, all I had to focus on were the dances Margo had choreographed for me, and we rehearsed those so incessantly I felt confident in my ability to perform them.

When our week-long run of performances was over and the blonde hair I'd been forced to endure for five weeks was colored back to resemble something less like a boy trying to turn tricks on Polk Street and more like the Donny Osmond I vaguely resembled, I flew back to New York and the familiar surroundings of SAB. I was too young to understand the symbolism behind *Death in Venice* or see it as anything other than what it appeared to be—my first professional job—but the pattern it established was right there in front of me at age eighteen, and the lesson it would teach me over and over and over again was this: to virtually every older gay man I would meet in my life (and there would be many), I would always be Tadzio.

New Boy in Town

There is a new boy in town, Michael Langlois, originally from Monterey and now studying at the School of American Ballet in New York. He and choreographer Margo Sappington breathed some life into Spring Opera Theater's *Death in Venice*, exhumed from two seasons ago. The opera remains deadly save for Sappington's dazzling dance sequences in which Langlois certainly stars. He is absolutely perfect as the beautiful blond object of Aschenbach's latent homosexual affection. In his stage debut, Langlois ably characterizes Tadzio so as to convey many metaphors of the dying Aschenbach's philosophy, not merely sexual fancy as represented in Visconti's shallow film. Ken Remo's Aschenbach is an admirable tour de force in a difficult opera, but it is Langlois who makes realization of Thomas Mann and Benjamin Britten's intentions.

AFTER DARK   June 1979

In San Francisco, dancer Michael Langlois breathed some life into Spring Opera Theater's production of Death in Venice *as Tadzio, the beautiful blond object of Aschenbach's latent homosexual affection.*

From After Dark Magazine 1979. Death in Venice. San Francisco Opera.

1976. Age 16.
Winston-Salem, North Carolina.

A S MY FIRST YEAR at the North Carolina School of the Arts progressed, I shed some of my piety, anger, and wariness of men and
became almost human. Almost. The solitude I embraced in order to
protect myself in public school was no longer necessary at NCSA, and
for the first time in years, I was able to let my guard down. I had built
some thick, high walls around myself and needed to learn to trust people again. I needed a break from the constant attention to dance and
homework. I needed to start enjoying life and acting like the irresponsi-
ble teenagers I generally scorned.

To get a sense of just how accidentally I embraced this idea, I'll
introduce Debbie. With her long brown hair, amazing body, and dust-
ing of freckles across her cheekbones, Debbie was a fourteen-year-old
ballet dancer many boys at NCSA fantasized about, myself included.
Imagine my surprise, then, when, one weekend night, she agreed to ac-
company me up to my room.

Not long after we sat down on my bed, we started kissing. My
mouth filled with her soft, raspberry-flavored tongue as I inhaled the
sweet smell of her hair and perfume. "Hold on," she said, pulling a
gigantic wad of bubble gum from her mouth and depositing it on my
nightstand.

I fell back on the bed. Debbie climbed on top of me. Moments later, she was unzipping her pants. Moments after that, she began unzipping my pants. Uncertain as to whether or not I should object to letting a stunningly beautiful fourteen-year-old girl seduce me, I thought it prudent to let Debbie do whatever Debbie wanted to do.

Whether it was the beer or the darkness or the potpourri of Debbie's flavors and smells, I was only vaguely aware that I was having sex for the first time, and it wasn't long after I came to this conclusion that I came to another conclusion and the whole thing was over. In short order, Debbie got dressed, kissed me on the cheek, popped her gum back in her mouth, and left. I fell back on my bed, staring numbly at the ceiling.

Following the loss of my virginity, I went into quite a depression. I thought that if all the adults in my life whom I desperately wanted to please knew what I'd done, they'd be sorely disappointed. And then, after some time had passed, I realized my life wasn't all that different. The people around me still treated me the same. I still got up early and ate my cereal quietly in my dorm room before traipsing over to *Studio A* for class with Mimi. And Mimi still looked at me through her gigantic glasses every morning with a touch of concern on her face as I wrestled my way through her barre, trying to hold onto my perfect turnout. It was then that I realized I didn't have to be such an unbearable bunhead in order to succeed as a dancer.

The funny thing about all the sex, drugs, and drinking NCSA was so paranoid about their students getting involved in and all the rules they'd made to prevent such things was that those were exactly the kinds of experiences I needed to have in order to help me grow up. When you walk around for so long convinced that staying up past nine o'clock in the evening is going to prevent you from succeeding, what you're really saying is that you have very little faith in yourself.

Indulging in these activities didn't make me any less of a dancer or any less of a person or any less determined to succeed. It didn't stop my teachers from caring about me or my mother or father from loving me or my friends from liking me, and once I realized I could have those experiences and emerge from them intact, I threw most of my puritanical ideas about the kind of person I thought I needed to be in order to succeed out the window.

1979. Age 18. New York City.

A MONTH OR TWO AFTER MY DEBUT as Tadzio in San Francisco, I was back in New York, standing in a dingy rehearsal room at the Ansonia Hotel, a historic building at 73rd Street and Broadway that once housed a gay bathhouse called the Continental Baths. (It later became a swinger's club called Plato's Retreat.) I was at the Ansonia in the spring of 1979 to rehearse *Lucrezia,* a one-act opera for the upcoming Caramoor Festival in Katonah, New York.

However noble this enterprise might have appeared to the powers that be at SAB, it was obvious to me when I saw how little the boys from SAB had to dance and how equally little we were given to wear that we were there primarily to provide a little eye-candy for Frederick Koch and his rich, gay, New York friends.

Frederick was on the board of the Caramoor Festival, but he was no mere figurehead. He knew a great deal about opera and was largely responsible, both financially and creatively, for the Respighi program that several boys from SAB were asked to participate in. Also on the bill were Peter Martins and Kay Mazzo from New York City Ballet. They would dance in a ballet by Robert Weiss called *Gli Ucelli.*

Given all this, it didn't entirely surprise me when I received an invitation to a party at Frederick Koch's Fifth Avenue apartment sometime after *Lucrezia* opened in mid-June. I suspected I'd been invited for the same reasons I'd been invited to Lincoln Kirstein's, but, just in case there were any doubts, I brought along my new girlfriend, Dana, a dancer from SAB.

Frederick's apartment was at once grand and cozy, full of beautiful paintings and books, all tastefully arranged to betray nary a hint of his true proclivities should his mom or dad happen to drop by. Dana was virtually the only woman at the party, but this didn't seem to faze her. "Come in here," she said to me with her Dallas drawl, luring me into Frederick's marble bathroom and locking the door.

"What is it?" I asked.

"All those cute gay men are making me horny," she said, pulling me in for a kiss.

When our sexual escapades in Frederick's bathroom were over, we returned to the party, whereupon Frederick asked if he could speak to me privately. I thought he was going to chastise me for misbehaving, but no. "I'm making a trip to London this summer," he said, "to visit friends and see the theater. I wonder if you'd like to join me for a week to ten days. All expenses paid, of course."

I was a bit taken aback, but not so taken aback that I couldn't already envision myself standing in front of Westminster Abbey. "Thank you for the offer, Frederick," I said. "That's very generous. But if you don't mind, I'd like to think it over."

"Of course," Frederick replied.

Before leaving the party, I asked one of Frederick's gay friends for some advice. "Frederick? He's totally harmless. Really. You've got nothing to worry about. He'll treat you very well, and I'm sure you'll have a lot fun. And, no, you don't have to sleep with him. I'm sure he just wants a pretty face to look at during intermission."

A week later, Frederick invited me over to his building for lunch to discuss the trip. I assumed we would be eating in his apartment, but it turned out there was a fully staffed and completely empty dining room on the ground floor of his building. After we sat down and ordered, the deafening silence was interrupted solely by the sound of our silverware scraping the occasional plate and my declaration that I would accept Frederick's offer with one proviso.

"I would like to see Paris and visit my relatives in Sweden before meeting you in London, if you don't mind."

"Well, no," he said, somewhat hesitantly. "I don't think that will be a problem. My travel agent will arrange everything. Just meet me in London on the agreed upon date."

Frederick went on to mention that his foundation would be paying for my trip under the guise of furthering my artistic education. I smiled, not bothering to question the legitimacy of this idea.

The more we spoke about the logistics of the trip and how everything would be taken care of by Frederick and his seemingly endless resources, the worse I began to feel about what I was embarking on. It was all so tawdry and dishonest. Frederick was using me for his own selfish reasons, and I was using Frederick for my own selfish reasons, and the whole thing was being written off like some tax-deductible contribution to Save the Children.

As lunch wore on, a few beams of sunlight pierced the gloomy confines of Frederick's empty dining room. Outside, it was a beautiful summer day, but there I was in the dark, whoring myself out to a Harvard-educated, middle-aged multi-millionaire who paid eighteen-year-old boys to go to Europe with him.

1979. Age 19. Europe.

S HORTLY AFTER MY NINETEENTH BIRTHDAY, I arrived in Paris for the first time. It was a gorgeous, sunny Sunday, and after stowing my bags at a youth hostel on the left bank, I set out to explore the city on foot. As I was standing in front of Les Invalides, an elderly man on a bicycle approached and asked if I was lost or needed any help. As we were chatting, he mentioned that he worked at the Swedish Embassy. "That's funny," I said, "my grandfather is from Göteborg."

A Swedish connection thus established, I let all thoughts of ulterior motives fall by the wayside, and when this gentleman invited me to lunch, I gladly accepted.

With his chiseled features and lanky physique, Sverker may have been adept at picking up teenage boys, but he was completely hopeless when it came to cooking, so, after arriving at the embassy, I took over, making us an omelet and a salad in their gigantic professional kitchen. When everything was ready, we retired to the garden.

"Where is everyone?" I asked.

"It's Sunday. The embassy is closed. Aren't you hot in those jeans?"

Why, yes, I suppose I am.

"Come upstairs. I've got a pair of swim trunks you can wear."

When I emerged from the bathroom wearing a pair of Speedos, Sverker looked at me and smiled. "Oh...that's *much* better."

Back in the garden, we sat down to lunch: me nearly naked, and Sverker, my very hospitable Swedish host, smiling at me over the top of his wine glass. In spite of my many questions, Sverker never told me exactly what he did at the embassy. It was all very dull stuff, he said, in comparison to my life as a ballet dancer. We discussed Sweden and my Swedish roots and, finally, my plans for a first visit to Paris (I had none). "Why don't you come and stay at my apartment?" he suggested. "It will be much more comfortable than some dirty, overcrowded youth hostel."

This seemed like just another one of Sverker's capital suggestions, like changing into a pair of Speedos, so, after lunch, we retrieved my bags from the youth hostel and returned to Sverker's apartment where he made another capital suggestion—a nap, just the two of us.

I hadn't slept a wink on the plane, so I lay down like Goldilocks in Sverker's bed. Everything was working out great on my first day in Paris: a free lunch, a new friend who seemed to have the run of the Swedish Embassy, and, now, a free place to stay.

Ooh...what's that?

Sverker's big arm wrapping around me.

And that?

Feels like Sverker's Swedish prick poking into my backside.

I lay there motionless, hoping my inertia might alert Sverker to the fact that I had no intention of letting him fuck me. He was very persuasive, however, and somehow guilted me into letting him hold me in his arms. I didn't have anything against affection, did I? No, I was no prude. Finally, unable to relax, I climbed out of bed. Much to my relief, Sverker mentioned he was going off to have dinner with friends. "You'll be alright on your own, won't you?" he asked. Obviously—I mean, look at how well I've managed thus far.

I spent part of my evening away from Sverker's penis having dinner on the Boulevard St. Germain, an area, I later learned, that was one of the more notorious cruising spots in all of Gay Paris. Perhaps that was why every other man who passed my table on the street stopped and stared at me.

After dinner, I headed for the Seine and stopped on one of its many bridges to admire the view of the setting sun. As I was mulling over the decidedly gay turn my European adventure was taking, a dark-haired Frenchman who looked to be about thirty years old approached. He had a camera around his neck and said he was a photographer. When he found out it was my first time in Paris, he suggested a tour of the city in his car.

As the stars came out, we arrived at Sacré Coeur. From there, we traveled back down to the Rue de Rivoli, up the Champs Élysées to the Arc de Triomphe, and down to the Eiffel Tower. As midnight approached, my guide suggested a stop for ice cream. Afterwards, we went back to his place to look at his photographs. Once inside his cramped little apartment, I realized that French men are a lot quicker off the mark than their Swedish counterparts.

"No," I said as he tried to kiss me. "You've got me all wrong."

This statement was translated in my French suitor's mind into, "You are incredibly handsome. Kiss me again."

After another aborted kiss, I opened the door and fled, back to the questionable safety of Sverker's apartment where I sacked out on the couch. Early the next morning, Sverker found me there. "My mother is ill," he said. "I'm afraid I must leave to be with her, so you won't be able to stay here any longer. But don't worry... I've found you a room in a very nice hostel near the Hotel de Ville. I will drive you there after breakfast."

Carl Sverker Åström was the Swedish Ambassador to France from 1978 to 1982. He was sixty-four years old when we met in Paris. He publicly admitted to being a homosexual in 2003 at the age of eighty-eight.

Between my many gay misadventures in Paris and my impending date with Frederick, I traveled to Sweden to visit my relatives. As the days passed in Göteborg, the date I was expected to be in London loomed like a ravenous, swelling cock in my mind. I found myself almost sick to my stomach at the thought of what lay ahead: yet another gay man who wanted to sleep with me. I called Frederick twice to postpone the inevitable, but there came a point when there could be no more delay. I'd made my bed. Time to lie in it.

When I finally arrived at Frederick's townhouse off of King's Road in London, he was just sitting down to lunch. A can of beef stew? Would I like some?

It was ghastly, the beef stew, and all the more so because Frederick could have been dining like the king that he was. But no, it was a can of beef stew warmed up on the stove—an apt introduction to Frederick's frugality and the fine cuisine of Great Britain in the late 70s.

When our regrettable lunch was over, Frederick showed me around our digs, a prospect I was dreading. The apartment where we were staying was owned by one of Frederick's many wealthy friends and was spread out over two floors: street and garden level (an English euphemism for "basement"). The bedrooms were down below. When I descended to view them, I noticed that the guest bedroom was unoccupied.

"You can sleep in here with me," Frederick said from the master bedroom as I was dragging my suitcase downstairs.

"Who's staying in the guest room?" I asked.

"No one. But the maid hasn't prepared the guest room."

"Oh, I don't mind," I said, veering past a bewildered Frederick and down the hall. "I'll make the bed."

There was a long pause, followed by, "Are you sure?"

"Yes! I'm sure."

That was the beginning and end of any discussion Frederick and I would ever have about sleeping arrangements.

Over the course of the next ten days, Frederick and I went to the theater every day, often twice a day. Most evenings found us at the Royal Shakespeare Company, and if we weren't there, we were dining together or with one of his many acquaintances, nearly all of whom were gay.

Frederick was a wonderful companion, actually; extremely knowledgeable, and I was eager to learn whatever he could teach me. As wealthy as he was, he was not an ostentatious person. He did develop a strange affectation when we were in London, however: he started speaking with an English accent. I found this utterly bizarre but managed, somehow, not to open my big fat mouth and tease him about it. He seemed to relish being in London and clearly wanted to be seen as just one of the locals, but I couldn't help wondering who the hell he thought he was fooling.

Two of Frederick's male friends lived on a sizable estate near Plymouth, and it was there that we found ourselves one weekend. The house we were staying in was a castle, essentially, minus the moat, and sat perched on a postcard-perfect hill overlooking the rolling countryside.

I spent much of the weekend alone as Frederick and his middle-aged pals scoured the countryside looking for gay adventure. They seemed particularly fond of hitchhikers and military men, and if it was a hitchhiker in uniform, so much the better. If I could believe half of what they said when they got home, nearly every guy in the English military was queer.

While they were thus occupied, I hung out with the very amiable (and gay) butler, who woke me up each morning by rapping on my bedroom door, then entering with a silver tray laden with coffee, tea, and various breakfast goodies. In the afternoons, I helped the butler pick herbs in the herb garden and chatted with him in the kitchen while he prepared our meals. Between times, I lay out by the pool, reading.

In spite of everyone's welcoming nature, I felt completely out of place with Frederick and his friends on their Brideshead-Revisited estate. It was obvious that I was Frederick's boy-toy, but even at that I was a fraud. I wasn't putting out for him, and I couldn't help but think this must have been an embarrassment. How hard could it have been, after all, for a man with all of Frederick's money and connections to find a cute, gay boy in New York to spend a week with him in London in exchange for a little sex?

January 1980. Age 19. Italy.

SIX MONTHS AFTER MY DEBUT in *Death in Venice*, Margo Sappington called and said, "How'd you like to go work with me in Italy?"

It was a six-month contract with a new company called Associazione Teatro Emilia Romagna (ATER) Balleto in Reggio Emilia, a few hours east of Milan—or so Margo's agent, Peter Diggins, informed me as I sat in his apartment on the Upper West Side signing a contract that included an extremely generous weekly salary, per diem, and free lodging. What I didn't have the nerve to tell Peter Diggins was that, salary aside, I still wasn't much of a professional dancer.

Italians, I would soon come to discover, are unpredictable artistes who see themselves as unpredictable artistes, even if they're not quite deserving of the moniker. As such, they like to wait for inspiration, for the right "moment" to do things. Who knows when the hell this will be? The point is, if you're not in the mood to work, you don't work; you take a nice lunch, you talk, you drink, you laugh, you enjoy life knowing that at any moment, inspiration might strike and something beautiful will happen because you are, after all, Italian, and to be Italian means you have some unwavering belief that if greatness doesn't already infuse every pore of your being, it soon will. And why not? When you look around, all you see is history and beauty and confirmation of this fact. They must be doing something right.

I assumed, given his eagerness to start work the morning after a twenty-four-hour journey from New York that involved snow storms and closed airports and an unexpected bus ride from Genoa to Milan, the director of ATER Balleto, Amodeo Amodio, was going to be a stern taskmaster—but no. The reason he wanted us in the studio that first day was because he knew how Italian he was, and three months to crank out a twenty-minute ballet would be just about enough time for his fickle muses to get the job done.

For the six months that I would live in Reggio Emilia, I occupied the same room at the Hotel Posta where I passed my first night. I did my laundry in the sink and hung my clothes up on hangers or over the furniture in my room to dry. There were no laundromats in Reggio; in fact, I never saw a one in the entire country. A good many Italians had washing machines, but apparently they were still putting the finishing touches on the Italian dryer. In the meantime, the population hung their laundry up in the bathroom or the kitchen or on some contraption with a million appendages made especially for the purpose. When they weren't hanging up their laundry inside, they were hanging it outside on a line wherever there was a bit of unused airspace. The country was one gigantic clothesline.

There was a small refrigerator in my room at the Hotel Posta, so in addition to doing my laundry, I prepared meals. Nearly every morning, there was an outdoor market somewhere in town where one could buy fresh vegetables, an infinite number of gigantic wheels of Parmigiano Reggiano, dried fruits, bread, you name it. I often went to these markets early in the morning, a time when a faint, grayish-yellow light colored the mist that hung in the air. It was through this strange, medieval atmosphere that I came to know Italy.

Monks dressed in heavy, brown robes that were cinched at the waist with thick rope often traversed the ancient cobbles, seemingly levitating across the ground. Stooped old men ambled slowly along, hands holding rosary beads clasped behind their backs as they approached the daily newspaper that was laid open and pasted to the old walls surrounding the town square. Meanwhile, the many coffee emporia of Reggio were churning out cup after cup of cappuccino and espresso as fast as they could make them, windows running wet with condensation against the chill winter air.

Just prior to this trip, I'd become a vegetarian, and although I wasn't working hard in rehearsals (I had a very small part in Amodeo's ballet), I started losing weight. About five people in Italy knew what a vegetarian was, so trying to explain why I was not ordering meat, given my limited grasp of Italian, was a real chore. It was like saying you didn't believe in the Pope. I drew far less attention eating alone in my room, and the longer I was alone, the thinner I became and the harder it was for me to socialize or connect with the other dancers.

Oscar, a fifty-year-old vegetarian and veteran of the Italian ballet world, was one of my few friends. We bonded for gastronomic reasons and began taking regular train trips to Florence to shop at what seemed to be the country's only health food store. It was quite a forlorn endeavor, but I was only vaguely aware of this. When one of the dancers asked me about one of these trips and whether or not I'd seen the *David*, I replied, "Oh, no, we didn't see *David*. We bought lentils."

I became increasingly isolated in Reggio, and it wasn't solely my diet that set me apart. The company brought in an ancient ballerina from Russia by the name of Alla Shelest to be our ballet mistress, and her classes, in my opinion, were abominable. I had no idea she'd been a ballerina at the Kirov for over twenty-five years and a student of Agrippina Vaganova, or that she had danced with Nureyev; all I knew was that launching into grand battements at the beginning of barre at ten in the morning during the Italian winter and then, in the center, doing promenades on demi-pointe were not approaches to ballet training I found very pleasant or useful.

With no alternatives in sight, I stopped going to company class altogether. Instead, I did a barre alone in a small studio at the theater every day. And as sometimes happens in life, but seems to happen more often in Italian life, a traveling carnival installed itself in a park next to the theater, where, each day, while I was holed up in my lair doing my lonely barre, they would play Pink Floyd's *The Wall*.

"We don't need no ed-u-ca-tion. We don't need no thought control. No dark sarcasm in the classroom. Teacher leave them kids alone... Hey! Teacher! Leave them kids alone."

I rather tired of this song after a few months but had to admit the 4/4 tempo was perfect for tendus and a great many other exercises.

Ironically, Michael Kamen, a friend of Margo's, had worked with Pink Floyd on *The Wall,* and it was his music she would soon be using for her Italian ballet.

The twenty or so dancers that constituted ATER Balleto were divided more or less into thirds: American, French, and Italian. Because of the strong unions in Italy, it was necessary that the company have a certain number of Italians, and, of those, several were nearing middle age because at age fifty-something, Italian dancers were entitled to a pension for life. I found this strange but not altogether unfamiliar.

At the School of American Ballet, there were a few older City Ballet dancers who still took class, collected salaries, and performed (primarily character roles) with the company. One of these was Francisco Moncion. He would've been about sixty years old when I was at the school, but he came to Stanley Williams's class on a regular basis along with Jacques D'Amboise, who was forty-four at the time but still dancing, doing pirouettes on a flat foot as they'd been done since the last century.

I had two disparate reactions to seeing these older dancers in class. Ignorant of their former glories, I saw them as hangers-on who took up valuable space at the barre and had no real business being on stage. Conversely, it was refreshing to think that someone like Balanchine or a country like Italy (with a push from the very powerful Italian unions) still cared enough to give these older dancers a job and not send them off to the Alpo factory just because they were over forty.

I was too young then to really appreciate how important this kind of treatment might be. My career, after all, had barely begun. The idea that the day would come when I would face a perilous future beyond the dance world hadn't occurred to me, but the day would come, and, unlike the dancers mentioned, my livelihood was not going to be protected by George Balanchine or the Italian government.

By the time Margo arrived in Reggio Emilia, three months had passed. As she began work on her ballet, the veil of the misty, dark Italian winter lifted, and with it came the realization that I was not going to be reliving anything remotely close to what we'd created together in San Francisco. Christian Holder, Jan Hanniford, and Christopher Aponte would be riding in Margo's star vehicle. I would be left standing beside the road with my thumb out. The only bright spot on my horizon was that spring had finally arrived and with it something that looked vaguely like sunshine.

With the restaging of Leonid Massine's *Parade*, for which I was cast as the head of the horse, my performing repertoire was complete, and we soon began traveling by bus to the many charming towns and cities of northern Italy. What I remember wasn't the performing, for I was doing pitifully little of that; it was the long, post-performance bus rides back to Reggio in the middle of the night, the ancient Italian opera houses with their raked stages, and the terrible feeling of isolation I couldn't shake. I was trapped in Reggio, unable to train as I wanted to or was comfortable with, unable to perform as I'd hoped, unable to enjoy the moment for what it was because I was simply too young to see beyond my petty frustrations.

And then, in early summer, my cushy contract with ATER Balleto expired and I decided to take some of my hardly-earned loot and travel around Europe. Why not? I had nothing to rush back to New York for.

I set out with Christopher Aponte and two French dancers on the overnight train to Paris, where I settled into a tiny attic room near Pigalle. I took some ballet classes at the studio of Matt Maddox, a former student of Jack Cole's, but was so rakishly thin at that point and had had so few real ballet classes, I was in no condition to be auditioning for any companies. I thought I looked fabulous, however, and for the first time in a long time actually liked the body I saw in the mirror.

After a week or so in Paris, I set off on my own, going wherever my mood took me: Amsterdam, Vienna, Salzburg, Innsbruck, Munich, Budapest. I went skiing in Zermatt and took long meandering walks around Venice. I was serenaded by gypsy violinists in the most expensive restaurants in Budapest and visited the disturbing remains of Auschwitz. I listened to Mozart in Salzburg and walked through the catacombs of Vienna, but after five or six weeks of vagabonding, I'd had my fill of frivolity. It's awfully hard to indulge yourself on holiday when you feel you've done so little to deserve that holiday. Such was the moral of that European vacation.

1980. Age 19. New York City.

WHEN I RETURNED TO NEW YORK, I was aware that my life as a ballet dancer had changed. However tenuous my technical foundation may have been, I could not legitimately call myself a student at the School of American Ballet any longer. I was a professional dancer who was getting paid to dance, and, while I could take class at SAB whenever I pleased and did so on occasion, I understood that I didn't belong at the school any longer.

In point of fact, there is no formal graduation from The School of American Ballet. The advanced level students, men and women, are simultaneously hoping to be offered a spot in New York City Ballet and auditioning for other companies during their last year or two at the school. If no job offers are forthcoming, the dancer in question is typically asked to leave, whereupon he or she begins studying with a private teacher while continuing to look for a job.

In order to sustain themselves, these former SAB dancers do whatever it takes to survive. They wait tables. They become hostesses in restaurants. They model or take temp jobs. They dance wherever and whenever a paying job arises. In my case, I began working part time at a small gourmet food emporium called The Natural Source and studying with Melissa Hayden, whose daughter, Jennifer, had been a classmate of mine at NCSA.

Bear in mind that, from the moment I left home, I had always worked. And I worked because I didn't feel as if my father owed it to me to support me. Yes, my parents paid my rent and utilities once I moved to New York, but beyond that I always felt it was my obligation to help out. My first part-time job when I arrived in New York was at a gourmet delicatessen across from Lincoln Center. After my return from Italy, not only was it clear to me that I was no longer a student at SAB, it was also clear that I could make my own living as a dancer, and from that moment forward I began paying my own rent and all of my own bills.

A former ballerina with New York City Ballet, Melissa Hayden had a studio on Broadway near 61st Street on the top floor of a decrepit old building above John Martin's Steak House, Jon Devlin's Dancercise, and Gabriella Darvash's ballet school. It was a sweltering, un-air conditioned space with two pillars and a wooden floor that bounced like a trampoline, and I absolutely loved it. I loved the floor. I loved the heat. I loved Melissa's no-nonsense approach to teaching and her rotating band of teachers: Willie Burmann, Alfonso Cata, and Bobby Blankshine.

It was at Melissa's studio in the summer of 1980 that I first laid eyes on Charles France, the former assistant to ABT's longtime co-director, Oliver Smith. Charles was about to become the assistant to the new director at American Ballet Theatre, Mikhail Baryshnikov. Misha had been asked to take over ABT in the fall of 1980 when Lucia Chase, the founder of the company, stepped down after forty years at the helm. On the lookout for new dancers, Charles came to watch class one afternoon, accompanied by Richard Tanner, a former NYCB dancer whom I knew from SAB. Dick, it turned out, had been hired by Misha to be a ballet master at ABT.

Charles and Dick walked into Melissa's studio as everyone did: straight onto the dance floor from the elevator at the back of the room.

Crossing conspicuously to the front, they plopped themselves down into a couple of chairs, whereupon Charles pulled out a beautiful, bright red Spanish fan, pushed his large glasses back up his slippery nose, and began wafting the fan madly about his face in the one-hundred-degree heat.

Weighing in at nearly three hundred pounds, Charles France was clearly very uncomfortable, and no amount of fanning was going to change that. After observing a few combinations in the center, he stood up, sweat dripping from his brow, and both he and Dick took their leave. Later that evening, Dick called.

"We'd like you to come to the ABT audition for Misha. It's going to be held at Robert Denvers's studio in a couple of weeks. It's by invitation only. There'll be about thirty other boys there."

On the day of the audition, I took morning class at Melissa's, then walked a few blocks over to Robert Denvers's studio in the old Sofia Storage building on Columbus Avenue across from New York State Theater. Dick Tanner was going to be teaching class that day, and he'd prepared me in advance for what to expect.

"Misha wants all the boys to be able to do double saut de basques to the left and right, as well as clean double tours to both sides; beyond that, I don't know what he's looking for." A saut de basque is a traveling air turn not unlike what an ice skater might perform, save that one leg is in a bent position with the foot at the side of the knee. A tour en l'air is a revolving air turn begun from a stationary position.

Dick's class turned out to be simple and straightforward, a page straight from the Stanley Williams' playbook that I could have done in my sleep. Once we came off the barre, I made certain to stay near the front of the room so Misha could see me. We ran through petit allegro and pirouettes, and the more we moved, the better I felt. By the time we reached grand allegro and the aforementioned saut de basques and double tours, I attacked each step and repeated them over and over again. I wanted there to be no doubt in Misha's mind that I was more than capable of doing the things he required.

And then, just as my determination was boiling over into something verging on the Napoleonic, class ended. Dick stood at the front of the room and thanked all of us for coming. We applauded, as is the habit after every ballet class, our shirts and the audition numbers we'd safety-pinned to our chests fading in our collective sweat. Misha thanked all of us for coming and said he had all of our names and phone numbers. We would be hearing from them.

I lingered around, hoping Misha would speak to me and give me some indication of where I stood, and, sure enough, he came over, and we shook hands. He knew me from the almost daily classes he took with Stanley Williams during his fifteen-month tenure at City Ballet. We weren't complete strangers.

"Nice to see you, Mikey," he said. "Tank you for coming."

"Thank you for inviting me."

And with that, he sauntered off, our penetrating conversation a harbinger of things to come.

⸻

While Dick didn't exactly give me the thumbs up, I knew I'd made a good impression, and, more importantly, I had no regrets. Whatever talent I possessed had been entirely exposed, and the outcome was now out of my hands.

"He hasn't made up his mind yet," Dick said to me over the phone later. "And he may not make a decision very quickly. That's a good thing. He liked you. He's just a bit concerned about your size."

"My size? I'm the same size he is!"

"I know. But he wants a bigger corps de ballet, and you don't really fit into the corps de ballet at your height, so there's a problem. One possibility is that we might take this other boy, Raymond Perrin. He's your size, and together you would look fine doing corps de ballet things opposite one another. He also has to find enough soloist things for you to do to justify hiring you. So it's not that simple."

"Soloist things. That sounds fine with me."

"Look, I'm doing the best I can. I'm working every angle. But you can't push Misha. Ultimately he's going to make up his own mind, and in the meantime you're just going to have to be patient. I'll call you when I hear something."

As the days passed, I tried to remain calm, but the longer it took, the less likely it seemed I would get in. My mother, needless to say, was on tenterhooks. My dad, as was his habit, said what he often said: "Well, Mike, if it's meant to be, it's meant to be."

I continued to go to class every day at Melissa's and work several evenings a week scooping ice cream at The Natural Source. It was the middle of July, the ice cream trade was booming, and my right forearm had grown to the size of a small tree. The only upside to this job was that it took my mind off Misha and ABT for a few nanoseconds every evening. And then, one afternoon, about a week after the audition, Dick called.

"Why don't you come over after work tonight?" he said. "I've got some news."

Around midnight, I left The Natural Source and walked up Columbus Avenue to Dick's apartment. I felt a little sick to my stomach, but at the same time I was practically flying. Dick's voice hadn't betrayed a hint of what the outcome might be, and when he opened the door to his apartment it was more of the same. He gave me a brief tour of the very stylish digs he shared with his boyfriend from New York City Ballet, then veered off into the kitchen. "Make yourself comfortable," he said.

"Dick," I replied, "about the only thing that would make me comfortable right now would be anesthesia."

I heard the refrigerator door open, then watched as Dick placed a bottle of Champagne and two glasses on the counter. "I thought you'd like to celebrate."

August. 1980.

AFTER BEING ACCEPTED into American Ballet Theatre, I returned home to my parents' seventeen-acre farm near Graham, North Carolina. While I was off becoming a ballet dancer and deflecting the advances of various and sundry homosexuals, my father had become the next Eddie Albert. By day he worked in the white-collar world of Western Electric; by night and on weekends he sat on his John Deere tractor, sculpting every inch of his seventeen-acre Haw River estate into a larger version of the suburban utopia he'd spent his entire adult life striving to cultivate.

I was relieved. Relieved that I was no longer expected to help my father keep nature in line (although I did on occasion) and equally relieved that all of my determination and hard work had finally paid off. The dream I'd harbored since age thirteen, when Terry Shields told me I needed to make a choice between sports and ballet, had come true. I was giddy. I was proud. I was afraid. I was feeling a hundred different emotions from one moment to the next. The one feeling I had above all others, however, was that now I was *someone*.

What I'd been before I was *someone* was, in my mind, just another struggling ballet dancer, one of thousands in New York who are always taking class, always auditioning, always hoping that soon they'll have a job that doesn't involve scooping ice cream or slicing Nova Scotia Salmon or sweeping out apartment buildings or staying up all night bussing tables at Studio 54—all jobs I had before I became a dancer who would forever be defined by three words: American Ballet Theatre.

Act II

Fall 1980. Age 20. New York City.

WHEN I JOINED ABT in September of 1980, it had no home. The historic old ABT studios at 61st and Broadway had been closed, the building demolished. The new studios at 890 Broadway were nearing completion, but until then, the company was forced to use spaces all over New York City. Radio City Music Hall was my destination that first day, and my new boss, Mikhail Baryshnikov, had asked my former teacher, Stanley Williams, to teach company class for the entire first week. This was, perhaps, the only thing I drew comfort from.

On a crisp, sunny Monday morning, I rode my bicycle from my apartment at 56th Street and 9th Avenue over to Rockefeller Center. This particular bike was a childhood treasure: an orange Schwinn ten-speed I bought with my own hard-earned yard-mowing money when I was ten years old. As I locked it on 51st Street near the backstage entrance to Radio City, I thought about how many times I had washed and waxed it over the years, fretting about its every blemish. It seemed fragile and out of place in New York City and even more so out there on the street, but I had a good lock, and it was in plain sight. It would be fine, I reassured myself.

After signing in with the guard, I found an elevator and rode it up into the heart of Radio City. Backstage areas of theaters are generally well-ravaged arenas of peeling paint; scuffed floors; and all manner of dramatic bric-a-brac sitting around gathering dust, rust, and ruin, and this part of Radio City was no exception. It was a windowless maze of dimly lit corridors, theater crates, and mysterious doorways that went to even more mysterious places, all of which I took in at a glance as I walked toward the dressing room, the old wooden hallways creaking beneath my solitary feet.

After changing into my dance clothes, I made my way to a studio that, like everything else at Radio City thus far, was utterly ghoulish. Dim lights cast long shadows across a room that must've been a hundred feet long but a mere twenty feet deep. Painted onto its wooden surface and traveling its length was a ragged black line. It was here, I surmised, that the famous Rockettes lined up to kick their legs and do whatever else Rockettes did.

I sat down on the floor and started stretching. I still had about forty-five minutes to kill before class started and figured I would need every second of it to gear myself up for the big event. After a few minutes, a beautiful, young black man arrived. He had dark, perfect skin and a lithe, muscular physique that glistened in the faint light. Carrying a portable barre into the center of the room, he put it down and looked over at me. "Guess I'm early bird number two," he said.

This was Ronald Perry, formerly of the Dance Theater of Harlem. Like me, he had just joined ABT. He was about to become one of Misha's favorites, dancing the lead in Balanchine's *Theme and Variations,* among many other principal roles. Ronald was ABT's only black male dancer and, unavoidably, someone who would be compared to one of the few black men to inhabit the classical ballet world—his former boss, Arthur Mitchell.

As ten o'clock drew near, more and more dancers arrived, and the atmosphere in the studio changed from suicidal to celebratory. The summer layoff was over, and everyone was giddily reconnecting, sharing vacation stories, and casting the odd glance at all the newcomers. Many of these dancers were people whose faces and names were familiar to me from the few performances of ABT I'd seen at the Met: Terry Orr, Cynthia Gregory, Jonas Cage, Jolinda Menendez, Marianna Tcherkassky, Fernando Bujones, Gelsey Kirkland, and Misha, of course.

Stanley Williams arrived in his usual outfit with his usual sense of urgency (five minutes late). Nothing had changed. He went through the ritual of lighting his pipe and chit chatting with Misha; his de facto pianist, Lynn Stanford; and some of the other ABT dancers he was familiar with.

When class finally began, I felt as if I'd been transported back in time to SAB, albeit an SAB without Peter Martins to put my particular tracing paper over, an SAB filled entirely with unfamiliar faces, all of whom could link steps together and dance with a cohesiveness and beauty I'd rarely seen before.

Once we got into the center, I was about as far from SAB as you could get. The room was packed and the dancers uniformly stellar. I tried to look like I knew what I was doing and portray some self-confidence, but, honestly, I felt overwhelmed. I stood at the back and found it virtually impossible to concentrate. I didn't want to be too pushy, so I waited for the older dancers to take their turns before I did. With eighty people in class, this meant that I hardly danced at all.

When class was over, I had my first rehearsal in the same Rockette room—a new staging of *Raymonda* divertissements that Misha was presiding over. I would be in the Mazurka. The Mazurka itself originally came from Poland, and the word is a reference to its musical structure; a ¾ time signature (which is a waltz) with an accent on the second or third beat. It is a folk dance or *character* dance, and as such, the dancers, both men and women, wear shoes with heels, rather than ballet slippers or pointe shoes.

I had had character classes throughout my training and always enjoyed them, so I felt as if I would enjoy working in character shoes again, but after about five minutes it became abundantly clear that our honeymoon with Misha was over.

"Meg! Vad you doink?" he hollered at Meg Potter. She looked at him like a deer caught in headlights. "Not like dat," he said, imitating her un-Mazurka-like movements, "like dis." He then demonstrated how he wanted her to do it, stomping his foot on the ground and rocking his body and head, before finishing with a flick of his wrist and an upraised arm.

We went through the same phrases over and over again, but no matter how many times we did them, Misha was rarely able to wipe that somebody-just-shot-my-cat look off his face. We weren't Russian enough, apparently, and he seemed perplexed by the fact that his new crop of personally-selected dancers couldn't grasp a simple thing like a Mazurka, a dance any five-year-old kid back in St. Petersburg could do in his sleep.

After that first eye-opening hour, I escaped the depressing confines of Radio City and biked uptown to Harkness House for a rehearsal of Antony Tudor's *Jardin Aux Lilas*. I arrived well before the appointed hour again so I could be warmed up and ready to make the kind of stellar impression I'd already made in company class.

And again I found myself in familiar territory, alone in a studio, albeit this time in a mirrored ballroom inside what was once the palatial home of Edward and Mary Harkness. I sat on the floor feeling as I often did at Harkness House: that Louis XIV himself might suddenly burst in and suggest we go for a hunt. But Louis never did burst in. In fact, no one did. I stretched for what seemed an awfully long time and at some point began to get worried. Surely, it was time for rehearsal by now? Finally, Danilo Radojevic opened the door. "Are you Michael? Rehearsal has started in another studio."

The hunt, obviously, was over.

Once I got to this second ballroom and apologized to Mr. Tudor, not much appeared to be happening. Tudor stood at the front of the room dressed in slacks and a dress shirt, his bald head and ramrod straight posture a perfect compliment to the calm, authoritative British tone he used to dissect what was happening. His only words to me were, "Follow Scott," i.e. Scott Schlexer, a boy in the corps de ballet. Everyone was moving in a circle. The movements were subtle. It seemed so simple, yet Tudor kept going over and over it, occasionally filleting a dancer with his sardonic sense of humor. Nothing was said about the technical aspects of the choreography, really—it was more about a feeling, a sense of the movement he was looking for, a tilt of the head, an inclination of the body. I was confused. After my earlier experience with Misha, this was dance on a completely different scale, and one that I was totally unfamiliar with.

I found myself getting cold, mimicking Scott's movements off to the side as the group went round and round. I tried to look diligent and hard working, but none of what I was doing seemed to matter one iota to Tudor. All I knew about dancing thus far revolved around executing the choreography to the best of my ability; that's what I thought dancing was about. Whatever Tudor was interested in had very little to do with the steps, but at the same time it had everything to do with the steps.

When rehearsal was over, I wasn't remotely tired physically. And while I might have learned a lot, I also knew I hadn't learned much. I hadn't a clue whether Tudor even noticed me.

From Harkness House, I biked back down to Radio City for a character class with Diana Joffe, a taciturn, raven-haired woman whom Misha had just hired and whose raison d'être in the new ABT seemed to be to spare Misha an aneurism and turn all of us ABT rookies into the Lakers and Celtics of the Czardas and Mazurka.

At the end of that first day, I went home perplexed. I had imagined beforehand that I was going to feel some sense of euphoria about this day, a euphoria that would lead headlong into eternal bliss because I was, at long last, in the great American Ballet Theatre, but all I really felt was baffled and bewildered. I consoled myself with the thought that at least I was getting to work with Mr. Tudor, one of the most important choreographers of the twentieth century and someone I'd always greatly admired. Sometime during the evening, Dick Tanner called.

"Michael, you don't have to go back to rehearsals for *Lilac Garden*. Tudor didn't think you were right for the part."

Not right for the part? What part? As far as I could tell, I didn't even have a part. I was just an understudy. Needless to say, I was crushed. How bad did you have to be to be excised as an understudy?

I went to bed that night feeling as if my first day at ABT had been much like that ragged black Rockette line on the floor back at Radio City: long and full of surprising gaps that no one was going to be filling in anytime soon.

And then, the following day, after another one of Stanley's classes and another hour of Misha pulling his hair out as we botched his beloved Mazurka and another one of Diana Joffe's character-less character classes, I exited the backstage door of Radio City and looked out at the bike rack on the sidewalk. It was empty.

ABT Primer

MIKHAIL BARYSHNIKOV WAS THIRTY-TWO years old when he became the artistic director of American Ballet Theatre. He had been dancing in the West for six years, four with ABT and fifteen months with New York City Ballet. He had no directing experience, but he was the most famous dancer in the world, and as that dancer, he was near the height of his physical powers. The knee surgeries that would begin in 1982 and continue for many years had yet to put a damper on his remarkable abilities.

When I joined Ballet Theatre, I knew nothing about the history of the company and very little about Misha. To my young eyes, Misha was simply the dancer I knew from the School of American Ballet, and Donald Kendall (chairman of PepsiCo and executive director of Ballet Theatre) was the rich old guy with white hair who, a few weeks after I joined the company, invited all of us up to the PepsiCo Headquarters in Purchase, New York. There, we had a huge picnic and ran around on acres of grass dodging piles of slippery goose shit, before heading back to the city with a slew of paraphernalia emblazoned with the Pepsi logo.

Lucia Chase, meanwhile, was the old woman I saw at the two unsuccessful auditions I'd had for ABT while she was still director of the company and then, after joining the company, on the rare occasion when she would unexpectedly appear at rehearsals or backstage.

Whenever this happened, the older dancers who knew Lucia would flock around to say hello, but nothing was ever said to the rest of us about her contribution to the company. This, I eventually came to realize, was just how things went at ABT.

One of the many surprising things I would learn about ABT was that they could not require any dancer to attend class. It was, however, made clear to me by Peter Fonseca, the boy I understudied in many ballets because we were the same size, that if I wanted to make a good impression on Misha and be asked back at the end of the year, I had best be in company class.

So when we finally abandoned Radio City Music Hall in the fall of 1980 and moved downtown to our unfinished home at 890 Broadway (where the men and women began taking class separately), virtually everyone—save a few of the principal dancers whose jobs were a certainty—came to Jurgen Schneider's men's class every morning at ten o'clock.

Despite our new union agreement and the $400 a week I was making as a new member of the company, I was ostensibly on "probation" and could be fired at any time for any reason. If I made it into my second year, I would be given the same job security that everyone else enjoyed—namely, I could only be fired for "just cause."

Just cause was a bit of a gray area at Ballet Theatre. It might mean gaining a lot of weight or losing too much weight. It might mean missing rehearsals or performances without a legitimate reason. It might mean drinking or doing drugs to such a degree that it was distinctly noticeable and compromised your ability to do your job. Doing the job and doing it well was what mattered. If you could manage that, you were given a long leash at American Ballet Theatre to do just about anything.

In a large ballet company like ABT or New York City Ballet, new dancers, even if they were soloists or principal dancers elsewhere, were generally given corps de ballet roles to dance, along with other roles of greater importance to understudy when they first joined. The parts you were given in either case were largely determined by your size, look, and body type, but also by what sort of future the director envisioned for you.

A girl like Susan Jaffe, who came from ABT's second company the same year I did and in whom Misha saw greatness from the get-go, was asked to understudy Gelsey Kirkland in *Pas d'Esclave* the moment she set foot in the door. The standout part I was given during the 1980-81 season was as the Gypsy Boy in *Don Quixote*, a small role I shared with the astounding Swedish soloist Johan Renvall.

Johan, who was essentially competing with Misha for roles, had already so thoroughly juiced the choreography for the Gypsy Boy with his helicopter jumps and otherworldly turning ability that I knew there wasn't a snowball's chance in hell I was going to impress anyone, but somehow I had to come up with something.

There were several moments in the first act of Misha's version of *Don Quixote* when the Gypsy Boy took the spotlight, and in each of those moments, something flashy was expected. There was very little set choreography per se, just a pattern on the stage to follow.

I asked Johan to teach me his helicopter jump, but his technical suggestions were so perfunctory and my initial attempts such a disaster, I gave up. After rummaging through my small bag of tricks, I came up with a few different jumps and turns, things I'd picked up at SAB from some of the boys in New York City Ballet.

When the time came for me to rehearse in front of Misha, I was very self-conscious. I knew I was going to be compared unfavorably to Johan, but the reality was no one had the time to teach me the types of acrobatic tricks I needed to learn, because none of the ballet masters at ABT knew how to do them. Male dancers of the previous generation didn't do helicopter jumps or barrel turns or double revoltads. (A helicopter jump, by the way, is essentially a traveling split jump wherein the legs scissor while the body rotates through a revolution or more in the air.)

The only people qualified to teach the types of tricks smaller men such as myself were expected to produce in Ballet Theatre were dancers such as Johan or Misha or Danny Radojevic—the dancers who knew how to do them. As a consequence, this type of teaching was very haphazard and generally reduced to what I got from Johan—a few suggestions after class.

I walked into Ballet Theatre thinking I would be guided through this process, because that was the pattern I had become accustomed to as a student. It would take me a while to figure out and accept the fact that, from the moment I signed a contract with American Ballet Theatre, it was all going to be up to me.

After several *Don Q* performances, I assumed everything was fine, but then Misha pulled me aside just before a show one night and said, "Mikey, vad you doink is too classical. Movement need to be sometink like Gypsy Boy vud do, naught Prince in Svan Lake. You understand?"

I nodded my head. Was I supposed to change everything *now*? Five minutes before curtain? I was stumped. I really had no idea how to make the double revoltads I was doing look like the double revoltads a gypsy boy would do, because gypsies, as far as I knew, didn't do double revoltads. But there you have it—I was expected to come up with something, somehow, even if it was five minutes before curtain.

I farted around, trying to make what I was doing look less "classical," and when the performance got under way, that's what I did. Misha never mentioned whether or not he was pleased with what I was doing, so I assumed it was okay. This, I eventually learned, was just how Misha operated. If he didn't like something, he would tell you. If he did, you weren't likely to hear much, if anything.

━━━━━━━━━━━━━━━━━━━

During those first few months of rehearsal in New York, I was an absolute wreck. I didn't let on that I was an absolute wreck, because I wanted to appear capable and hardworking, and I wanted to be more than just a "one and done" dancer at ABT, but the daily ordeal of men's class with Misha and Misha's favorite teacher, Jurgen Schneider, was almost more than I could bear.

Without a doubt, Jurgen, who came to Ballet Theatre from the Munich Opera, was a likable man who could be very funny at times, but we never hit it off. I found his class archaic and his manner condescending. In spite of how I felt about Jurgen, I knew I had a lot of work to do if I was going to stay in the company, much less get out of the corps de ballet. I'd been able to get through my classes at SAB because I'd had two years to get accustomed to the teaching at SAB and I was good at covering up my weaknesses, but there was no covering up of weaknesses at American Ballet Theatre.

With all due respect to Stanley Williams, nobody in ABT cared whether you turned without turning or jumped by going *ovah.* Could you dance? Could you sustain your focus and your energy and link movements together no matter how awkward so the choreography looked seamless and effortless? Could you present something clearly with all the parts of your body operating in harmony? And could you do all of those things on the exact place on stage where you were supposed to be and in unison with any number of other dancers? And, finally, could you get through Jurgen Schneider's men's class without Misha wincing and saying something to you like, "Mikey, vad you doink?"

Mikhail Baryshnikov
photographed by Kenn Duncan
with the company mascot, Chelsea

ABT Souvenir Program 1980.
Photo credit: Kenn Duncan

Peter Fonseca

A S THE 1980 REHEARSAL PERIOD PROGRESSED, the weather in New York grew predictably more ominous. The days grew shorter and colder. The sky was always gray, or maybe it just seemed that way to me as I stared out the grimy third-floor windows of American Ballet Theatre toward the ABC Carpet store across the street.

Every morning, I woke up in my apartment at 56th Street and 9th Avenue filled with a feeling of dread. I was intimidated by the caliber of the dancers at ABT and continually fretted about the impression I was making on Misha. I hung on his every word, tried to interpret his every glance. I wasn't accustomed to Jurgen's class or his style of teaching, so my body felt out of sorts. I struggled to get warm and stay loose. One of the few bright spots on my ABT horizon was Peter Fonseca.

Peter joined American Ballet Theatre in 1976. Of Costa Rican descent, he trained with his mother, Hortensia, at the Washington Academy of Ballet and later at the American Ballet Theatre School. His most distinguishing moment prior to Misha's arrival took place during a performance of *Don Quixote* at the Metropolitan Opera House in September of 1979.

Jennifer Dunning, a dance critic for *The New York Times*, wrote: "This production of *Don Quixote* is notoriously jinxed, and, at the start of the wedding pas de deux, Mr. Radojevic developed cramps in both legs and was unable to continue. Yoko Ichino, his Kitri, collared Peter Fonseca, who was dancing one of the wedding guests, and called to him, 'Fake it,' and together they finished without a single major partnering flub. Mr. Fonseca sailed through an extemporized variation with touching eagerness and the technical bravado of a seasoned principal. Charles Maple alternated in the coda with great aplomb."

I first saw Peter at the School of American Ballet in 1977. He came to Stanley Williams's class every few months, dressed in a startling array of tropical colors; set against his café-au-lait skin and the black-and-white dress code the SAB boys adhered to, he looked like a macaw among a sea of penguins.

Peter did not possess a great jump, but he could turn like a top in both directions, and in Stanley's class, where turning was a central focus, that ability drew attention from everyone, Stanley included. When I asked him once where he learned to turn so well, he said, "In my mother's kitchen, on the slippery linoleum floor, in my socks."

It wasn't merely that Peter could turn, however. He was incredibly coordinated and could tackle the most difficult combinations with ease. What further distinguished him from the SAB students and the New York City Ballet dancers I was accustomed to seeing was that he was in American Ballet Theatre, the company with the international roster of superstars that traveled all over the country and the world and performed at the grandiose Metropolitan Opera House, a place few of us at SAB had ever set foot in because SAB never handed out free tickets to see American Ballet Theatre, they handed out free tickets to see New York City Ballet.

After I joined the company, Peter took me under his wing, carefully teaching me his roles and making sure I understood the counts, the spacing, and the important nuances in the choreography. When I mentioned the struggles I was having in Jurgen's class, he said, "When we have a free afternoon, we're going to go uptown and take class with my teacher, David Howard."

David Howard. There was that name again. It had been, what, seven years since that moment in my parents' bedroom back in Andover when Fred Alexon advised me to go to New York and study with David Howard? Seven years of struggling to figure things out on my own because I was too stubborn and too stupid to take a step back, too mistrustful to believe the sound advice of someone like Mimi Paul.

David

ORN AND RAISED IN ENGLAND, David Howard, née David
Charles Edwards, performed in radio shows, films, and commer-
cials as a child, before joining Sadler's Wells Theatre Ballet (now the
Royal Ballet). At the invitation of Rebekah Harkness, he came to New
York in 1966 to teach and later direct the Harkness Ballet School. It
was there that he met Jo Anna Kneeland.

While working on the film *Great Moments from the Dance*, Jo Anna
Kneeland began using a device called a Movieola, an editing machine
that allowed film editors to slow films down and cut them at exactly the
frame desired. During this process, she spent hours and hours watching
dancers move in slow motion. What this revealed to her was that what
most teachers were saying about technique was completely contrary to
what dancers were actually doing. This discovery was the beginning of
a kinesthetic approach to the teaching of classical ballet, an approach
David adopted and built his reputation around.

When I met David, his studio was located on the third floor of a
small building on West 62nd Street between Broadway and Columbus Avenue. It was a large rectangular space with a white Marley floor
and a couple of pillars near the back wall. A number of gigantic, colorful posters of women from the world of dance and theater were hung

around the room. Yma Sumac, the Peruvian soprano with a four-octave range, was featured in one. David knew her personally.

During my first class with David (and the fifty to sixty dancers who attended every one of his classes), I felt better physically and emotionally than I had in weeks. The barre exercises were simply constructed and moved sensibly towards more complex rhythms and difficulty. Lynn Stanford, the pianist who played for Stanley Williams's classes at SAB, also played for David, and his gift for selecting popular music, standards, classical, and jazz was just as helpful and entertaining as it had been in Stanley's class.

Unlike most of the ballet teachers I'd had in my life, David offered up no mysterious metaphors about animals, vegetables, or minerals; or ridiculous entreaties to copy someone else. He didn't point out the obvious. He didn't tell you to do something because *that's just how it's done* or *that's how I did it*. He led you with the structure of his class and his exercises in directions that allowed your body to work more efficiently. There were logical explanations as to why things worked or didn't work, and encouragement to use energy patterns and gravity to help facilitate movement. If those explanations didn't suffice, David didn't pretend he had all the answers. "Figure it out for yourself," he'd say.

In the classroom, David was authoritative but good-natured. He didn't patronize or mock the students unless someone was really misbehaving. When he got to know me better, he would walk by during the barre and mutter something suggestive, but this was always done with tongue firmly implanted in cheek. He had a wry sense of humor, which he used to great effect, allowing the class to laugh at their fears and foibles. On the rare occasion when he was perturbed by a dancer's approach or behavior, he wasted no time putting them in their place, or quietly telling them after class not to come back or to move to a less advanced class.

After that first class with David, I knew I had found a teacher in whom I was willing to put my complete faith and trust, and I put my faith and trust in him because I knew that he would be able to fill the gaps in my porous technical foundation with logic and reasoning, not smoke and mirrors.

This, essentially, is the great hurdle every ballet dancer has to overcome: that of putting the development of their body, technique, and, ultimately, career into the hands of one particular individual and his or her approach. It is like a marriage, in this respect, and for a ballet dancer, it carries nearly as much import.

David Howard and Michael Langlois outside of Steps.
New York City. Around 2008.

Revelations

ONE OF MANY THINGS THAT SURPRISED ME about American Ballet Theatre was just how much I was expected to learn on my own. There was no organized mentoring or coaching system for new dancers. You observed the older dancers you were often called upon to understudy and learned through a combination of mimicry and baptism by fire. No one ever sat me down and told me what my weaknesses were or how I might remedy them or what I needed to do to get ahead.

Individual coaching within Ballet Theatre was generally reserved for soloists or principal dancers, many of whom also received private coaching with their favorite teachers in New York over and above what they got within Ballet Theatre. If you were in the corps de ballet, there generally came a moment when you were offered a standout role or were thrown into the spotlight because of an injury to another dancer, and, depending on the importance of that role and/or the availability of a ballet master, you might get some individual help, but you might not.

If no coaching or rehearsals were offered, a dancer was forced to rely on someone who knew the role or on videotape, if it existed. The dancers at Ballet Theatre, by and large, were accustomed to doing things this way, and they almost always stepped forward to help those who needed help (for the good of the company, of course). This help, however, was generally limited to teaching the choreography and the spacing. The rest was up to the individual.

I didn't give any of this much thought at the time, because I was thinking what most dancers who get accepted into American Ballet Theatre or New York City Ballet are thinking: *Pinch me! Am I really here?* And besides, it's human nature to want to look like you know what you're doing, so you rarely bother admitting how much help you probably need.

In Ballet Theatre's defense, there was never enough time, money, or personnel to handle the myriad issues individual dancers and the company faced on a daily basis. When principal dancers at a company like ABT were complaining about having to fight to get coaching or rehearsals, you realized that as a corps de ballet dancer, you were truly on your own.

━━━━━━━━━━━━━━━

One of the greatest misconceptions about the ballet world is that it's rife with limp-wristed queers running around in pink tutus and tiaras singing "It's Raining Men." The fact is there were twenty men in American Ballet Theatre's corps de ballet in 1980, and of those, ten were gay. Four years later, there would be twenty-five men in the corps de ballet, and of those, eight would be gay. A few short weeks after joining Ballet Theatre, one of those gay men invited me over to his loft for dinner, and from that moment forward I became immersed in his world.

Peter Fonseca's closest friends in Ballet Theatre were Robbie La-Fosse, David Cuevas, and Greg Osborne. All of these boys were gay. More importantly, they were older and more experienced in the company, so I looked up to them. They, in turn, looked up to Peter, someone who always seemed to be one or two steps ahead of just about everyone at ABT.

While most of the dancers in the company lived in quasi-civilized rental apartments, Peter bought a loft in the Garment District long before loft living was fashionable and began renovating it himself. He ripped down walls, stripped the ceilings, and refinished the concrete floors. With what remained of his free time, he sewed costumes, made headdresses, and created fantastic masks. He collected Fiestaware long before it became popular, was a phenomenal chef, and bought his clothes and shoes at New York's most exclusive men's boutiques. As the holiday season approached, he began making his own Christmas ornaments for the sizable tree he always bought. In addition, he made big batches of his own eggnog, a Costa Rican concoction he called Rum Popa. He bottled this in old glass flasks and gave it away as gifts, and none of this, as far as I could tell, was done for show. It was done because Peter appreciated quality and beauty in every facet of his life.

As the long rehearsal period in the fall of 1980 progressed, Peter and I became almost inseparable, and I began to suspect he was falling in love with me. I wasn't harboring concerns that I was in the closet myself, because every day that I was with Peter, I was forced to confront the fact that, no matter how much I liked him, I simply wasn't attracted to him in a sexual way. I knew our relationship was lopsided, but I didn't know what to do about it, so I did nothing. I let it go on, hoping Peter would come to accept the fact that I would be his friend and nothing more.

═══════════════

After three months in American Ballet Theatre, I had learned a number of corps de ballet roles, and when December rolled around, I packed my bags; said goodbye to my roommate, Jeff; and boarded an Amtrak train at Penn Station with most of the dancers in the company. Our destination: the Kennedy Center in Washington, D.C.

My repertoire was as follows:

Understudy: *Voluntaries*, Glen Tetley

Understudy: Red Cowboy: *Billy the Kid*, Eugene Loring

Corps de Ballet: *Concerto*, Kenneth MacMillan

Drinking Companion: *Prodigal Son*, George Balanchine

Gypsy Boy: *Don Quixote*, Mikhail Baryshnikov

Fakir: *La Bayadère*, Natalia Makarova

Corps de Ballet: *Les Noces*, Jerome Robbins

Corps de Ballet: *Les Patineurs*, Frederick Ashton

Understudy: *Push Comes to Shove*, Twyla Tharp

Cowboy: *Rodeo*, Agnes de Mille

Soldier, Child, Buffoon: *Nutcracker*, Mikhail Baryshnikov

Corps de Ballet: *Theme and Variations*, George Balanchine

Peasant: *Giselle, Swan Lake*

Opening Night

THE KENNEDY CENTER IN WASHINGTON D.C. is a gigantic, white complex of three theaters overlooking the Potomac River: the Concert Hall, the Opera House, and the Eisenhower Theater. The Opera House, where Ballet Theatre performed, had one very large rehearsal space where the entire company could take class, along with one smaller studio. Including the stage itself, the company had a total of three spaces for rehearsals and class. With six studios at our disposal back in New York, this arrangement on tour was insufficient, so the company rented space in local ballet studios. It was impractical to get a large group of dancers to and from these outside studios, so they were used exclusively for the soloists and principal dancers.

Because opening night was just days away, the majority of our rehearsals at the Kennedy Center were dress rehearsals on stage with a full orchestra. One of these rehearsals was for *Pas d'Esclave,* an excerpt from *Le Corsaire* that would showcase the phenomenal talents of Gelsey Kirkland and her partner, Patrick Bissell. When neither dancer showed up for their dress rehearsal because they were back in New York on a cocaine bender and couldn't get on the train to Washington, Misha fired them. This caused quite a stir within the company, but that stir had little affect on me. I had my own worries, and Susan Jaffe, who stepped out of the corps de ballet to dance with Alexander Godunov in *Pas D'Esclave*, had quite a few more.

The program for my first performance with American Ballet Theatre on December 10, 1980 was Ashton's *Les Rendezvous*, Balanchine's *Prodigal Son, Pas D'Esclave,* and Twyla Tharp's *Push Comes to Shove*. I would dance the role of a drinking companion in *Prodigal* and understudy Warren Conover in *Push Comes to Shove*. Warren, as you may recall, was the mysterious blonde dancer (boyfriend of Fred) who appeared at my local ballet school back in Andover when I was just twelve years old.

Prodigal was set to go on around nine o'clock. My plan was to begin my preparations ninety minutes before I had to be onstage, allowing half an hour for makeup and an hour to warm up. My warm-up consisted of a barre I gave to myself or did to a taped recording of one of David Howard's barres, scores of which I made back in New York before the tour began. Many dancers in Ballet Theatre traveled with audiotapes of their teachers' classes, Maggie Black and David Howard being the two most common. During the long months on tour, these taped barres and classes were a comforting reminder of home. They made the nightly chore of warming up for a performance a bit easier. They also made it possible for the Maggie Black dancers (Martine Van Hamel, Kevin McKenzie, Robert Hill, etc.) or the David Howard dancers (Cynthia Harvey, Peter Fonseca, Wes Chapman, myself, etc.) to band together for a barre or an entire class should they feel the need.

At seven thirty p.m. on opening night, our wardrobe master, Bob Holloway, handed me a costume and a bald cap, and I was on my own. I had no idea how to do my makeup as a drinking companion and sat there wondering if anyone at all was going to be helping me through the process. As one of the smallest boys in the corps de ballet, I was the lead Goon, as we called ourselves—the one responsible for leading the other boys out and initiating much of the choreography, so I was, understandably, a bit nervous.

We had rehearsed this Balanchine masterpiece extensively back in New York with John Taras and Richard Tanner, both of whom hailed from City Ballet and knew the ballet inside and out, but those rehearsals had all been conducted with solo piano. I would soon be hearing Prokofiev's devilishly complex music with full orchestra for just the second time, and I was nearly apoplectic about losing track of the counts, none of which were remotely similar to the tried and true 4/4s, 2/4s, and 3/4s that are the bedrock of classical ballet. And I knew that if I lost track of those counts, the whole ballet was going down the shitter and my career at ABT along with it.

No one at Ballet Theatre suggested I get the orchestration and listen to it at home to familiarize myself with the music, but, as I mentioned earlier, this was standard operating procedure at ABT. By the same token, no one had given me a list of makeup supplies I should buy or bothered to ask if I knew how to apply makeup, let alone the very particular makeup the Goons were expected to wear.

I had pancake, mascara, eyeliner, shadow, and lipstick, but in my brief performing career, I had never really been taught how to put any of it on correctly. Thankfully, Peter Fonseca saw the look on my face, and, though he had his own concerns getting ready to dance one of the Prodigal's servants, he took the time to show me how to erase my eyebrows using good old-fashioned Ivory Soap, then helped with the basics of foundation and shadowing. When all was complete, he said, "I know a great makeup store here in Washington. I'll take you there."

It struck me as a bit presumptuous that a company as prestigious as ABT would place so much responsibility on my shoulders, but by the time the curtain had risen, the music was playing, and Robbie LaFosse was out onstage plowing through ABT's world premiere of *Prodigal*, it was a little late in the day to be pointing this out to them.

When the musical phrases arrived that signaled the entrance of the nine Drinking Companions. I stood at the front edge of the downstage right wing, feeling sick to my stomach. It had been my dream to dance in American Ballet Theatre, and in about fifteen seconds that dream was about to come true. What a nightmare.

Raymond Perrin, my bookend in the corps de ballet, stood behind me. He put his hands on my waist, and we inched forward. The other seven boys were lined up behind, waiting for me. Eight, seven, six, five, four, three, two...

And out I came, stomping out the rhythm in my absurdly deep, absurdly turned-out second position as Prokofiev's music lurched forward, its odd timbre a perfect reflection of the off-kilter characters that were then making their presence felt. Lights from the opposite wing glared into my eyes. I could make out a few body shapes, dancers who were watching or waiting to make their entrances.

I'm sure I was almost mouthing out the counts as we marched across the apron of the stage like a drunken caterpillar and circled back towards the center. Time slowed, and as it did, I tried not to get ahead of myself. It seemed to take an eternity to get back around to the center, but finally we arrived and, right or wrong, I leapt downstage toward the audience on what I hoped was the correct count.

A vast, empty blackness appeared before me, speckled with bits of red (the exit signs). I could feel a wave of cool, air-conditioned air wash over me and realized I must have landed just outside of the battery of side lighting that heated the stage. Lean right, lean left, booga booga boo!

From there on out, it was mostly a blur. I was hurled high into the air by the eight other Goons, then went about my business with the well-rehearsed efficiency of a trained monkey. After several minutes, I no longer felt nervous. I started to actually listen to the music. I was not continually worrying about what came next. And while on the one hand I was out onstage "performing," it appeared to me that I was quite alone and that this was a little charade my friends and I were indulging in for our own amusement.

In spite of my fears about screwing up, I was right about the counts and managed to get through *Prodigal* without ruining my coming-out party. My job was safe, at least until tomorrow, and the fact that I'd gotten through that first performance gave me a much-needed boost of confidence.

We would dance *Prodigal* many times over the course of that tour, and while I always enjoyed the dance aspects of this Balanchine masterpiece, it took me a long time to appreciate Prokofiev's music.

My first performance with ABT. Drinking
Companion, Prodigal Son. Dressing room
of the Kennedy Center. December 1980.

Musical Appreciation

L IKE MANY BALLET DANCERS, I came to classical music indirectly; it was simply part of the process. As a youngster, I studied the
piano briefly, but that was the extent of my musical training. As a ballet
student, I was subjected to all types of music in the classroom, most of
it bastardized versions of Chopin or Tchaikovsky played on scratchy
old records or by less-than-gifted local pianists. There were waltzes and
polkas and tangos and more variations of *Nutcracker* than you could
shake a stick at, little of which appealed to me.

When I was young, I had a difficult time learning to dance "on the
music" as my first ballet teacher, Paul Wallace, referred to it. I was so
wrapped up in trying to figure out how to get my body to move in a
balletic fashion, I had no space left in my little brain for music. Consequently, I was often bounding around the room completely unaware of
the tempo while Mr. Wallace clapped or stomped on the floor. "Listen
to the music, Michael! Listen to the music!"

When I became more proficient as a dancer, I actually prided myself on my ability to hear tempos and phrasing. I was the type of dancer,
like many in Ballet Theatre, who became very good at counting musical phrases and memorizing movements that corresponded to those
numbered phrases. Occasionally, I encountered dancers who eschewed
counting altogether, relying instead on their ability to "memorize" the

music so they didn't have to count. I was at once envious and suspicious of these dancers, for I felt that dancing to counts was a crutch and, ultimately, simply not how ballet should be done. On the other hand, it seemed amateurish to eschew counting musical phrases.

In my opinion, the whole point of dancing is to lose yourself in the music and marry the movement you've been taught to the particular nuances in the music as it is being played by a living, breathing orchestra. A dancer's phrasing and interpretation of the music is what gives them their personality, their artistry. Silently ticking off numbers and phrases in your brain is no way to express anything, or at least it never seemed that way to me.

When it came to learning ballets in a company like Ballet Theatre, we were expected to learn ballets via counts because that's how the ballets were taught. On *two* you do this, and on *three* you do this, and so on and so forth. There simply wasn't room for half-measures. If you were dancing in the corps de ballet, everyone needed to be on the same count, and on that count you needed to be in a very specific spot on the stage. Bits of glow-in-the-dark tape were placed at the center and quarter marks running upstage and downstage so we could map out our movements correctly. Of course, there were times when, musically speaking, things were left up to interpretation, but by and large the counts were extremely precise. In fact, we were so good at counting, we didn't even have to hear the music. The ballet master could just start counting, and, as long as they counted the phrases correctly, we could dance an entire ballet to numbers.

As a result of learning ballets to numbers, I relied on counting until I felt comfortable enough with the choreography or the music to relinquish those numbers, but that was by no means an easy thing to do. Learning ballets to counts ingrains those counts in your mind, and forever after you associate movements with a number. In some cases, I would blend the counts and the melody into a musical-arithmetical hybrid, singing the counts alongside the musical melody. When the music was particularly uneven in terms of phrasing (Stravinsky, Prokofiev) or the movements that corresponded to the musical phrases were very dense and irregular (Twyla Tharp), I never abandoned counting.

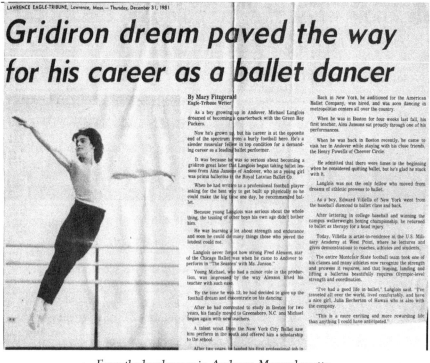

LAWRENCE EAGLE-TRIBUNE, Lawrence, Mass.— Thursday, December 31, 1981

Gridiron dream paved the way
for his career as a ballet dancer

By Mary Fitzgerald
Eagle-Tribune Writer

As a boy growing up in Andover, Michael Langlois dreamed of becoming a quarterback with the Green Bay Packers.

Now he's grown up, but his career is at the opposite end of the spectrum from a burly football hero. He's a slender muscular fellow in top condition for a demanding career as a leading ballet performer.

It was because he was so serious about becoming a gridiron great later that Langlois began taking ballet lessons from Aina Janson of Andover, who as a young girl was prima ballerina in the Royal Latvian Ballet Co.

When he had written to a professional football player asking for the best way to get built up physically so he could make the big time one day, he recommended ballet.

Because young Langlois was serious about the whole thing, the teasing of other boys his own age didn't bother him.

He was learning a lot about strength and endurance and soon he could do many things those who jeered the loudest could not.

Langlois never forgot how strong Fred Alexson, star of the Chicago Ballet was when he came to Andover to perform in "The Seasons" with Ms. Janson.

Young Michael, who had a minor role in the production, was impressed by the way Alexson lifted his teacher with such ease.

By the time he was 13, he had decided to give up the football dream and concentrate on his dancing.

After he had commuted to study in Boston for two years, his family moved to Greensboro, N.C. and Michael began again with new teachers.

A talent scout from the New York City Ballet saw him perform in the south and offered him a scholarship to the school.

After two years, he landed his first professional job in

Back in New York, he auditioned for the American Ballet Company, was hired, and was soon dancing in metropolitan centers all over the country.

When he was in Boston for four weeks last fall, his first teacher, Aina Jansons sat proudly through one of his performances.

When he was back in Boston recently, he came to visit her in Andover while staying with his close friends, the Henry Powells of Cheever Circle.

He admitted that there were times in the beginning when he considered quitting ballet, but he's glad he stuck with it.

Langlois was not the only fellow who moved from dreams of athletic prowess to ballet.

As a boy, Edward Villella of New York went from the baseball diamond to ballet class and back.

After lettering in college baseball and winning the campus welterweight boxing championship, he returned to ballet as therapy for a head injury.

Today, Villella is artist-in-residence at the U.S. Military Academy at West Point, where he lectures and gives demonstrations to coaches, athletes and students.

The entire Montclair State football team took one of his classes and many athletes now recognize the strength and prowess it requires, and that leaping, landing and lifting a ballerina beautifully requires Olympic-level strength and coordination.

"I've had a good life in ballet," Langlois said. "I've traveled all over the world, lived comfortably, and have a nice girl, Julia Becherton of Hawaii who is also with the company.

"This is a more exciting and more rewarding life than anything I could have anticipated."

From the local paper in Andover, Massachusetts.

First Positions

THOSE INITIAL WEEKS AT THE KENNEDY CENTER at the end of 1980 were a time I spent becoming accustomed to ABT and its incessant performing routine. Company class for the men and women together was at ten a.m. four days a week. The other two performance days were matinee and evening performance days, and on those occasions, company class was at noon and the matinee performance began at two p.m. One half hour before every performance, we were required to be in the theater unless we had no ballets to dance. If we were understudying a ballet, we could sign in and leave the theatre, provided the stage manager knew how to get in touch with us in case of an emergency.

Throughout most of our performance days in Washington, we had rehearsals for ballets that were upcoming, but because of union regulations limiting the number of rehearsal hours to two on a performance day (beyond which the company had to pay us overtime), we rarely went beyond this threshold. This meant there were a number of hours during the day when I had time to go shopping, sightseeing, or visit a museum, and that's what I often found myself doing. In retrospect, what I should have been doing was seeking out some private coaching from one of the ballet masters or taking a class at Washington Ballet or working on strengthening my body, but I did none of those things. None of us did, really, because doing any of those things on tour was difficult if not impossible, and, as I mentioned earlier, no one was encouraging us to do those things.

Christmas was fast approaching, and, for Ballet Theatre, this meant what it perennially means for every ballet company in America: money. Money for an American ballet company is spelled N-U-T-C-R-A-C-K-E-R. Though I'd been cast as a Buffoon in the second act, the Buffoon dance had been axed by Misha (it would be reinserted in subsequent years). So in the first act I played a Child in the party scene and a Toy Soldier in the battle scene, while in the second act I dressed as a Buffoon but did no actual dancing.

As half-baked as this was, I couldn't realistically expect my parents and grandparents not to drive up from North Carolina to watch me perform for the first time with American Ballet Theatre, so I awaited their arrival with mixed emotions.

I was ashamed to have so little to dance, but this feeling was buried beneath the novelty of the moment and the time between classes, rehearsals, and performances, when my parents were able to see snippets of what my life was like. And what they saw was their son walk into their hotel room dressed in a turquoise Missoni sweater, blue-green Versace suede pants, and a pair of black Maude-Frizon tuxedo pumps. Meanwhile, behind me stood my new best friend, the very similarly attired Peter Fonseca, a dark-haired, Latin-flavored, more colorfully dressed version of me.

Believe it or not, everything about this scene appeared perfectly natural in my eyes. I was the me I'd slowly become back in New York under Peter's influence, and Peter was Peter, a Latin dandy. I will say this: Peter managed to say all the right things and put my entire family at ease (or so it appeared). They had loads of questions about the company and Washington, D.C. (probably because they were nervous and trying to avoid the obvious question: are you fucking our son?), and Peter, who was from Silver Spring, Maryland and knew better than most how ABT operated, impressed them with his knowledge and sense of humor. As they were chatting, I could practically hear the gearbox grinding in my mother's head.

Well, I can't think of a nicer boy for my son to fall in love with. When's the wedding?

As for my father... I think Peter's arrival was confirmation of the fact that this ballet business his son had gotten involved in was exactly what he suspected it was: a world filled with limp-wristed queers running around in pink tutus and tiaras singing "It's Raining Men."

Whatever my parents and grandparents may have been thinking, they didn't share their thoughts with me. If they believed Peter and I were lovers, well, that was just one of those things people assumed— something I probably would have assumed as well had I not known better. Who, after all, would have believed that a straight boy and a gay boy could spend so much time together without being lovers?

By the time the company decamped to Miami Beach just after the New Year, my mother was practically drawing up the adoption papers. She gave Peter a big hug and a kiss goodbye. "Take care of my son, would you?" she said as they were driving away. "I will, Mandy," Peter replied, glancing at me with a mischievous look in his eye.

As the company traveled south to Miami, north to Chicago, and westward to San Francisco and Los Angeles, it dawned on me that in order to be an ABT dancer you had to be incredibly resilient. I suppose for the older Ballet Theatre dancers, the national tour had its own kind of routine, but within that routine there were wild variations on everything from climate to classrooms. One of the most dramatic changes for me was that of having to take class onstage.

This shift away from the classroom mirror to a gigantic, empty theater was terribly disorienting at first. Accustomed as I'd become to staring at my feet and legs in a mirror every day for the past ten years, the first hurdle I had to overcome was figuring out what the hell to look at. Of course I knew what my head positioning should be because this was part of the ballet lexicon, but even at that I was like most ballet dancers—obsessed with the mirror—and ergo, often peering out of the corner of my eye at my line in the mirror as I danced.

Without the magnetic pull of the mirror, I became more aware of my entire body and began dancing with a completely different focus, feeling, and mindset. I had no way to gauge what I looked like onstage, so I had to rely on feel, and what I started to feel was liberation. Dancing became more of a pleasure because I wasn't continually finding fault with what I saw in the mirror.

The more frequent ABT classes onstage became, the more I preferred those to being in the classroom, an environment where I felt my body and perspective shrink back into a narcissistic, incredibly self-critical little box. In fact, when we returned to a normal classroom with mirrors, I tried to forget they existed. But they were like a drug; no matter how much I tried to resist their pull, the mirrors sucked me in, and eventually I found myself staring at some part of me and not liking what I saw.

The final weeks of that first, long four-month tour with Ballet Theatre were a blur of gray winter days and bus trips between hotels and theaters in Detroit and Minneapolis. And then, finally, it was back home and on to upstate New York, where we performed in Syracuse, Rochester, and Buffalo in order to fulfill some state artistic funding guidelines. I became ill during this upstate journey and missed several performances. As I lay in my hotel room with a high fever, all I could think was, they're going to fire me, they're going to fire me, they're going to fire me.

Peter became my nursemaid, reassuring me that everything would be all right, that I wasn't going to be fired for being sick. Between his trips to the theater where he was dancing one of the most demanding roles in our repertoire, the Boy in Green in Ashton's *Les Patineurs,* he brought me soup and juice and kept his eye on my fever. Those were moments when I realized life with Peter would've been so much simpler if I'd been gay.

By the time the company returned to the Kennedy Center in late spring, the cherry trees were in bloom and Peter was well on his way to becoming a soloist. After four years of treading water under Lucia Chase, Misha gave him the lead in *Flower Festival at Genzano* and *The Guards of Amager.* He was also given important roles in *Les Rendez-vous, Push Comes to Shove, Nutcracker, Concerto,* and *Raymonda.* Every soloist role he was given was a tremendous success, and the more he proved capable of handling those responsibilities, the more Misha gave him.

Peter and I stayed at his family's home in Silver Spring while we were in Washington. He slept in the room he'd had since he was a young boy, and I took one of his four older brothers' rooms. His mother, Hortensia, who ran a local ballet school, was quite a worrier, and she doted on both of us like we were kids at a sleepover. And, much like kids at a sleepover, Peter and I stayed up late every night talking, much as we had in New York.

During one of our conversations, I asked him how old he was when he realized he was gay. Quite young, he said, maybe five or six. He never told his parents. His older brother Paul, who was also gay, knew, but Peter said he never felt the need to have that discussion with his parents. He assumed they knew and was certain it didn't matter to them.

After our late night gabfests, we had a hell of time getting to class on time. Peter, even on his best days, was no slave to the clock, whereas I was accustomed to arriving for class at least half an hour early in order to stretch; with Peter in charge of the driving, this was virtually impossible.

Every morning, we found ourselves racing along Rock Creek Park in the family car, pulling into the Kennedy Center minutes before class was about to begin. But then something surprising happened. In spite of my fears about abandoning my routine or making the wrong impression on Misha, I had wonderful classes. Whether it was the panic of the moment that warmed me up or not I can't say, but running in at the last minute taught me a valuable lesson: I didn't necessarily need my rigid pre-class rituals. I wasn't that fragile. My body knew what to do. I just had to trust it.

Another important lesson I would learn during that first tour was that there was an accepted model for how an American Ballet Theatre dancer operated. You were expected to take class every day. You were expected to show up for rehearsals on time (not five minutes late). You were expected to learn the counts and the choreography you were given and be adequately prepared to perform. You were expected to look good, not get too thin or too heavy, and, most importantly, you were expected to perform up to the ABT standard.

As dancers in American Ballet Theatre, it was assumed we knew what was best for our bodies. This meant training with whatever methods or teachers we deemed appropriate. If there were exercises within company class we didn't like, for example, we could make up an exercise of our own choosing or not do the exercise at all, provided it was not a distraction to the other dancers. If you wanted to give yourself a class or take class elsewhere, that was generally fine. Above and beyond this, we were often allowed to "mark" rehearsals (not dance full out) because it was assumed we all had arduous performing schedules to consider.

The implication here was a confusing one for me. On the one hand, I was supposed to be this incredibly strong athlete, a dancer at the very highest level of my profession; on the other hand, I was this fragile creature who shouldn't tire himself out too much before the big show.

What I would come to discover is that every ballet company develops a certain way of doing things. In some companies, dancers—of their own accord or because the director insists on it—dance every rehearsal full out, regardless of what lies ahead of them that day. In other companies, "marking" is practically the norm, while in others it depends on the circumstances.

In American Ballet Theatre, we did, of course, dance rehearsals "full out" on many occasions—while we were creating ballets or in the midst of a rehearsal period, for example—but as soon as we began performing, we were supposed to be saving ourselves for something, even if—as in my case—that something was not a whole hell of a lot.

The distinction here is actually gender based because, in a company like ABT or New York City ballet, the corps de ballet women work twice as hard as the men. In fact, the women work so hard and have so few nights off relative to the men in most big ballet companies, ABT once considered paying the women more. This idea never went beyond the talking stage, but it certainly would have been justified.

PETER FONSECA

Shown here in the male variation from the pas de deux Flower Festival in Genzano, Peter Fonseca was born in Washington, D.C. and began his ballet training with his mother, Hortensia Fonseca. He also studied with Mary Day at the Washington Academy of Ballet and at the American Ballet Theatre School. He joined Ballet Repertory Company (now ABT II) in the Summer of 1975. Mr. Fonseca joined American Ballet Theatre in the Spring of 1976 and was appointed a Soloist in December, 1981.

His roles with the Company include the leading male roles in Les Rendezvous and Theme and Variations, the pas de trois from The Guards of Amager, the pas de deux from Flower Festival in Genzano, and featured roles in Airs, Concerto, The Nutcracker, Prodigal Son, Raymonda (Divertissements from Act II and Act III), and La Sonnambula.

During the summer of 1982, Mr. Fonseca, with other members of ABT, appeared in "An Evening of Ballets by Jerome Robbins" in Spoleto, dancing in N.Y. Export: Op. Jazz.

ABT Souvenir Program 1981.
Photo credit: Gregory Heisler

Metropolitan Opera House.
Spring Season. 1981.

IN THE SPRING OF 1981, I entered the right side of the lobby at the Metropolitan Opera House and descended an escalator opposite the box office. At the bottom, I pushed open a pale, non-descript double door. In the next instant, I was standing in a dank, dark garage with low ceilings. Pools of light illuminated bits of darkened pavement. A few parked cars sat in recessed spaces adjacent to a singular empty drive. About fifty yards away, toward a square of daylight spilling in from Amsterdam Avenue, I spied an illuminated sign that looked as if it might mark the stage door. Passing along a soot-stained wall, I came upon a slight recess and walked up a few stairs through another set of doors. There, I found myself in a windowless room with a seating area, some phone cubicles, and a lectern-like perch where a black security guard sat under a singular pin spot with a clipboard. I showed him my ABT identification, and he checked my name off a list. "Through that door," he said, pressing a buzzer that unlocked a gray metal door to my right. Once inside this door, I stood at the end of a long, brightly lit, red-carpeted hallway. To my left was the ABT callboard and various alphabetically arranged cubbyholes for mail to company members.

A few older boys arrived. I followed them down the hall and around the corner to the left, where we mounted a flight of stairs. On the second floor, in the back left corner of the building, we found the men's corps de ballet and soloist dressing rooms. Narrow windows around the perimeter looked down onto Damrosch Park on one side and Amsterdam Avenue at the back.

The corps de ballet dressing room was an enormous, white-tiled space with rows and rows of white, Formica-topped dressing tables as well as a gigantic, white-tiled bathroom. The last aisle of the dressing room along Damrosch Park was occupied by Bob Holloway and Bruce Horowitz, our wardrobe personnel. These two men were responsible for repairing, preparing, and delivering individual costumes to their respective dancers prior to each and every show.

I walked up and down the aisles of the dressing room and found, adjacent to Peter Fonseca's elegantly arranged spot, a white paper towel from the bathroom with my name scrawled across the top.

After locating my theater case downstairs near the loading dock, I came back upstairs and arranged my makeup table with the same degree of fastidiousness Peter did. Everything had its place. I laid down a bright red towel to cover the surface of the makeup table, around which I put containers for my brushes, lipsticks, eyeliners, mascaras, and pancakes in various shades. Beyond the practicalities of makeup, I accessorized my area with photos and little tchotchkes, stuffed animals, mementos, and "merdes," the gifts dancers give to one another on opening nights or special occasions. And last but not least, there was always a vase or two for the flowers that become a continual presence in every dancer's life.

The Met season, I was about to learn, was a special time of year for the corps de ballet men of ABT, many of whom found themselves with little to do on tour but drink and chase ballerinas. It was during the Met season that most of us found ourselves standing around in a rehearsal room at 890 Broadway or uptown in the gigantic basement rehearsal room of the Metropolitan Opera House (C-3), trying to remember the counts and choreography to a remarkable ballet by Jerome Robbins that was performed but once a year: *Les Noces*.

This ballet about a Russian peasant wedding to music by Igor Stravinsky was first choreographed by Bronislava Nijinska for The Ballets Russes in 1923. Robbins created his version in 1965 for ABT's 25th Anniversary. The reason *Les Noces* was only performed once a year and only at the Met was that it required four grand pianos, four tympani, and a full choir, all of which was placed onstage behind the dancers. It was a huge expense to mount, but if there was any ballet indicative of ABT's belief in art for art's sake, it was *Les Noces*.

Terry Orr, a former principal dancer with ABT, was the ballet master in charge of setting *Les Noces,* and, as far as I could tell, it was like an annual circumcision for him. Terry was nearly forty years old then and had been in Ballet Theatre since 1965. He became a ballet master in 1978. More character dancer than classical dancer, he was known for his roles in ballets such as *Rodeo, Billy the Kid,* and *Fancy Free.* He'd been married to Cynthia Gregory, one of Ballet Theatre's most renowned *American* ballerinas, but that hadn't worked out, and he had subsequently settled down with another Ballet Theatre ballerina, Marianna Tcherkassky.

Slight of build and full of energy, Terry's ruddy complexion brightened easily when he was excited or angry, which happened with some regularity. He was a proud man and wanted to do a good job, but he was also a bit insecure, particularly when it came to *Les Noces*. He didn't have the photographic memory for choreography and counts that his counterpart, Susan Jones, had, and as a result, he became testy or irritable when confronted by some detail he couldn't quite remember (and there were many, many details in *Les Noces*).

Most of the dancers had a hard time recalling the nuances of *Les Noces* after a year. Stravinsky's music, for starters, is very complex and had to be counted from beginning to end. In the final analysis, no one cared whether Terry remembered every step or every count—we just wanted to make sure we got it right so that when Jerry Robbins showed up for final rehearsals he wouldn't blow a gasket or fall ass over teakettle into the orchestra pit. I wanted Jerry to be pleased, not simply because he had a reputation for being difficult and falling into orchestra pits, but because I'd become quite fond of Terry, and I knew he needed all the support he could get.

Peter Fonseca, like Susan Jones, had a remarkable memory for counts and choreography. Consequently, many of us turned to him for answers. To his credit, Peter didn't lord this ability over Terry, and while I think it pained him at times to admit it, Terry seemed to accept this. A truce of sorts was reached, and this was evidenced by the fact that Terry would occasionally solicit Peter's advice. In not-so-subtle ways, however, Terry seemed intent on making certain Peter knew, and more importantly, that we all knew, that he, Terry, was not going to have his masculine authority called into question by a flaming queen like Peter Fonseca.

What made *Les Noces* so fantastic for me as a newcomer to the company was that it brought everyone together like an actual wedding might have. The ballet was so big and the music so powerful, it merged life and art. It was a rare treat to be able to dance with a large group of men, and strangely reminiscent of playing on a football team, complete with all the butt- and back-slapping bravado. I absolutely loved it and, at the same time, found it utterly hilarious given that the world outside the doors of 890 Broadway or the Metropolitan Opera House, for the most part, considered all of us a bunch of faggot ballet dancers.

On Fire

D URING A LONG HOLIDAY WEEKEND while we were performing at the Met, Peter suggested we go out to Fire Island. He and a few other boys in Ballet Theatre had rented a house somewhere in the Pines, a gay enclave where Calvin Klein, among others, had a home.

I didn't know it at the time, but Peter was quite the party boy. He enjoyed his drugs and was very promiscuous, but either he stopped behaving this way after we met or he kept that part of his life hidden from me, because as far as I could tell, he was practically a saint, albeit a saint who enjoyed a good hit of marijuana every now and then.

I had never been to Fire Island, but it was obvious from the clusters of handsome, well-muscled young men packing the train out to Sayville that its reputation as a Mecca of homosexual depravity was well founded. Queer or not, when we disembarked the ferry, I was completely awestruck by the beautiful, fairytale nature of the Pines. There were no cars whatsoever. Elevated boardwalks meandered like yellow-brick roads through a landscape of small trees. Occasionally, a house or wild deer would appear, but otherwise all one encountered was silence interrupted occasionally by the sound of a wagon being pulled along the boardwalk. Little red wagons were ubiquitous in the Pines, being the most popular method of transporting groceries and such things.

After reaching our house, Peter and I changed into bathing suits and headed to the beach, where we found Robbie, David Cuevas, and a few other boys from Ballet Theatre. The water was still frigid at that time of the year, so we lay around on our towels most of the day, smoking weed and talking. That night, we all pitched in to make dinner. Peter filled the table with candles, then ran out to pick some wild-growing things to make a bouquet. When all was ready, we sat down. I gazed around the table at the handsome, candlelit faces of all the gay men assembled, and it suddenly struck me that this might have been a scene straight from the Last Supper.

We woke up late on Sunday, and by the time we had eaten breakfast and showered, it was early afternoon. "We're all going to tea dance," Peter said. "I brought some Quaaludes. Would you like one?"

Tea dance was a Sunday afternoon party, a daylight rehash of the Friday and Saturday night clubbing that goes on in every gay community. At what seemed to be the only club in the Pines, I downed my Quaalude, ripped off my shirt, and danced like one of The Village People. Everyone was soooooo beauuutifullll!!!! As fucked up and vulnerable as I was, and as fucked up as Peter probably was, he managed to control himself, and in the early evening hours, he took me back to the house and put me to bed.

The following morning, as we were sitting out in the sun on the deck of the ferry back to Sayville, I looked over at Peter. I knew he loved me, and I knew he wanted to sleep with me. I also knew after what happened at tea dance that he was going to let that be my decision. My view of our friendship crossed a real divide at that point, and on the other side of that divide was the realization that I loved Peter. I wasn't *in love* with him, but I loved him, and I didn't care what anyone might think about the two of us. I never had. When we were walking down the street together, I often held his hand or put my arm around his shoulder. Perhaps I should have cared what others thought. Who knows? I was certain Misha didn't care one way or the other. He didn't have prejudices in that regard, and it was obvious he didn't, because he was championing people like Robbie LaFosse, Peter, Johan Renvall, and Ronald Perry—and they were all gay. As if that weren't evidence enough, he'd chosen one of the most polarizing queens in the entire ballet world to be his closest confidant: Charles France. My feeling about Peter was this: the only influence he was going to have on my life or my career at Ballet Theatre was a positive one.

⸻

Sometime during my weekend in Fire Island, my mother received a telepathic message about my escapades in New York and sent Thad, an old family friend, up to New York to investigate. I say this because, just prior to Thad's arrival, she said to me on the phone, "You know, dear, if you're questioning your sexuality in any way... Well...I just want you to know that your father and I will love you no matter what."

Thad was my first swimming coach, a job he had held at our local pool while pursuing his law degree at Wake Forest. Tall and lanky with wispy blonde hair and angular features, he was a lively, alluring presence, and as a young boy, I idolized him. Our paths hadn't crossed much over the past few years. He was busy with his law practice in Greensboro, along with his second marriage to an extremely wealthy older woman. I was busy dancing in New York. Nevertheless, when I heard his voice on the phone inviting me to dinner, I felt like a kid again.

I knew things had changed dramatically in Thad's life since his recent marriage, but I wasn't sure how dramatically until I saw the black stretch limousine parked out in front of my building in Hell's Kitchen.

When I climbed inside, I found Thad in his element: dressed in an impeccable suit with a colorful shirt and tie, cocktail well in hand, his face a bit flushed.

"Well *how the hell* are you?" he boomed, his southern drawl scotch-scented. "Come over heeahh!" he said, pulling me to his chest and giving me an ample squeeze. With my face smooshed against him, I could feel the familiar tremor in his bony arms, an ailment he'd long suffered from and seemed intent on medicating with massive doses of alcohol.

An hour later, we were sitting at Windows on the World at the top of the World Trade Center. Between cocktails and dinner, we spoke about the renovation of his palatial home in Greensboro, my life in Ballet Theatre, and my friendship with Peter. "I'd like to meet this boa!" Thad said at one point. "Your mother tells me he's quite a dressah."

After dinner, Thad suggested we visit a bar he knew on the Upper East Side, so we headed uptown in the limo, arriving at what looked like a residential building in the middle of a block somewhere in the east 60s. I followed Thad as he approached an unmarked door on street level.

Inside, a long bar stretched back to the rear wall. The décor was decidedly masculine, lots of dark wood paneling and comfortable leather chairs. Clustered around the smoky bar was a crowd made up entirely of middle-aged men in suits and ties, their starched collars loosened after a long day of money-making. They all looked like my father, a thought I tried to push out of my mind as quickly as possible.

As Thad ordered drinks, I looked at the clientele, and the more I looked, the more looks I got in return. Thad seemed completely oblivious and completely at home. When he caught me staring at him, he smiled. "What is it?"

"Nothing. Do you come here much?"

"When I'm in New Yawk. I can walk here from the Carlyle. Convenience is everything in a bah."

"I see." And in fact, I finally did see. I saw a man in a suit who had a secret, surrounded by lots of other men in suits who harbored secrets about who they really were. I realized then just how lucky I was to know who I was and who I wasn't.

By the time Thad's limo pulled up in front of my building, it was early morning. I gave him a big hug and thanked him for a wonderful evening. "By the way," I said. "You can tell my mom that Peter and I are just friends."

ABT Souvenir Program 1981. Photo credit: Francesco Scavullo.

Romeo and Julie

S OME NEW DANCERS DESCENDED on Ballet Theatre in the spring of 1981, apprentices from ABT's junior company, ABT II. This wasn't unusual. The Met season was a time of year when injuries from the long tour had taken their toll on the company, and extra girls were often needed for ballets that required large numbers of women—*Swan Lake* or *La Bayadère*, for example. One of these dancers was cast opposite me as the Gypsy Girl in *Don Quixote*.

A couple of weeks before *Don Q* was scheduled to be performed, I was called to rehearsal in Studio C-3, the largest rehearsal room at the Met. C-3 was like a gigantic bunker, four or five floors beneath the stage. One arrived there via one of two banks of military-gray elevators. Like most of the backstage areas at the Met, C-3 was scarred by years of theater crates or bits of scenery being carted to and fro, by dancers and singers and the comings and goings of massive opera and ballet companies. A special sprung floor had been placed over the original wood floor, and its scuffed, gray Marley, along with the rips in the gigantic, red Dufy canvas that hung along the back wall, served to enhance a sense of the passage of time and the "show must go on" atmosphere that infused the Met.

When I arrived for *Don Q* rehearsal that day, I saw an unfamiliar girl sitting on the floor in the corner. She had long, dark hair and brown eyes. Very cute, I thought. She must be the new Gypsy Girl. Our roles demanded that we act like children, and it was apparent as rehearsal wore on that this girl knew how to have fun. When rehearsal ended, I was going to ask her if she wanted to go out on a date, but in the midst of mustering up my courage, she disappeared.

Days went by. Finally, I decided to get her phone number from Florence Pettan, Misha's secretary. Why I felt the need to lie about my intentions to Flo, I don't know, but it just seemed like she might balk at giving out the personal information of a young female apprentice she didn't know to a boy in the corps de ballet she knew only slightly. Lying seemed like the best approach, and, though I could tell Flo was a bit suspect when I asked her for the phone number, my work-on-*Don-Q* excuse was right up her alley. She adored ABT, after all, and had devoted most of her adult life to furthering its cause. If I needed a phone number for the good of the company, then, well, by golly, here it is. And I was right. Less than five minutes after arriving in the Green Room, I was walking out with the treasure I'd been seeking.

Phone number in hand, I set about planning a menu and doing the shopping, certain this girl would leap at the chance to have dinner with me, a handsome young man in the Main Company. Unfortunately, she never answered the phone.

After a couple of days, the food was getting stale, so I thought, to hell with it, I'll just have to make the dinner, date or no date. To get the process underway in proper Julia Child fashion, I opened a bottle of wine and started drinking. About an hour later, the meal was nearing completion and I was depressed and drunk. My roommate, Jeff, was thrilled, however, as he was about to be the happy recipient of my elaborate feast.

"Why don't you call her again?" he said. "What have you got to lose?"

"Hello?"

"Hello, who is this?"

"Michael, from ABT."

I was so taken aback, I didn't know quite what to do, so I just vomited up the whole saga, telling her how I'd gotten her phone number from Flo by lying about having to discuss *Don Q*. I went on to describe my big plans to invite her over for dinner, confessing that said dinner was then being eaten by my roommate as I was finishing a bottle of wine. She seemed to find my story amusing, so, not wanting to waste the opportunity, I said, "What are you doing right now?"

"I'm doing my laundry, actually."

"Would you like some help with that laundry of yours? I'm quite a folder."

Without a moment's hesitation, she said "Sure."

And that was that. I grabbed the last of the wine (and another bottle just in case), told Jeff to enjoy the dinner, and hopped in a cab. Fifteen minutes later, I was sitting on a ratty, old couch in her apartment in Chelsea.

─────────────

"You know," she said, as she began pulling bits of clothing from the massive pile on the couch and folding them, "I remember you from SAB."

"When were you at SAB?" I asked, certain I'd never laid eyes on this girl in my life.

"The summer of '78."

"'78? I was working at Studio 54 that summer. I got fired by Steve Rubell."

"Why did he fire you?"

"I was given an album they were promoting at some party. Employees weren't supposed to accept gifts, but it seemed innocent enough.

Anyway, Steve must have seen me take the album and he confronted me in the dishwashing room. 'Get the fuck out of my club!' he screamed, breaking the album over his knee and tossing it in the garbage."

She laughed, then picked up a pair of her underwear and placed them in the small pile she'd been creating as we spoke.

"Where are you from?" I asked.

"London. Both my parents are English, but I lived there very little when I was growing up. My dad is a linguist at the University of Hawaii. We traveled a lot when I was young so he could do his research. I lived in Africa and South America, and then we ended up in Honolulu. I studied ballet there, then went to a performing arts school in Champaign, Illinois before coming to New York with my parents. They moved into this apartment with me when I came here."

"For a girl from England, you don't have much of an accent."

"I forced myself to get rid of it. When I was at Punahou—that's the school I went to in Honolulu—the kids made fun of my British accent. Most people think you're so lucky when you tell them you're from Hawaii, but it was an awful place for me in many ways. It's hard to be white in Hawaii, but it's twice as hard being a white girl with a British accent who studies ballet."

I looked at this enchanting girl, her long, dark hair cascading down over her shoulders. She could have been my sister, and her itinerant childhood seemed a near duplicate of my own, albeit far more exotic.

When she finished folding her laundry, she moved closer to me on the couch. In the valley our bodies suddenly created, her miniscule pile of underwear spilled into my lap. "You don't have to go anywhere, do you?" she asked.

Julie and I rarely spent an evening apart after that. And while it probably appeared a bit hasty to most of our friends and family, it seemed perfectly natural to us that after being told we were both going to be dancing with American Ballet Theatre the following year, we began talking about moving in together.

━━━━━━━━━━━━━━━━

There was one downside to falling in love with Julie that I hadn't considered: Peter Fonseca. Foolishly, I thought Peter would be happy for me, because I knew I would have been happy for him were the situation reversed. What I had forgotten was that Peter had, in fact, met someone and fallen in love. And that someone was me.

Peter responded to my attempts to include him in our lives with silence. As dismayed as I was by his reaction, I was so busy over the summer flitting between my parents' house in North Carolina, and Julie's parents' home in Hawaii, I didn't have much time to see Peter. When I did think about him, I came to the conclusion that our friendship was never going to work in its present format. I assumed, because Peter was older, that he should have known better than to fall prey to that stereotypical gay assumption that inside every straight man is a gay man itching to get out of the closet. And I was naïve enough, perhaps, to believe that a gay man and a straight man could be close friends—a belief I refused to abandon in spite of what happened with Peter.

Julie and I at her parent's apartment in Honolulu. 1981.

Fall. 1981. Age 21.

THE BEGINNING OF MY SECOND YEAR with American Ballet Theatre was an indication that Misha was eager to put his stamp on the company, and there was no better evidence of that stamp than the sledgehammer he took to our repertoire: seven new ballets and three revivals. To shake things up even more, he selected none other than Francesco Scavullo, of *Cosmopolitan* magazine cover fame, to shoot the souvenir program.

Scavullo's windblown photographs seemed symbolic of the moment, for our rehearsal period was nothing short of a hurricane. There were four restagings of previously created work: Balanchine's *Bouree Fantasque*, Roland Petit's *Carmen*, Merce Cunningham's *Duets*, and Eliot Feld's *Variations on America*. There were three entirely new ballets: Choo San Goh's *Configurations*, Lynne-Taylor Corbett's *Great Galloping Gottschalk*, and Kenneth MacMillan's *The Wild Boy*. And, finally, there were three ABT revivals: Balanchine's *Apollo*, Eugene Loring's *Billy the Kid*, and Tudor's *Pillar of Fire*.

Misha and Robbie LaFosse would alternate the leads in Kenneth MacMillan's *The Wild Boy*, while I, along with many of the men in the corps de ballet, would be one of the animal-like creatures who populated the imaginary jungle where the Wild Boy lived.

I knew little of Kenneth MacMillan or the impetus for his new ballet, a work that seemed to be a synthesis of *Tarzan* and *The Rite of Spring*, but from the very first rehearsal, I could see that this famous English choreographer had little intention of breaking a sweat during the creative process.

He was, to be quite blunt, a slug, particularly as it pertained to ironing his clothes, most of which looked as if they'd been slept in for several days. They hung off his large droopy frame in irregularly creased peninsulas, his belt cinching a divide in a soft belly that sat like bowl of pudding in the middle of his body.

Thus attired, *Sir* Kenneth, as we jokingly referred to him at times, would sit in a chair at the front of the room day after day and watch while we rolled around on the floor creating his ballet for him. Kenneth's assistant was Monica Mason (the woman who would later become the director of the Royal Ballet), and for the few weeks it took him to concoct this straight-to-DVD cult classic, he would continually get her attention by uttering her name in a mournful, nasally whine: "Maaawwwnica, I say, Maaaawwwnnn...ica, thair, thair, what that boy's doing, I like that, have them do that."

While it might have seemed thrilling on paper to create an entirely new ballet with the man who gave birth to one of the most renowned versions of *Romeo and Juliet* ever choreographed, the men of American Ballet Theatre were no dummies, and most of them soon realized that if they stood around long enough, myself and a couple of the other teacher's pets would knock ourselves out coming up with all the steps, and then, once Kenneth had approved those steps, they would set about learning them.

There was an attitude among the dancers at Ballet Theatre that it was not our job, nor were we getting paid, to create ballets. We were willing to help, certainly, and there was a certain degree of pleasure to be derived from having our ideas embraced by a choreographer, but we weren't the Joffrey Ballet, and Kenneth MacMillan wasn't our Gerald Arpino, a man famous for creating ballets on the backs of his dancers and taking all the credit for them.

What Kenneth MacMillan thought about our behavior, I have no idea. He seemed resigned to the fact that only a handful of us were willing to help him, and in our own dysfunctional manner, we managed to cobble together the kind of ballet that makes critics scratch their heads and say to themselves, "What the hell was this guy thinking?"

In the midst of creating *The Wild Boy*, we were treated to a lengthy visit by Roland Petit, the director of the Ballet de Marseilles. Petit had come over from France to set his 1949 version of *Carmen* on Ballet Theatre although it was, for all intents and purposes, a vehicle for Misha and Natasha Makarova. We were their Pips.

Carmen was a piece of dance theater that appeared quite scandalous to English audiences when it premiered in London in 1949 with Zizi Jeanmaire dancing the lead opposite her future husband, Petit, but to my contemporary eyes it seemed almost hokey. The problem from the outset was that Petit still seemed to be living in 1949. He was incapable of communicating to us how we could embrace his ballet as contemporary dancers, so we were mostly left to chuckle in private over his smugness and his choreography. He might have assumed we were aware of his reputation, *Carmen's* history, and the stir it initially caused, but that wasn't the case. No one at ABT, as I'm sure I've mentioned before, thought it might be important to explain who Petit was and the historical significance of his ballet.

Rehearsals with Petit were subtle battles waged in a no-man's land of professional politesse. We pretended we liked Petit, and Petit pretended he liked us. We did the steps and executed them in a manner

Petit found acceptable, but it was an entirely soulless endeavor, as far as I was concerned.

The relationship between the dancers of American Ballet Theatre and those who came in from "outside" the company was one I would come to observe over and over again as the years went by. For the most part, I liked and respected the choreographers or stagers who came to work with us, because the people who were invited to stage or create work at Ballet Theatre were, by implication, accomplished.

Ballet dancers are no different than any other artists, however. They will give everything of themselves for someone they genuinely like or believe in. If, in the case of someone like Petit, they don't particularly warm to a person, they still give it their all when they get out on stage because dancers have pride—in themselves and the reputation of the company they represent. When you represent a company called American Ballet Theatre, that pride is enormous, and it is embedded in your soul.

Whatever had gone wrong with Petit, it hardly mattered. We knew we were mere window dressing for Misha and Makarova. We came to understand the work solely from the steps we were given, and we went out on stage and executed those steps with the same degree of superficial bombast Petit exhibited in the rehearsal room.

One of the highlights of the 1981 rehearsal period for me was an appearance by Eugene Loring, the creator of *Billy the Kid*.

Loring was one of the original members of Ballet Theatre; prior to that, he was a member of Ballet Caravan, the company that would eventually become New York City Ballet. He choreographed *Billy* in 1938 for Ballet Caravan (Lincoln Kirstein wrote the libretto), and it would remain his most successful ballet, compared often to another cowboy ballet: Agnes de Mille's *Rodeo*. Loring's work, however, was a far bleaker depiction of the West than De Mille's, chronicling as it did the life-and-death struggles of a notorious outlaw.

Loring was seventy-one years old the day he walked into the studio. In less than a year, he would be dead. His face drooped on one side, possibly the result of a stroke, but he was a feisty old character who seemed to be facing his mortality with a pitchfork. He commanded respect, and I gave it to him, openly and willingly.

At one point early on in the rehearsal, he silenced the piano and stood up. Looking slowly to the left and the right, he took the measure of everyone in the room. Then, in a voice trembling with emotion, he said, "Ladies and gentlemen...this is *not* a ballet about Sylphs and *Wilis!* This is a ballet about *real* people. And I expect you to dance it that way."

For a few moments, there was complete silence. Loring let what he'd said sink into our brains for a moment, then looked again at each of us, seemingly willing us to absorb the import of those words—*real people*—and what they might possibly mean to us, children of the television era whose sole knowledge of the old West was a combination of *Roy Rodgers* and *The Lone Ranger*. Finally, after what seemed an eternity, he sat back down and said, "Let's take it from the top."

The other new creations that would begin to take shape that fall were Choo San Goh's *Configurations* and Lynn Taylor-Corbett's *Great Galloping Gottschalk*. I was given a nice role as part of the small ensemble in the first movement in *Gottschalk,* and, although I was initially just an understudy for *Configurations,* I would get many opportunities to perform that ballet after it premiered in Minneapolis.

With all these new ballets to learn, I felt things were progressing for me as a dancer in the company. I was beginning to realize that life with my new girlfriend, however, was going to be a bit more dramatic than I anticipated.

Julie was an extremely emotional person, and while those emotions were often fascinating to behold, they were indicative of issues I was incapable of dealing with. Not long after we met, for example, I came home from rehearsal one day and found the bedroom window thrown open and Julie sitting on the ledge, looking down to the street below.

"What's going on?" I asked.

She mumbled something about wanting to kill herself.

Our apartment was on the third floor, which meant, as far as I was concerned, that if she did actually jump, she'd only succeed in landing in the bushes down below and seriously hurting herself. A few interminable minutes passed. Finally, after a great deal of coaxing and cajoling, I managed to talk her off the ledge. Later, when she calmed down, I asked her what was going on.

"When I lived in Honolulu with my parents, they used to go out a lot. They often left me at home with my middle brother, and he loved to torment me. I mean *really* torment me, to the point where I honestly thought he might kill me. So as soon as my parents left and I knew it was just going to be him and me, I would lock myself in the bathroom."

"Didn't you tell your folks about this?"

"They didn't listen. They thought I was exaggerating. They had no idea what he was capable of—no idea."

I thought this incident on the window ledge was going to be a mere aberration, but a couple of weeks later, it happened again. And the result, thankfully, was much the same as it had been the first time. When it happened a third time, I said, "I'm not going through this again, Julie. If you want to kill yourself, go ahead. I'm not going to stop you."

I walked away wondering if she was going to call my bluff, if she'd do it just to spite me or to prove to her parents once and for all that she was telling the truth. Thankfully, that didn't happen, and when Julie realized I wasn't going to react or try to save her, the window-ledge dramas came to an end.

What did not come to an end, however, was Julie's use of our bathroom as her own private sanctuary.

"Hey, Jules!" I hollered as I stood outside the bathroom door one night not long after moving in with her. "Open up, I have to pee!" I could hear the shower running, but either she couldn't hear me or she chose to ignore me. When she finally emerged, I said, "You know, you don't have to lock the door with me here."

"It's an old habit. Makes me feel more comfortable."

Moments later, as I stood over the toilet, I smelled vomit. When I found her in the kitchen pouring herself a glass of ginger ale, I said, "Are you okay? Are you sick?"

"I'm fine, why?"

"Because I smelled vomit in the bathroom, that's why. Were you throwing up?"

"No, I was taking a shower."

"Are you sure you weren't throwing up?"

"Yes, I'm sure."

This brief exchange was the beginning and end of any discussion Julie and I would have about bulimia for a long time. And while I suspected she was lying, I felt I had little choice but to trust her, and that meant trusting she would tell me the truth when she was ready to. Until then, I wasn't going to second guess her or badger her about it. Where, when, and how she threw up after that I never really knew. She ate twice as much food as I did and was still skinny as a stick—something we used to joke about, actually. Of one thing I was certain: I never smelled vomit in our bathroom again.

Tour of Duty

A N AMERICAN BALLET THEATRE TOUR in the 1980s was noth-ing short of a military operation. With about ninety dancers and fifteen to twenty support staff, a few tireless, overworked members of the administration organized everything from booking flights and hotel rooms to bringing our mail from New York each week.

During the 1981-82 season, the company logged 12,945 miles during nineteen weeks on the road. Anywhere from six to thirteen forty-foot trailers were used to transport lights, scenery, and costumes from one city to another. We spent over $260,000 on transportation and nearly one million dollars on lodging and food.

A tour booklet was, much like the tour itself, magically produced every year and given to every dancer, multiple copies if need be. In this book was a list of every city on tour, repertoire, flight times, company hotels, theaters, backstage phone numbers, local banks where we could cash our checks, doctors, chiropractors, hospitals, local health clubs, anything and everything ABT thought we needed to know.

One of the many perks of being a dancer in American Ballet The-atre was that it was entirely up to us whether or not we wanted to travel on the company flight or stay in the company hotel. We were free to do as we pleased, just like real adults. As long as we showed up for rehears-als and performances, the company didn't really care how we got from point A to point B, or what we did in between. If we stayed elsewhere on tour, we could pocket our hotel money and our meal allowance, and this money, coupled with whatever overtime pay we might make, meant that my weekly tour paychecks were often three times my typical weekly salary.

Tours in the 1980s invariably began in December with three to four weeks of performances at the Kennedy Center in Washington, D.C. This was a time when the company was getting accustomed to performing again after a summer layoff and several months of rehearsals in New York. It was a time when certain dancers would get longed-for opportunities and new ballets were waiting around every corner. The company was filled with a mixture of hope, resignation, and, in some cases, despair, as those who left loved ones back in New York girded themselves for the long bouts of solitude that lay ahead.

For those who'd been in the company for at least a year, we generally knew what to expect. We knew what parts we would be getting to dance and what parts we wouldn't. We knew each city and what the hotels and theaters would look like, although those cities and theaters would change on occasion. To our regular repertoire of American cities (Washington, Miami, Chicago, Los Angeles, San Francisco, Minneapolis, Detroit) we would eventually add Boston, Philadelphia, San Diego, Houston, and Atlanta.

December in Washington was a time Julie and I spent watching the nation's capital gear up for the Christmas season while we performed eight shows a week at the Kennedy Center. Initially, these performances would be repertory programs, but as Christmas drew near, there would be *Nutcracker* or, later on, *Cinderella*. Eventually, sandwiched between the Christmas Eve matinee and the evening performance on Christmas

Day, we celebrated, many of us with trees and decorations and friends or family who came in from out of town. By late afternoon on Christmas day, however, our brief stab at the holiday would come to an end as we turned our attention once again to the theater where we lived our lives. By the time we got back to the Kennedy Center for the evening show on Christmas Day, took class, and had put on our makeup and costumes one more time, it always seemed to me as if Christmas was a more realistic detour around the make-believe world I actually lived in.

It had long been a New Year's Eve tradition at New York City Ballet to take the *Nutcracker* they'd been performing for a month or more and add some unlikely twists to the well-worn narrative. It took very little coercion to convince us to do the same. These twists generally involved a fair amount of cross-dressing in the party scene and cameo appearances by various members of the staff. And always the battle scene between the mice and soldiers would offer up a degree of mayhem and retribution not seen in Tchaikovsky's day. Just about anything went, really, and often did, most of it entirely beyond the purview of the audience.

The dancers, all of whom were more than a bit weary of listening to "Waltz of the Flowers" and seeing giant mice battle toy soldiers for the umpteenth night in a row, became giddy to the point of apoplexy at the prospect of skewing this old chestnut and leapt at every opportunity to do something unexpected.

I was a relative newcomer to ABT, but I soon realized that Misha did not enjoy nor take kindly to anything the dancers might cook up on New Year's Eve. Understandably, he had some uneasiness about just how overboard we might go; visions of a run on the box office and cries of outrage over what the dancers of American Ballet Theatre had perpetrated undoubtedly kept him up late the night before New Year's

Eve. As a result, every year, he would get on the theater PA system prior to the show to warn us not to do what we were about to do. He sounded like a broken record, really, and our reaction was always the same; we laughed, then went about putting the finishing touches on our makeup and our plans, all of which we considered utterly brilliant and hilarious.

Who, I used to ask myself, did Misha think we were? Did he honestly think we had no sense of integrity or appreciation for the forty years of great dancing that preceded us at American Ballet Theatre? Did he think we had no respect for tradition or had learned nothing by continually striving to rise to the standard he expected of us? Did he not trust us?

Clearly, we didn't know Misha very well, and he didn't know us very well, because not only could he not stop us, he would never admit that what we did was often funny and very clever. It was all done in the spirit of the evening and with a great deal of concern on our parts for how far we could or, for that matter, should go. It was our moment to have a bit of fun, to laugh, to wrest of bit of control from Misha's iron-fisted grip on our lives and the company.

If Larry Peck rollerblading down the *La Bayadère* ramp like a ski jumper while dressed as a giant mouse during "Waltz of the Flowers" wasn't a brilliant New Year's Eve spoof, I don't what is. In any event, after a couple of years of trying and failing to put a stop to our fun, Misha eventually decided to step in and choreograph the New Year's Eve show, thus taking every ounce of the evening's joy away from us and putting it firmly into his lap, which is exactly where he seemed to want it. I will admit, the multiple casts of Princes making surprise entrances was an amusing touch, but the whole thing lacked the one ingredient that made the New Year's Eve show so memorable and so hilarious: it was *our* creation.

Not long after the annual New Year's roasting of the *Nutcracker*, Ballet Theatre usually headed south for a two-week engagement at the Jackie Gleason Theater in Miami Beach. During our second visit to Miami in January of 1982, Misha came up to me after class one day and said, "Mikey... Jerry Robbins and I...vee are taking some dancers to Spoleto Festival in Italy dis summer. I vant you to learn First Sailor in *Fancy Free* and *Opus Jazz*. Okeea?"

"Okay, Misha, sure. Thank you."

Stunned, I walked outside into the piercing Florida sunshine and stared in disbelief at the brightly colored Lichtenstein sculpture reclining in the grass. Nothing I'd done at Ballet Theatre up to that point had prepared me for the opportunity Misha was offering. His belief that I was capable of dancing a role as important as First Sailor in *Fancy Free* felt like a gram of Miami's finest cocaine shooting directly into my bloodstream.

Created by Robbins in 1944, it's impossible to overstate the impact *Fancy Free* had on American Ballet Theatre or the ballet world. It was a short ballet based on contemporary characters that everyone in America at the time could relate to: three sailors on shore leave, hanging out in a bar, trying to outdo one another in order to pick up two girls. The music was composed by Leonard Bernstein, the set designed by Oliver Smith, and the whole of it put the twenty-five-year-old Jerome Robbins on the map. *Fancy Free* was, as Eugene Loring so aptly put it, a ballet about *real* people, and it, along with the works of Anthony Tudor and Agnes de Mille, came to characterize a style of psychological and dramatic ballet that would define American Ballet Theatre.

The casual way Misha asked me to learn *Fancy* led me to believe that I was expected to do it on my own, so I got hold of a video and started learning the steps. No rehearsals were scheduled. No ballet master was assigned to teach me the part or coach me up. Obviously, I was excited, but in the back of my mind I felt like a bit of an afterthought, a back-up sailor in case someone got hurt.

Whatever Misha's expectations were, he did not share them with me. He had presented an opportunity, and I knew I had best make the most of it, with or without help. Throughout the remainder of tour, I tried, whenever possible, to find a space to work on *Fancy Free*, but it wasn't easy. The solo wasn't particularly difficult to learn, but it presented some technical challenges I was having a hard time with.

With a great deal of excitement and trepidation over the task at hand, I set to work. Meanwhile, the company departed the blue-haired splendor of Miami Beach for Chicago. We had changed theaters and hotels from my first year in the company and would now spend two weeks at the Americana Congress Hotel overlooking Lake Michigan, performing directly across the street at the Auditorium Theater.

For the duration of our stay in Chicago, I awoke each morning to a frosting of ice on the windows and gazed out at the glacial emptiness of Lake Michigan. After a cup of coffee and a muffin, or no muffin, I would head down to the banquet room on the ground floor where the company had installed a sprung floor and some portable Mylar mirrors in what would become virtually our sole classroom and rehearsal space.

During matinee days in Chicago, company class was held on the Auditorium Theater stage—a slight improvement over the Windsor Ballroom at the hotel (a space with all the Windsorian charm of a Motel 6). There was more room on stage for class, and I was not faced with the strange versions of myself that the Mylar mirrors presented. In one of these "mirrors" I might appear waiflike, for example, and in the next, obese, all of which begged the question: is there anything more sadistic one could do to a bunch of ballet dancers, all of whom have tremendous angst about their weight and bodies, than put them in a room where they will see themselves looking fifteen pounds overweight or fifteen pounds underweight? In the latter case, one might logically assume this would make us feel great and in the former, suicidal, but we were no fools. We knew the thin Mylar mirror was lying. We weren't so sure, however, about the fat one.

When we finally returned to New York after our long tour, a group of dancers from Ballet Theatre assembled in the very same studio where I had first auditioned for Misha, that of Robert Denvers. An actual bar similar to the one in *Fancy Free* had been brought in, and both Jerry Robbins and Misha were there along with all the boys who were cast in the ballet. When my moment arrived, I got about three-quarters of the way through the solo before Misha said, "Mikey, Mikey, iss okay. Vee don't need to see entire solo. Iss fine." And that was that. I fell back to Earth where I belonged.

Spoleto

DESPITE MY DISAPPOINTING SHOWING in *Fancy*, I managed to go home that evening with some "parting" gifts. I was asked to learn *Opus Jazz* and come to Italy as an understudy. And in early July, not long after the Met season was over, that's where I found myself, alone in a small apartment down a steep hill from Spoleto's central piazza.

The atmosphere at the Spoleto Festival was, well, festive! The town seemed as if it had been put together by Disney to look like an ancient Roman playground for the rich and the beautiful. Shops were selling the most gorgeous clothes, exotic foods, and regional wines. Many of these places existed only during the festival and were wedged into ancient stone buildings along cobblestoned alleyways. There were outdoor cafes and restaurants and gelaterias in abundance. Everything I saw and tasted was magnificent. It seemed almost criminal that we had to work in that setting, and, apparently, I wasn't the only one who felt that way, because both Jerry Robbins and Misha seemed content to work us as little as possible.

Most of our days began with class followed by a few hours of rehearsal, then it was off in a cab to the local pool, home for a nap, a leisurely lunch, or a stroll through town to do some shopping. We'd come to Italy having prepared all of the ballets back in New York, so there was little to do once we got to Spoleto save tie up a few loose ends and get accustomed to the dreaded Italian raked stage. I was already well acquainted with Italy and raked stages and had no actual dancing to do as of yet, so for me it was a veritable paid vacation.

I stood on the sidelines, marking the choreography to *Opus Jazz* as Susan Jones, our ballet mistress from ABT, ran rehearsals. When I first joined Ballet Theatre, Susan often taught company class, but as her responsibilities for managing ballets and making up the daily rehearsal schedule (a herculean task) mounted, she didn't have the time or energy for teaching.

In 1980 when I joined the company, Susan was just twenty-eight years old, but already two years into her retirement from ABT's corps de ballet. She seemed like one of us. She was affable. Her class was enjoyable and thorough. She didn't seem to have an axe to grind. She'd taken on responsibility for Twyla Tharp's *Push Comes to Shove* and, later on, ballets like Paul Taylor's *Airs,* Merce Cunningham's *Duets,* and a number of other ballets I was either involved in personally or wanted to be.

What struck me most profoundly about Susan was that, in the short time I'd known her, she added a considerable amount of weight to her diminutive frame. In addition to this, her dark hair had gone prematurely gray—or she simply stopped coloring it, I don't know. The result of these two phenomena was that she seemed to age before my eyes. I say this not be cruel, but because in a ballet company where eating disorders are commonplace and people are obsessed with youth, beauty, and bodies, it is striking that someone with the discipline to devote their life to making the body beautiful and maintaining it could so quickly toss that discipline aside.

The reason I began to wonder about Susan more than I otherwise might have was that, after the Spoleto Festival began and everyone was comfortable on stage, I wanted an opportunity to dance. It seemed ludicrous that I should stand in the wings night after night. I knew *Opus Jazz* backwards and forwards, but, more to the point, I believed I was fairly adept at it. When I asked Susan whether or not I might be able to dance, she was less than enthusiastic. "We'll see," she said.

Nobody, it seemed, really much cared whether I got to dance *Opus Jazz* or not, despite the fact that there seemed ample time for a couple of extra rehearsals to get me in on the action. I knew this because most of the dancers spent their days as I did, lounging by the pool, sitting in cafés, or shopping, and it became obvious as the end of the Festival neared that Susan's "we'll see" wasn't going to amount to much.

What Susan neglected to tell me was that while Jerry Robbins might have been on his best behavior where Misha's treasured Ballet Theater dancers were concerned, he had no qualms about treating Susan to a dose of his infamous charm, and she was on the verge of hopping on a plane and high-tailing it back to New York. My request for consideration and extra rehearsals, as innocuous as it might have appeared to me then, was simply impossible for her to contemplate. Unfortunately, Susan didn't share this information with me at the time, and I was left to conclude what any ballet dancer would, i.e., that I simply wasn't worth the time or that Susan just didn't like me, or both.

On the bright side, the Italians won the World Cup three-nil over Germany while I was busy not dancing in Spoleto. The performance I would watch, yet again, from the wings was postponed until after the match was over, owing to the fact that everyone in the entire country was glued to a television set. In the square behind the theater, dancers, orchestra, townspeople, and tourists gathered round to watch one of the many TVs that had been dragged out into the streets. Around eleven that evening, it was all over; the Italian Davids had somehow managed to vanquish the mighty German Goliaths, and, as a line of cars circled the town, horns blaring, Misha stormed through another brilliant performance of *Other Dances* with Susan Jaffe while I gathered dust in the wings.

When at last the curtain came down on the final performance, a few jokes about my wallflower status were made, and it seemed only fitting that I should laugh along with those jokes. Better to laugh than cry, I suppose. But back in the privacy of my room and in the solitary weeks that followed, I realized the entire experience had cut me to the very core.

With about a month left before ABT resumed rehearsals in New York, I went to Rome, rented a car, and set off on an Italian road trip. As thrilling as this idea might have seemed, my vacation from my vacation was not exactly the pleasure cruise I imagined. No matter where I went in my microscopic Autobianchi, I couldn't get away from myself. Florence, Pisa, Elba, Corsica, Capri—in each and every instance I was awed by the beauty of these places, but even more awed by how lonely I felt and how distressing it had been to spend three weeks in Spoleto watching other dancers do things I believed I could have done just as well, if not better.

Despite many good reasons for swallowing large doses of anti-depressants, I tried to spin this entire event into a positive. I had been invited to Spoleto, and this was, in and of itself, indicative of something. And then one night in Capri, I found myself dining with two strangers, an older couple who gave me some unsolicited advice.

"Do you really want to make it in this company, ABT?" the woman asked, after listening to my tale of Italian frustration.

"Yes, of course."

"Then commit yourself to that. But *really* commit yourself to it. Don't just *think* it's something you'd like to do. You have to want it and be certain that you want it." And then, just as I was falling under her Tony-Robbins spell, she said, "But be careful what you wish for."

Admittedly, this was an awful cliché, but she said it, not me, and at the time I was young enough and naive enough and had had just enough Barolo to believe she was Anne Landers, the Dalai Lama, and Nostradamus all rolled into one. As I walked back to my little hotel on Via Sopramonte that balmy summer night in Capri, the solution to my problem seemed stunningly immediate, and it was this very immediacy that made it so captivating. I realized that what I needed to propel myself out of the dung heap of ABT and get Misha and Susan Jones to notice me (in addition to some good, old-fashioned hard work) was a good old-fashioned eating disorder. If I can't get anyone's attention with my dancing, my thinking went, maybe I can get it by being carried out of Ballet Theatre on a stretcher.

It wasn't so much that I stopped eating in Capri, though I came close to it. I simply didn't eat anything until dinner. What I hadn't bargained for was that by the time I sat down to my reward for a day of abstinence, my stomach had shrunk to the size of a pea. After three bites of pasta, I sat back, looking dispiritedly at the delicious food I knew I wasn't going to finish. My Italian waiter looked on, horrified, his entire Mediterranean worldview smashed like a watermelon dropped from a ten-story building.

This went on night after watermelon-smashing night, my evening repast pushed aside in lieu of too much wine and the inevitable drunkenness that followed. And each night, as my waiter removed my barely-eaten plate of food, he would look at me, his eyes a mixture of confusion and despair. I knew what he was thinking. *What the hell is wrong with you?*

1982

FAST FORWARD. SEPTEMBER. ABT's rehearsal period has just begun, and this is my first men's class after returning from Italy. As I'm finishing an exercise and walking off the floor, Misha says to me, "Mikey, Mikey, vaad you doink?"

I look over at him and think to myself, my name isn't Mikey, it's Michael. And as for vaad I'm doink? Vaad I'm doink? What the fuck do you think I'm doing? I'm taking this awful class from your ballet master du jour, Jurgen Schneider, the man who's at least partly responsible for that first of many knee surgeries you recently had because he's too afraid to tell you you're wrenching the hell out of your knees at the barre trying to turn out your feet. And even though I think he's got nothing original to say and I'd much rather be uptown taking class with David Howard, I'm here so you can *see* me, and you and Jurgen and the legendary ghosts of American Ballet Theatre can mold me into a worthwhile piece of clay.

In the meantime, I am toiling away, hoping to get some foothold on that slippery outcropping called the balletic ideal. On a highly irregular basis I delude myself into believing that I've actually grabbed hold of that ideal, because in order to be the greatest ballet dancer in the world, I have to believe I'm capable of becoming that dancer, one with a name like Misha or Sasha or Rudolf, a dancer born in a country like Russia and nurtured by the likes of Pushkin, the Kirov, and the entire Soviet Empire, before I defect to the West where I'm immediately anointed a star, a superior being with talents far beyond any American's, a fantastic creature whose country can build a war machine capable of destroying the entire planet yet still manage to produce some of the finest examples of that trivial, elitist little thing known as ballet. All of which is a roundabout way of saying that I look at Misha with utter bemusement.

And then he does what he usually does: he mocks me. "Mikey, vhy you do like dis?" he says, contorting his arms into some grotesque position that might conceivably require surgery.

I shouldn't be surprised. How many dancers, after all, have any idea what they really look like? None. Ask a ninety-five-pound corps de ballet girl from ABT or New York City Ballet what she sees when she looks in the mirror, and she'll tell you a big fat cow who needs to stop eating so fucking much.

Apart from mockery and being an all-around killjoy, the behavior Misha indulges in most often is expecting instantaneous results of the highest order. He simply cannot comprehend why you would place your arms *here* instead of *there*, especially when *here* is correct and *there* is wrong or unworkable or awkward or, even more unforgivable, ugly. And because he can do pretty much whatever he wants to with his body, it's difficult if not impossible for him to grasp the fact that you can't.

"Vhy can't you do dis?" he invariably seems to be thinking. "Eet isss so eaasy."

And because he is capable of making that leap between what he envisions a movement should look like and its execution—with every nuance of shape and amplitude and musical luster his mind and body can instantly conjure up—he is impatient and often pissed off because,

God damn it, there simply aren't enough Mishas in ABT to do things the way he wants them done. For that matter, there aren't enough hours in the day to take care of all the shit he has to take care of as director, womanizer, actor, and world-famous dancer.

In the final analysis, he is Misha, and I am not. I am a dancer for whom those two things—the vision and the result—must be bridged by more time, work, and disappointment than Misha will ever comprehend. No matter how many caveats I come up with, however, I am left with one irritating and unavoidable fact: Misha is what I aspire to be; what every man in ABT in one way or another aspires to be and measures himself against. And not only would we like to be able to dance like him, we desperately want to please him because his pleasure, which is so rare, is irrefutable proof that you have done something well. And not *well* relative to what you are typically capable of doing, but well within the bounds of Misha's definition of wellness, and that is, for just about any normal living human being and, without a doubt, every dancer in American Ballet Theatre, a staggering achievement.

Funnily enough, I am secretly thrilled to be the object of Misha's attentions, even when it means having my fragile technique or my even more fragile personality dissected. *At least he is noticing you,* some little voice inside me whispers. This whisper, however, is often drowned out by the screaming feeling that when it is happening and I am standing there quietly being filleted in front of the entire class, I want more than anything else to become the opposite of me, the non-me, the black hole of me.

Misha's parody of my port de bras makes a few of the boys in class chuckle: Victor Barbee, Gil Boggs, Ross Stretton, and Danny Radojevic, all of whom stand with Misha at a portable barre in the center of the room. They are his groupies, his Greek chorus. They laugh whenever he laughs and get serious whenever he isn't in the mood for fun and games (which is most of the time) and just generally act as if they've gotten past the velvet rope and all the rest of us are still standing outside in the rain.

But who can blame them for laughing, really? When you've got the most physically gifted dancer in the world doing the mocking, the results speak for themselves.

"Brilliant," gushes Anna Kisselgoff in *The New York Times*.

"Stunning," writes Clive Barnes in *The New York Post*.

"A Quasimodo for the ages," opines Arlene Croce in *The New Yorker*.

As cruel as he can be at times, it is my belief that Misha was rarely, if ever, *intentionally* cruel. His cruelty was something that completely escaped him. I imagined that, in his experience back in the old country, it was normal to exaggerate, to caricature, to refrain from giving compliments, to focus on the negative no matter how much progress a dancer might be making, to say things like, "You look like a boiled chicken." You're not supposed to take any of that seriously. Come on! You're supposed to laugh. A boiled chicken? Ha ha! That's a good one! A real knee slapper.

And because it was so memorable and so funny, I'm sure Kristi, the girl in the corps de ballet he said this to, will never forget it as long as she lives. But Misha? Five minutes after he said it he won't remember it. He'll have no idea how hurtful it was or how long it might linger in her mind.

Six weeks after my Tony-Robbins epiphany in Capri, the results of my hunger-artist initiative weren't exactly going according to plan. On the positive side, I was down to a hundred thirty-five pounds, a number I pledged to keep an iron-fisted grip on via the use of every anorexic's favorite household implement: the bathroom scale. I would soon be taking it on a four-month tour of the United States, compliments of American Ballet Theatre.

Another positive is that I managed to get some attention above and beyond Misha noticing my ghastly port de bras. David Richardson, an ABT ballet master long associated with New York City Ballet and, one could only assume, a veritable orgy of eating and behavioral disorders, saw me looking like a tanned cadaver in class that first day back and came over immediately.

"Michael," he said, sashaying up with a ravenous look in his eye, "you look fabulousssss."

I realized from David's reaction that I was well down the road toward my goal (or insanity, take your pick), and suddenly it felt like Christmas.

Yes, all I could think about was food and not eating and the few morsels I would reward myself with after a day of starvation. Yes, I occasionally felt faint, but that slight dizzy feeling was one I created all by myself, and that was exactly the kind of control I savored to its fullest. Because deep down, what any person in my position was looking for is the belief that they are finally, at long last, in control. I couldn't control Misha. I couldn't control Susan Jones. But there were two things I knew I could control in that crazy, mixed-up world called American Ballet Theatre: a knife and a fork.

The one other thing I knew I could control was my ability to keep this a secret from Julie. When she saw me upon my return from Italy, she remarked that I was thinner, quite a bit thinner, but she had no idea that my future happiness on a day-to-day, second to second basis would revolve entirely around a number on a bathroom scale.

In order to avoid breaching the arbitrary, one-hundred-thirty-five-pound levee I created and the inevitable forfeiture of food that must surely follow as night follows day, I continually hedged my bets. You could never eat too little in my book. Everything became a game of diminishing returns. I stockpiled an absence of food, built up an armory of hope from one meal to the next, reassuring myself with each spoonful I didn't put on my plate or that I tossed down the drain or "saved" for tomorrow that I had been a "good" boy. I would make my target weight.

What I didn't bank on was the fact that the less I ate, the more I thought about food and the slower my metabolism got, making me tired and often irritable. During the duller stretches of ballets like *Don Quixote* or *Giselle,* my mind wandered to the checklist I kept in my head of every morsel of food I had consumed during the day and the something or nothing I would allow myself when I got home.

Those were the moments in my life when, confronted with the absurdity of what I was doing, I came face to face with the ridiculous notion that I had taken control of my body and my career. Nothing could have been further from the truth. Anorexics don't take control, they give it away—completely, willingly, wholeheartedly—to a morsel of food or a mirror or a number on a bathroom scale.

But sweep that little observation under the rug as quickly as possible and move on. Tomorrow's another day, and with that comes a newfound sense of purpose to redouble one's efforts and focus on the positives. I am getting thinner. People are noticing me. My jeans are so loose now, I can buy a new pair. I'm still too fat. I've got a headache. My arabesque looks great. I'm really not hungry. I'll just have a salad and a glass of water or, no, make that a glass of wine. A margarita? Sure, why not? No one seems to notice me. I hate my thighs. Why did I just eat that? I hate myself. One drink and I'm shit-faced. This is awesome. Five more pounds. Why won't my ass go away? I feel great. I look pretty good at this weight. I look like shit. I'm a piece of shit. I suck. I'm fat.

I went home after class that first day back and vacuumed Julie's entire apartment. As I sucked up the dust and bits of dirt and lint that marred the surface of her old, rose-colored, wall-to-wall carpeting, I felt as if those minor imperfections were my imperfections and that by making them disappear, my feelings of dirty, fat inadequacy would disappear, and for a few fleeting moments, I felt clean and perfect and whole.

This is my penance.

This is my world.

I am its master.

Carpet, you are mine.

Charles the First

A S A BOY IN THE CORPS DE BALLET of American Ballet Theatre, there were very few instances, if any, where I had to speak to Misha's infamous assistant, Charles France. I had no reason to. I wasn't a soloist or principal dancer, and I wasn't a corps de ballet dancer who had a drug problem or an eating disorder so dire that it required his attention. Those were the kinds of issues and people Charles France dealt with, not boys in the corps de ballet on the verge of losing their minds.

Charles was believed by many, both inside and outside of Ballet Theatre, to be the true power behind Misha's throne. Years later, I asked Charles about this.

"I'd been at Ballet Theatre for ten years, and I felt that what I had to do was tell Misha exactly what I thought and then let him decide what he wanted to do. He *always* made the final decisions. Sometimes I would say things like, 'You want to do this, but if we do this, this is going to happen. Are you aware of this?' Those were the kinds of things I would say. Nothing ever happened in secret. I always told Misha everything.

"Misha couldn't do things like the programming or all of the casting. He did the first cast of everything, and he chose the repertoire, and I did the programming because I was very good at it and could do it quickly. I'd make sure subscribers weren't getting the same ballets or dancers they'd had the year before, things like that.

"What caused some people to misinterpret my role was that Misha was completely terrified about speaking to dancers he suspected were going to make trouble. He would talk to people he thought were reasonable, but sometimes his antennae were just quivering away, so he'd ask me to speak to them. In many instances, what these dancers wanted to talk about were things he and I had already spoken about, so I would usually say, 'Misha and I have spoken about this, and he's just not going to change his mind. If you still disagree, I think the best thing you can do is to make an appointment with him yourself.' And strangely enough, they rarely did.

"My theory was that some dancers would rather hear no from me than no from Misha, because when Misha said no, it was like this earth-shattering, never-to-be-changed thing. Some of these dancers would then come back to me and say, well, what about this or what about that; and sometimes I would say, I'll ask, or sometimes I would say, you'll have to see him about that."

When Charles came to New York as a young man, he went to Columbia University. He was working on his graduate degree in French when he took a summer job at ABT. That job led to his becoming assistant to Oliver Smith, a set designer and the co-director of ABT from 1945 until 1980.

"When I came to New York, I would go to the ballet quite a bit," Charles said. "I had a friend who worked in Sol Hurok's office, and one evening she invited me to go see *The Dream* with Antoinette Sibley and Anthony Dowell.

"So I was sitting there, and I began to feel sort of odd. And when the curtain came down, I was in this open-eyed coma. I had the feeling that I suddenly understood ballet as a whole thing—the technique, the lyricism, the acting. Somehow, I came to understand what was great and what wasn't, and why.

"I had those feelings about everything I saw at that time, starting in the late 60s. It was truly an epiphany. I knew who was a star and who wasn't, and I could explain why. Consequently, when I started working in the press department at ABT, I knew everything about what was being done and who was doing it, and I did a very good job."

All of this may have been true, but when you're a rakishly thin member of the women's corps de ballet at American Ballet Theatre and an incredibly affected, bespectacled, obese man who was never a professional dancer in his entire life peers over the top of his glasses and down across a gigantic belly to tell you in a fey, nasally whine that a pointe shoe is merely a "theatrical *device*" and that you should not make so much noise when you run around on stage in them, the loathing for and paranoia about Charles France reached gargantuan proportions at American Ballet Theatre.

The dancers in the corps de ballet talked about Charles as if he were some sort of Svengali, but I never believed that. "He's an evil man," Julie would tell me, before reiterating that every girl in the corps de ballet dressing room thought he was the devil incarnate, a big fat queen who didn't know the first thing about what it took to be a professional dancer.

Charles was intelligent, certainly, and very very opinionated. He often said things to dancers with little regard for their feelings, and this, coupled with the fact that he was as fat as he was and had never been a dancer, made it virtually impossible for most of us to respect him, let alone like him.

Like most of the men in the corps de ballet, I had an inordinate amount of time to dwell on things like Susan and Charles, and in my most vindictive states, I would look at the two of them hovering on either side of Misha at the front of the rehearsal room and say to myself, "How on earth did those two fat people come to stand in judgment over so many skinny little lives?"

1982. Locked Out.

According to the 1982 ABT Annual Report, during the previous season, ABT toured to eleven cities and staged 203 performances. We sold 570,000 tickets that totaled over twelve million dollars in revenue, and yet, by the end of that year, the company would still have a $287,000 shortfall. What made this figure particularly noteworthy was that it was the first such shortfall in four years, and it immediately preceded the 1982 labor negotiations between ABT management and our union, The American Guild of Musical Artists.

Despite the shortfall (an amount more or less equal to ABT's expenditure for pointe shoes), Lenny Leibowitz, the dancers' labor lawyer, would file charges of unfair labor practices with the National Labor Relations Board and accuse ABT management of financial deception.

"If they can't afford to pay the dancers," he said, "let us see the books. If they can, then why not pay?"

ABT's response to this insinuation wasn't a curt "fuck you"; rather, it was a 1.3 million dollar offer to increase salaries and other forms of compensation. This was deemed insufficient by our union reps, and, because they told us to, we voted against it. The timing of the ongoing negotiations meant ABT would have to cancel our engagements in Washington, Boston, and Paris (the only time I would ever have the opportunity to dance at the theater for the Paris Opera, Palais Garnier, in my life). Our union reps and Lenny thought management would cave to our demands in order to save those performances. They were wrong.

The people on the board of American Ballet Theatre were like the people on most other boards: they were rich. The chairman of the board at that time was Donald Kendall (CEO of PepsiCo), and he and the other wealthy members of the board were not the sort of folks who were accustomed to being strong-armed. They certainly weren't going to be intimidated by a bunch of ballet dancers. Unfortunately, Lenny and our union reps hadn't thought very deeply about this or the deficit the company was running, and the day after the ABT board rejected our final offer, not only were we not going to Paris, we were not going to work.

For the most part, Misha was in complete agreement with our demands. A first-year dancer at ABT made $405 a week in 1982. A second-year corps de ballet dancer made $405 a week. A third-year corps de ballet dancer made $410 a week. (Who the hell, one had to wonder, negotiated those salaries?) Soloists started at $540 a week, and principal dancers made $650 (though most of the principal dancers negotiated their pay individually). Per diem at ABT was $24 a day.

Understandably, $405 a week, even in 1982, was not a hell of a lot of money, so it wasn't surprising that we asked for increases in year-to-year salaries that might amount to more than five dollars over three years. We also asked that any dancer have the option to room alone on tour should they wish, and a few other incidental things having to do with per diem and overtime pay—money issues I've long since forgotten.

As an ignorant, lowly member of the corps de ballet, I thought the principal dancers in ABT were making a fortune. In 2010, I asked Cynthia Harvey, an ABT principal dancer in the 1980s, about her salary. "I made, maximum—before I stopped in 1996—$885 a week after taxes. When I was guesting [dancing with other companies], I never earned more than $2,000 per performance. I earned more touring with Misha on his summer tours in the 1980s than I did in an entire year with ABT."

Our labor lawyer, Lenny Leibowitz, had made a career out of exacting revenge on management, and before we knew what was happening, it was US against THEM. The one point Lenny neglected to drive home was that ballet companies are not like General Motors. They don't *make* money. They *lose* money. $287,000 in 1982, to be exact.

What we should have had the good sense to realize was that in a ballet company, you're all in it together: dancers, administrators, board members, everyone. Nobody's doing any of it to make money. They're there because they believe in the art form or have been touched by it enough to open their wallets and, in some cases, devote their professional lives to it, even though it's a loss leader and pays peanuts.

There's no use pointing fingers and saying to a board member like Jackie Onassis or Donald Kendall, "You're hiding money from us! You're cheating us in some way!" But that was the type of thing our union reps and Lenny were accusing management of doing. They believed we were being duped, but, honestly, did we really want ABT's finances called into question by the IRS or the NEA? What good could that possibly lead to for the company, or us?

I was twenty-two at the time. What the hell did I know about how ABT operated? Like many of the dancers, I got caught up in the moment, in the power we suddenly found ourselves with. We could actually bring ABT to its knees! Of course, when you follow that thought through to its logical conclusion, you realize that ABT isn't just the board of directors or the executive committee or Charles France or Misha or Susan Jones or all the mysterious ABT hobgoblins who stand between you and your dreams—it's YOU.

ABT Cancels Third Booking

As the American Ballet Theatre labor dispute went well into its second month, ABT announced cancellation of its four-week season in Washington, scheduled to open Dec. 7. Unless a last-minute change occurs, the Kennedy Center season will thus become the third casualty of the dispute, having been preceded by cancellations in Paris and in Boston.

Meanwhile, ABT's dancers have scheduled a benefit to be held Nov. 15 at Roseland in New York. The

benefit, called "The First American Ballet Theatre Dancers Ball," will have the theme "Would You Like to Swing With a Star," and will cover the era of the '20s to the '50s. Dick Cavett and Jim Dale will be M.C.'s and ABT principals scheduled to appear include Natalia Makarova, Martine van Hamel, Marianna Tcherkassky, Cynthia Harvey, Danilo Radojevic and Kevin McKenzie. New York City Ballet dancers will join the festivities. Dinner

(Continued on page 12)

American Ballet Theatre dancers bringing attention to their plight during the Columbus Ave. street fair Festival. Among them were Cheryl Yeager, Elaine Kudo, Lisa Rinehart (first three girls on platform) and Michael Langlois (on the right)

Patricia Barnes

Lockout Fundraiser. 1982. New York.

All we were really doing with this lockout business was biting the hands that fed us and causing irreparable damage to the goodwill the members of the board and management had for the dancers of ABT. But for a few moments, the corps de ballet, who outnumbered the principal dancers and soloists by a margin of nearly two to one, felt empowered in ways we never did before, and, like most people who've become accustomed to feeling manipulated by circumstances seemingly beyond their control, we were intrigued by this power and wanted to know what it felt like to wield it.

And wield it we did. Without understanding the situation entirely, we circled our proletariat wagons and garnered a fair amount of publicity for our efforts during the lockout, much of which I was personally involved in as a member of the publicity team. We made the nightly news and marched in parades. Julie and I went to Washington and protested in front of the Kennedy Center. We met with NFL players who were, likewise, involved in their own labor negotiations. And while this was going on, we presented ourselves as poor, starving artists who were being taken advantage of by a bunch of rich, social-climbing New York millionaires.

I never mentioned this to anyone, because it seemed important to present a united front, but I felt like a hypocrite in the midst of this dispute. I really didn't need any more money to dance for American Ballet Theatre. I was doing fine. I was thrilled to be where I was. I didn't care about getting a single hotel room on tour or most of the other demands we had on the table. Yes, $405 a week as a starting salary at ABT in the New York of 1982, where the average two-bedroom, one-bath apartment rented for $625 a month, was not enough money to live comfortably on, but no one was really disputing that fact.

Our dancers' representatives had our best interests at heart and so did Lenny—of that I'm certain—but there was no need for the rancor or the work stoppage.

Charles France's reaction to our behavior at the time was this:

"It was completely unnecessary. And Misha was very sanguine about the whole thing. We talked a lot about it, and he knew that most of the dancers' requests were perfectly normal. However, as far as the timing was concerned, we all thought it was shocking. We were supposed to be on our way to Paris the next week! And yet nobody said, okay, let's go to Paris and come home and figure this out. It wasn't that big of a deal."

By the time the smoke cleared four months later, we had accomplished the following: first-year corps de ballet salaries actually went backward to $400 a week (this figure would increase to $425 a week in 1984-85). Second-year corps de ballet salaries increased from $405 to $425, with $25 weekly increases in succeeding years. Soloist salaries jumped from $540 a week to $625 a week and reached $700 a week in 1984-85. Principal salaries increased from $650 to $750 a week and reached $825 a week for the 1984-85 season.

To put this in perspective, the dancers at the heart of ABT's corps de ballet (fifth-year dancers) could expect to make $4,704 more per year beginning in 1982 for a forty-two-week annual contract. If they stayed into their seventh year, they would make $5,250 more per year. The salary I lost during the four-month lockout amounted to $6,480.

Postscript: In July of 2009, Lenny Leibowitz, our labor lawyer, was arrested and charged with embezzling approximately $150,000 from the independent union representing the dancers and stage managers of American Ballet Theatre.

Woytek

ONE OF THE UNEXPECTED BENEFITS of the labor dispute in 1982 was that after it began, one of our new ballet masters, Woytek Lowski, agreed to work with me privately. I knew I needed to make an extra effort (beyond starving myself) if I was going to go anywhere in Ballet Theatre, so when the lockout became a reality, I turned to Woytek. He had the time, and he was willing. We started the day after the lockout began.

Virtually every day for as many hours as studio time allowed or it took for me to reach a point of exhaustion, Woytek and I worked on the many weaknesses in my dancing. Five hours at a stretch was not an uncommon amount of time for us to work, and it didn't matter to Woytek whether I was tired or feeling sick or if it was ten in the morning or ten at night or the only free-of-charge space we could find to work was a dingy, dark studio buried somewhere deep inside Carnegie Hall.

Woytek pushed me, and he pushed me hard. He believed I could do the work, and the fact that I actually got through those marathon sessions and made significant progress in spite of how I sometimes felt proved to me that I had more strength, determination, and ability than I realized.

No self-help books, psychotherapists, or pep talks from Misha or Susan Jones could have accomplished what those solitary sessions with Woytek made possible. I had to feel it in my body. It was the only way I was ever going to believe in myself, and, oddly enough, this was Misha's philosophy as well.

"Any dancer will always be his own sternest critic," he wrote in *Baryshnikov at Work*, "but real work means knowing how to invest the time, first to see yourself clearly for what you are, and then to recognize what you might become."

Woytek was a thin, muscular, strikingly handsome man. Born in Poland, he was a graduate of the Vaganova Academy who danced with Béjart, and later with the Boston Ballet. Serious in the classroom, he nevertheless had a terrific sense of humor and laughed easily in spite of the chronic hip pain he suffered.

In 1982, Misha hired Woytek to be a ballet master at ABT, to teach men's class or joint company classes primarily, and right off the bat, I got the distinct impression that he and Misha would have an uneasy alliance. Woytek, though I could tell he wanted to, was loathe to correct Misha in class. This wasn't surprising. Most, if not all, of the teachers at ABT were wary of Misha and never corrected him in class. Perhaps Jurgen Schneider corrected him when they worked alone together, I don't know. What I do know is that Misha, while obviously needing guidance and probably wanting guidance, was left to his own devices in class.

I began working as Woytek suggested, contracting my lower abdominal muscles to flatten my lower back such that I often felt like I was dancing in a vice, an approach completely divorced from that of David Howard. This distortion came not simply from Woytek—it came from Pilates, something I began doing regularly with Robert Fitzgerald at Woytek's suggestion.

Robert was a soft-spoken, sadistic man with twiggish limbs and a soft, round belly. He wore diamond studs in his earlobes and owned two gigantic afghan dogs that lay around his spacious Upper West Side apartment like a couple of area rugs.

Several mornings a week, I would arrive at Robert's studio and climb onto one of his medieval exercise devices. While I was sweating bullets to achieve the exact positioning he demanded, Darci Kistler, my old classmate from SAB, would be lying beside me, waltzing through the exercises with an ease that made me hate her. Bitch.

In spite of how much I despised Pilates initially, I gradually became stronger and more proficient at it. I hated Darci less and liked Robert more, and before long, my spine was virtually as straight as the wooden rod Robert often placed along my back as a benchmark for correct alignment.

This ramrod straight approach was odd and unnatural, and some voice inside me kept telling me this was no way to dance, really, holding so much tension in the core of my body, but at the same time, I felt tremendous power when I flattened my lower back. It was as if all of my thrust went directly down through my body. As a result, my jumping ability increased immeasurably.

My reservations about Woytek's methods aside, as I got stronger and stronger, I began to see glimpses of what I was capable of, and those glimpses both thrilled and frightened me. My ability to keep my focus while turning was like getting a new bicycle for Christmas. I no longer struggled merely to execute steps and instead began observing myself moving through space, thinking about how I wanted to dance, where I could push the music, or where I wanted to hold back. I moved into the third person.

Woytek was not merely my coach—he became my Henry Higgins. When he realized I was eager to learn about more than just ballet, he began bringing me books on various painters. He took me to the opera and introduced me to classic foreign cinema. He began teaching me about the great male dancers of the past by showing me films of Vladimir Vasiliev, a great dancer from the Bolshoi, and Edward Villella, his New York City Ballet equivalent.

I smiled while watching those bits of Villella, recalling our meeting in Andover when I was young. Nothing about seeing him dance at Phillips Academy had prepared me for the Villella I saw on film. He was an animal. A marvel. An amazing force of nature who commanded my attention.

After seeing Vasiliev and Villella, my concept of what great dancing could be, or should be, changed. I realized, for the first time, that my fascination with perfect line and beautiful feet and legs did not a dancer make. What made a dancer was something else, something that was only marginally related to technique. The execution of the steps was important, certainly, but both Vasiliev and Villella had a certain rawness, an intensity of focus that altered my notion of what constituted the ballet beautiful.

Woytek taught me so much that, at times, I felt as if it was almost too much. He was giving me all that he knew and could impart as a teacher because that was just his nature, and in me, he'd found a willing and eager acolyte. Finally, the amount of time we spent together began to affect my relationship with Julie. She was not only upset by the hours Woytek and I spent together; she suspected he was in love with me. I realized this might actually be true, but I didn't want to throw the work away because of it. Fortunately, I didn't really have to make a choice between Woytek and Julie, because four months after the lockout began, it ended.

Woytek had been talking to me about our return to work for a while. He said that the first impression Misha would have of me in class was crucial. The old Michael had to perish under mysterious circumstances. Another dancer would have to step in. A dancer capable of being a soloist or principal dancer or President of the United States. I was, understandably, nervous.

Woytek was scheduled to teach class our first day back at work, and while this should have felt like just another one of our many private coaching sessions together, there were strange dissimilarities that made me uneasy. Woytek was clearly not himself. He was trying to teach while simultaneously giving me his usual raft of corrections, albeit with all sorts of surreptitious glances and gestures. *Put your foot here. Don't forget your arm position there. Good. Not so good. What are you doing?* All of these thoughts were being communicated to me, and I took them all in silently, nodding my head like the dutiful student that I was.

When we came off the barre and into the center, Woytek looked at me, implying that I should take a spot toward the front rather than where I usually stood, which was somewhere in the second or third row of dancers. After demonstrating the adagio, he divided the class into two groups. Without a word, I knew to wait for the second group so that Misha, who was dancing in the first group, could marvel at the new me.

When it was my turn, I moved to the front. The music began to play, and though I wanted desperately to be calm, I could not relax. I gripped my abdominal muscles and fought my way through the movements. Instead of transitioning smoothly from one position to the next and feeling the ground under my feet, I went in little fits and starts. I struggled to find my center, but it seemed to have taken an extended holiday in Bermuda. I tried to exude confidence, but felt no confidence whatsoever.

Woytek and I both knew I could execute this adagio in my sleep, but for some reason, with Misha's eyes upon me and the knowledge of what was at stake, I became completely unsure of myself. It was as if some part of me wanted to justify Misha's low opinion of me by showing him just how bad I was. Look, Misha, you were right. Silly me. Who did I think I was? I'm awful. In fact, I'm even worse than before I did all this work with Woytek.

When the adagio ended, I started to walk off the floor. Misha looked at me.

"Mikey, Mikey, vad you doink? Vhy you hopping all over de place?"

Gee, you tell me. You're the dance genius, remember?

After my horrible adagio, I could barely look over at Woytek. When I did, I knew I had failed him. The blemish was on the page. I couldn't erase it. Misha's view of me would be the same as it had always been.

When class ended, I was as silent as I'd been throughout the entire ordeal. Woytek, who was very old-fashioned, was no help. He said little. I said little. And then, as had been his habit for some time, Misha came over and handed me a new pair of his leather ballet slippers.

"Tank you, Mikey," he said, walking away.

I slipped off my soft canvas shoes and wrenched his tight leather versions over my sweaty, bare feet, the better and quicker to break them in.

This shoe thing was a habit Misha and I arrived at when, for some reason, he tried a pair of my shoes on one day and decided he liked the way they fit him. Since then, I'd become his shoe whore.

My wide, size-eight foot was a perfect compliment to his own, and, given the old-fashioned tautness of the hard leather shoes he preferred, it took a while before that type of shoe was broken in to its ideal state. This was where I came in, speeding up this unpleasant process so that after wearing his shoes around for a few days, they were soft and pliable while still giving him the support he liked.

I hated Misha's shoes, however, and didn't know how he managed to dance in such antiquated leather creations. They were constricting. They were stiff. They were uncomfortable; nothing like the soft, modern, canvas shoes most of the men of my generation favored.

As much as I despised having to break Misha's shoes in for him, I could not deny I felt special having his shoes on my feet. They gave me some connection to him that I otherwise would not have had. At the same time, I felt even more like a peon because I realized how trivial this shoe business really was. He didn't need me to do this. Before I came along, did he have some minion somewhere, at City Ballet or the Kirov, who broke his shoes in for him? I doubted it. I made some part of his life a bit easier, and that was fine; it made me feel good to be helping him out in some way because, in reality, there were a microscopic number of ways I might conceivably help Misha do just about anything. He didn't need me. He had an assistant and a business manager and a secretary and a physical therapist and any number of people, men and women, who were only too eager to do his bidding for whatever it was he might need at any hour of the day or night.

After working Misha's shoes in for a while, I stowed them in my dance bag and headed to the dressing room. I didn't have much on my rehearsal plate that day, so I walked home to Chelsea feeling so sorry for myself I could barely pull my eyes from the blackened bits of bubblegum smooshed into the New York City sidewalks.

When I got home to our apartment at 25th Street and 8th Avenue, I dragged my beloved vacuum cleaner out of the closet. Pulling Misha's shoes from my dance bag, I slipped them on my bare feet and turned on the machine. Thus attired, I canvassed the entire apartment, kneading Misha's shoes with my toes as I picked up all the errant pieces of lint and dust and dirt that didn't belong, feeling more and more satisfied the more spotless the carpet became. When at last the wall-to-wall had that freshly mowed look I treasured, I put the vacuum back in the closet and began wiping down the kitchen floor with a wet rag.

For a while I'd been obsessed with clean floors, perhaps because, as a corps de ballet dancer, I'd become so accustomed to sitting on them. We did, after all, spend much of our lives sitting on the floor watching other dancers do more important things. A girl in the corps de ballet once said to me when I complained about having to sit around so much, "Hell, this is nothing. I spent so much time sitting on my ass my first year in the company, I got hemorrhoids."

After the floors had been cleaned to my satisfaction, I lay down on Julie's old couch and looked down at Misha's shoes on my feet. They were finally starting to feel less like straightjackets, and I was thinking that by tomorrow or the next day they should be ready to stop torturing me and start shaking the dance world from its moorings. I stared at them and imagined myself back in Woytek's class.

I saw myself hopping around, saw Misha's face, heard the consternation in his voice. He always wanted to know why I was doing something wrong when the right way was so obvious, any idiot should be able to do it. And the answer to Misha's eternal question *was* obvious, it was so obvious he didn't really need to point it out—but point it out he did, because deep down inside he wanted to help, and some part of him thought he was helping. All he ever really succeeded in doing, however, was reminding me that I fell off balance instead of staying on balance or that my arm was too high when it should've been lower or that I went to the right when I should have gone to the left. Most of the time, I knew what he was going to say before he opened his mouth.

After ruminating on that day's disaster for a while, I got up and went to the dining room table where I found a piece of paper and a pen. Writing was something I'd been doing since I was young. My Swedish grandfather, Björn, was enthralled with language, the English language in particular, and the two of us began exchanging letters when I was a child. As an adult, I kept notebooks, and when I wasn't writing letters to my grandfather or to friends or family, I began recording snippets of my life.

That day, I began with what was foremost in my mind.

I hate myself. I hate myself. I hate myself.

Solitary Confinement

ONCE THE DISAPPOINTMENT OF HAVING FAILED to impress Misha with the new and improved me was behind us, my private coaching sessions with Woytek came to a virtual halt. We tried to muster some enthusiasm for continuing, but I think we both realized our hearts were no longer in it. We used the excuse of rehearsal and studio constraints and touring to mask what both of us were feeling, which was that we'd reached a plateau. I didn't want to continue working if it was going to mean the destruction of my relationship with Julie, and Woytek might have realized that I simply didn't have what it took to get to the next level. In point of fact, I don't know what he was thinking. We never spoke about it.

What I realized later, apart from the fact that I had more potential as a dancer than I imagined, was that my relationship with Julie was coming to compete with ballet for importance in my life. I had always believed my success as a dancer was truly a life or death issue. Everything about who I was and my value as a person revolved around whether or not I was going to "make it." This fear of failure propelled me through many of the difficult moments.

But what exactly constituted success or failure? At one point, I might have said that just getting into Ballet Theatre would have been success enough, but once that milestone was reached, I could see that languishing in the corps de ballet for the rest of my career was never going to be enough. The problem then became, what could I realistically do in Ballet Theatre beyond the corps de ballet?

After what happened with Woytek, I realized that ballet was going to come to an end one day, and when it did, what would I be left with? Many ballet dancers were willing to sacrifice virtually everything for professional gain (look at Misha, Makarova, and Nureyev). They were willing to leave countries and marriages and family and relationships behind for their career, but I was no longer sure if I was one of those dancers.

As Julie's boyfriend, I knew I was loved. Our relationship was, more often than not, a romantic fairytale. When we weren't lavishing one another with extravagant gifts, we spent our vacations on the beaches of Rio de Janeiro, scuba diving in Key West, or hanging out in Hawaii or the south of France with her parents. The flipside of this fantasy life was another fantasy life, a life based on an amalgam of Ozzie and Harriet, June and Ward Cleaver, and most of the millionaires living on the East Side of Manhattan.

To wit: a couple of years after Julie and I met, I took some of the salary I'd been able to save at ABT and bought a small summer cottage on a lake in Pennsylvania. This cottage became our "country" house. And while it might have appeared to some that I was way out of my league buying a house at twenty-three years of age, it seemed perfectly normal to me. Both Julie and I cherished that little house and spent countless weekends there, swimming, boating, and sitting in front of the fireplace.

Our fairytale life aside, it was evident that both Julie and I had serious problems and secrets we were keeping from one another, not the least of which were our respective eating disorders. The reason I never told Julie what was really going on in my life in that respect was that

I didn't understand, nor was I willing to admit, that I had a problem. I was playing a game, a game in which I established the rules and no one else knew what they were—not Julie, not my parents, not even me much of the time because the rules were ever-changing. I believed those kinds of "issues" didn't affect me. Anorexia, bulimia, and drug addiction affected people like Gelsey Kirkland or Patrick Bissell or some over-wrought girl in the corps de ballet. Admitting I had a problem would've been akin to admitting I had weaknesses, and that was not something a stubborn, ambitious ballet dancer trying to convince himself he's strong enough and talented enough to make it in American Ballet Theatre is apt to do very easily.

After the lockout ended in January of 1983, the company went through a whirlwind rehearsal period before beginning our annual tour. We headed to the Kennedy Center in Washington for a week, then went on to Miami, Chicago, and the West Coast as was the norm. I found myself falling into a severe depression as tour began. I needed time to regroup from what had happened with Woytek. And then, as I was swimming laps at the Di Lido Hotel pool in Miami Beach, I realized this career of mine, however flawed or disappointing at times, had oc-cupied half of my life and deserved everything I had to give it. The only reason I was swimming laps was because I was bored and because I had energy to burn—energy I needed to burn—so I could stay under my target weight. But expending my energy in a swimming pool when I should have been using it in a ballet studio suddenly seemed like an absurd waste of time.

The next day, with no private coaches in sight, I began working on my own in whatever space or studio was available. If one wasn't available, I worked on the sides of the studio or in the back of the studio or in the wings of the theater. I made up steps. I practiced whatever I could. I did barres alone. I turned alone. I did petit allegro alone. I jumped alone. I took bits of choreography or classroom exercises and ran through them alone.

These solitary sessions became, like most everything else in my life at the time, an obsession, alongside portion control and weighing myself every morning. At first I was a bit self-conscious about what I was doing, not wanting to distract from rehearsals or draw too much attention to myself, but I managed to push those feelings aside because I was determined to do whatever was necessary to improve. I was discreet. I was so discreet, pretty soon I was invisible.

Throughout the entire tour, no one ever said a word to me about what I was doing every day in the back of the studio or in the wings at all hours of the day and night. Part of what I was doing was my way of saying to Misha, "Look at me! I'm not giving up! No matter how much you ignore me or how little you give me, I won't give up!" It was my quiet little fuck you, and perhaps people sensed this—perhaps that's why they avoided me. But never, ever, did anyone approach or ask what I was working on or if I'd like some help or if I was losing my fucking mind.

Perhaps some people sensed my desperation, but hell, if you weren't desperate, you weren't in American Ballet Theatre. Everybody was desperate, and many people were seriously disturbed, drinking to excess, snorting coke, smoking too much weed, swallowing bottles of Advil, starving themselves, dancing in constant pain, throwing up, or otherwise going through all sorts of psychological hell in order to cope with the demands of the profession or their private frustrations. As dancers in American Ballet Theatre, we were accustomed to craziness and pushing ourselves to the very brink while living in a fantasy world where aberrant behavior was not only an everyday occurrence, it was practically encouraged. Rarely was any of this confronted. It was avoided until it became so detrimental to the dancer or the company there was no choice. I've got my own problems, everyone in ABT seemed to be saying to themselves, I don't have time for yours.

The fact that no one said anything to me was no great surprise. I didn't really expect anyone to say anything. I didn't really expect anyone to offer to help, however much I secretly wanted them to. The truth was, I didn't respect most of the classroom teaching that went on in the company, and among the ballet masters, about the only one who might have had the time to help me besides Woytek was Michael Lland.

Michael, however, was an oddly volatile man at that point in his life. He was overweight. He hobbled around with a cane, wearing strange, black orthopedic shoes. He smoked and drank and ran *Theme and Variations* rehearsals like a bipolar Patton. He was prone to screaming, and when he screamed "D'Agoberto! What the hell are you doing!" it was so mind-bendingly loud and full of vitriol, I worried he was going to give himself a heart attack.

At fifty-eight years old, Michael was an icon of the company. He had joined Ballet Theatre as a soloist in 1949 and been a ballet master since 1971. By the time the 80s rolled around, however, he had very little to do; he was only responsible for a handful of ballets, and this lack of work clearly seemed to be getting the better of him. He accompanied us on tour, but I had no idea how he spent all his free time. I got the sense he drank quite a bit, but I could've been wrong. When I tentatively approached him and asked if he would coach me, he said yes, but I found myself reluctant to follow up for all sorts of reasons. I didn't really know him. He almost never taught class, and when he did, it was a strange brew, a confusing mix of time periods and ideas layered with the ever-present sense that he might explode at any minute. I felt as if I had asked him to help me out of pity because I knew he needed something to do, so I wasn't altogether comfortable with that, and when he didn't follow up on the offer, I let it go.

═══════════════

The company's arrival in Chicago in February of 1983 was a telling reminder of my place within American Ballet Theatre at the time. A page from our tour booklet:

FOURTH WEEK - CHICAGO

Theater: Auditorium Theater
                 50 East Congress Parkway
                 Chicago, Illinois 60605
Backstage: 939-9780
Hotel: Americana Congress Hotel
                 520 South Michigan Avenue
                 Chicago, Illinois 60605
                 (312) 427-3800
                 $26 single, $26 double plus tax

Bank: Illinois State Bank
                 300 South Michigan Avenue
                 Chicago, Illinois

Rehearsal: Windsor Ballroom in hotel,
                 theater and some at Ruth Page,
                 1016 North Dearborn, Chicago

Performances:

Tue Feb 8   GALA   SYMPHONIE CONCERTANTE   8 PM
                   DUETS

                   PAS DE DEUX

                   PAS DE DEUX

                   GOTTSCHALK

Weds Feb 9   SHADES   8 PM

                   APOLLO

                   OPUS JAZZ

Thu Feb 10   NEW TAYLOR-CORBETT   8 PM

                   LA SYLPHIDE

Fri Feb 11   DUETS   8 PM

                   PAS DE DEUX

                   LA SYLPHIDE

Sat Feb 12   PUSH COMES TO SHOVE   2 PM

                   LA SYLPHIDE

                   OPUS JAZZ   8 PM

                   LA SLYPHIDE

Sun Feb 13   FREE DAY

What I saw when I glanced at this week in our schedule was this:

On Tuesday evening, I would dance *Gottschalk*, the last ballet in the gala. I would not perform on Wednesday, Thursday, or Friday nights. I might go into the theater and watch *Opus Jazz* because I was an understudy and needed to be available in case of an injury. But I could, technically speaking, be just as available back in my hotel room. In all likelihood, I would not watch the show on Thursday or Friday, in which case I might go out to dinner with someone who also had the night off or see a movie or hang out in my hotel room. On Saturday, I would dance a miniscule part in *Push Comes to Shove*, the first ballet in the matinee. On Saturday evening, I would be off again. On Sunday, I would have the entire day off to recover from my taxing week of work.

What Julie saw when she looked at this week in our tour booklet was this: In the gala on Tuesday, she would dance *Symphonie Concertante* and *Gottschalk*. On Wednesday, she would dance *Shades*, the first ballet on the program. She would be done after that, so perhaps we would go out to dinner, unless I decided to be in the theater because I was understudying *Opus Jazz*. On Thursday and Friday, she would dance *La Sylphide*. During Saturday matinee, she would dance *Push Comes to Shove* and *La Sylphide*. On Saturday night, *La Sylphide* again. Sunday would be a day off to do laundry, sew pointe-shoes, and have sex, because our day off was virtually the only day of the week when we both had the energy or enthusiasm for it.

In spite of how little I was doing in Ballet Theatre at that point, I loved touring. Life on the road was a seamless extension of my life with Julie back in New York. In fact, it was easier than my life back in New York with Julie because my sole responsibilities on tour were class, rehearsals, and performances. Beyond that, there was little Julie and I thought about save what restaurants stayed open after the show, where there might be some good shopping, and how we might spend our upcoming day off.

Tour meant paring down life to its essentials, and in this respect it was very much like ballet, an endeavor that lays bare what the body is capable of and what the dancer has learned about those capabilities. I grew to love touring so much, I often used to think I would like nothing better than to spend the rest of my life moving from city to city and hotel to hotel, never having to make my bed, never having to sort through bills or waste a moment of life attending to the trivialities of daily existence. Trivialities didn't exist on tour.

Spring. 1983. New York.

MY GLORIOUS NOMADIC LIFESTYLE ASIDE, by the time this particular tour was over, I felt like I might barely be able to avoid a trip to Bellevue, the infamous psychiatric hospital where Gelsey Kirkland once found herself. I resumed classes with David Howard, and we spoke frankly about my work with Woytek, my hopes for the future, and my disappointments at ABT.

David was a good listener, and the more we discussed what he had observed in my dancing while I was working with Woytek, the more convinced I became that my instincts were right. Yes, I was a stronger dancer in many respects, but my dancing had become forced and rigid. I was so concerned about being perfect and pleasing Woytek, I couldn't move, couldn't relax. I felt like I was dancing with a load in my pants.

"Tell you what," David said, "why don't we start working together? I think I can help you."

And so it went. All my beliefs about not being worthy of David's time were a folly. All I'd had to do was ask. Hell, I didn't even have to ask.

―――――――――

David generally taught two to three classes a day, so we began working at his studio late in the evening whenever I had a performance off.

Occasionally, we would do some barre work to warm up, but we never spent long at the barre. I'd had class and some rehearsals during the day, so there was little need to rehash the barre. We moved into the center as quickly as possible, and it was there that David gently exposed my weaknesses and pushed my mind and my energy in new directions.

These weren't the grueling marathon sessions I'd become accustomed to with Woytek. They were opportunities for David to spend time with me, the kind of time he couldn't afford to spend in class when there were fifty dancers to attend to. We would take snippets of movements and break them down, discussing their energetic components. In spite of my many frustrations and withering self-criticism, David was always encouraging. He was giving me the keys to his kingdom one evening at a time. It was up to me to figure out how to use them.

David believed that every movement had a predominant energy pattern. A glissade, for example, has an "over" energy, while an assemblé has an "under" energy. There were other patterns—spirals, for example—that might predominate with movements of the upper body. David said that he didn't think of steps per se when he was creating exercises; he thought of the predominant energy patterns in any one movement and how those patterns could be combined to both challenge the dancer and help facilitate a series of movements.

An example of the tension between opposing energies that he often spoke about is apparent in a very basic movement such as a plié, something that looks like a simple knee bend. As the body descends with the bending of the knees, there is a sense of energy rising up through the top of the head, and, likewise, as one ascends from the bottom of the plié, there is a sense of driving energy down into the ground. The body is working in two directions at once, and it is this dynamic feeling of opposing energies that gives a dancer a sense of life, of having "tension" without being "tense," as David often said.

Jumping is another example. Jumping isn't about trying to hoist the body up into the air; it's about thrusting downwards quickly and rebounding from the ground. You simply cannot jump slowly, David often said. One of the biggest revelations I had while working with David was coming to understand that all the emphasis on turnout in classical ballet is largely a façade. Dancers moving through space simply don't stand on the perfectly rotated legs you see them using at the barre. Watch a dancer's standing foot when they are actually dancing in the center of the room. Forty-five to fifty degrees of rotation is the norm. Furthermore, if you slow down film of a ballet dancer jumping, you will observe that classical ballet dancers, in spite of their belief that they are dancing in turned-out, classical positions, jump off of an inwardly rotated leg.

The more I worked with David, the more I came to understand that ballet really is an illusion, and that different dancers required different things. What looked good on one body would not necessarily work or look good on another. Longer arms required different positioning than shorter arms, for example.

David wanted me to look at my body and my dancing as unique. For a dancer like myself, someone who'd spent two years at SAB trying to dance like Peter Martins and two years at ABT trying to dance like a combination of Misha, Gelsey, and Fernando Bujones, this was a revolutionary idea. "Be yourself" was David's inherent message, and he maintained that that was the only unique thing anyone had to offer as a dancer or, for that matter, as a person.

―――――――――――

Two days before American Ballet Theatre's opening night at the Metropolitan Opera House in the spring of 1983, George Balanchine, the founder of New York City Ballet and the most renowned choreographer of the twentieth century, passed away. On May 2, after our opening night gala, Anna Kisselgoff wrote this in *The New York Times*:

"Dressed in black and wearing the makeup that suggested the harlequin mask needed for his own performance on the program, Mr. Baryshnikov said, 'I wish I could toast Mr. Balanchine with a shot of vodka the way he would like, but I have to dance.' Referring to Mr. Balanchine's own company, the New York City Ballet, he added: 'Mr. B. does not just look out for the company across the plaza, he looks out for us and all the companies.' Mr. Baryshnikov then asked the audience 'to listen in his honor to the final moments of the second movement of Mozart's *Symphonie Concertante*, music that Mr. Balanchine loved very much.' And as the conductor, Kenneth Schermerhorn, raised his baton, John Taras, Mr. Balanchine's longtime associate and ballet master of the City Ballet, rose and stood in the audience. Some 3,999 other persons followed suit."

During every Met season, the opportunity to speak to Misha about your year and your hopes for the future was made available to every member of the company. I can't say for certain how many dancers in the corps de ballet took advantage of this opportunity, but I suspect very few did.

After my first year in the company, I never let a Met season go by without speaking to Misha. I felt he owed me five or ten minutes a year. He was my director, after all, and I wanted him to know what my aspirations were and ask him what he felt I needed to do in order to achieve those aspirations. Most of these conversations were arranged in advance through Flo, Misha's secretary, and took place prior to an evening's performance in an empty principal dressing room at the Metropolitan Opera House.

I was always a bit nervous about these talks and fretted about them for weeks beforehand, going over in my mind what I felt I should say, what I felt I could realistically ask for, and so on. It seemed to me that Misha was only slightly less uncomfortable with these chats, and while I wanted to make that discomfort go away, I had no idea how. In an entire year, I rarely had a conversation with him that lasted more than a minute. In fact, if it weren't for those annual torture fests, no more than a handful of words would have ever passed between us.

Here are some examples of exchanges I might have with Misha during the course of a year:

#1. Misha: Mikey, vad you doink?

#2. Misha: Mikey, you go here.

#3. Misha: Mikey, you come in here and you do dis.

#4. Misha: Mikey, vad you doink?

#5. Misha: Mikey, not like dis. Like dis.

What Misha would tell me in our first tête-à-tête about my esteemed place at the bottom of the company fishpond was that of all the things I needed to work on, my arms were at the top of the list. "Vatch Danny," he said, referring to the port de bras of Danilo Radojevic, one of our principal dancers and a boy who was my size.

What Misha didn't realize, however, was that I'd spent more than two years at the world-famous School of American Ballet without being told that my arms were actually attached to my body. And while I thought I should have been forgiven for not focusing too heavily on my port de bras because of what I wasn't taught at SAB, it was, at the end of the day, no one's fault but my own.

I spent the bulk of my time at the school staring at my legs and feet, only occasionally glancing upward to see how my arms might be doing. When I noticed they were flailing about somewhere close to where Petipa or Vaganova or Cecchetti or Bournonville or my teacher, Stanley Williams, thought they ought to be, I would go back to staring at my legs and feet. Stanley, it must be said, almost never mentioned where your arms were supposed to be and spent the bulk of class gazing down at his own feet with his arm stuck out to the side somewhere above his shoulder. Not an ideal example for ballet students, nearly all of whom end up copying their teacher's mannerisms.

My arms sucked. That's essentially what Misha was telling me. Of course, Misha didn't use the word "suck" in reference to my port de bras. Suck was one of those words that wasn't in his vocabulary. "Hell" was about as far as he went in the profanity department, and as such, it was a word he used rather often.

"Vad de hell are you doink?"

He should have had that phrase tattooed on his forehead.

Ignoring the obvious, I said to him, "You know, Misha, I understand I'm competing with Gil and Johan and Danny for parts and that at this point I'm not at their level, but there are parts that I think I'm capable of doing or at least understudying, yet Gil always seems to be the one who gets cast. He's dancing everything."

Gil, i.e. Gil Boggs, had recently come to ABT from the Atlanta Ballet, and since then he'd been the flavor of the week. He had danced every role in the repertoire, save Albrecht, that might conceivably have suited a boy who was 5'7" (which just happened to be the number corresponding to Misha's height, and mine).

Misha sat up from his slouched, woe-is-me position on the ottoman like I just told him he'd won the Latvian Lottery.

"Isss true," he said, as if this was the first time anyone had brought this fact to his attention. "You right. Gil hass many parts. May-bea too many."

I felt victorious. I had said something Misha agreed with and, more importantly, something he didn't seem to have even considered. And why would he? He was used to dancing every role he ever wanted or could get his hands on, so why shouldn't Gil? Or Danny? And suddenly I felt that, even though I might not have been a great dancer in his mind, at least he respected my intelligence. Sensing he had arrived at the end of that thought of his, I leapt in to fill the potentially explosive void.

"Misha," I said, "I'm not going to sit here and ask for things I don't think I deserve or don't think I'm capable of doing, but I'd like to be in one of Mr. Tudor's ballets. Just call me to the rehearsals. I don't mind understudying. And I don't care which ballet it is. I just want to work with him."

What I didn't spell out to Misha, but what should have been abundantly clear, was that I loved Mr. Tudor. He symbolized ABT, in my opinion. He was our Balanchine, and he was still alive. At 74, he wasn't getting any younger.

"I vill talk to Richard," Misha said, meaning Richard Schafer, the dancer closest to Tudor at the time and the person largely responsible for rehearsing his ballets—along with Sallie Wilson when Tudor wasn't around to do it himself.

Misha then began moving around on his seat in a way that told me it was time to wrap things up, he had bigger fish to fry.

"Okay, Misha," I said in response to his meek assurance that he would speak to Richard. "Thank you. I'd appreciate that."

In spite of what Misha said, I was convinced nothing would come of my desire to be in a Tudor ballet. We both stood. I could feel Misha's relief that it was over, sense his mind churning toward the million-and-one things he must attend to that evening.

After leaving the Met that night, I felt rather smug. I'd gone to the top for an answer, and I'd gotten one. Gee, I found myself saying, once I get my arms going the way Danny's are, then, by golly, everything will be fine. The only problem with this was that I didn't particularly like Danny's arms. Yes, they were in the right places at the right times, and they didn't distract too much from what he was doing, but there was no lyricism or poetry to them. Yet, according to Misha, they were clearly a step up from whatever the hell I was doing. Yikes.

By the time I got on the subway at Lincoln Center and headed downtown, I realized that something was amiss. I was beginning to question Misha's judgment, and that was not something I needed to be doing, because if there was one thing I could count on in Ballet Theatre, it was Misha's eye, the integrity of his dancing, his vision, and my respect for that vision.

Once off the train, I stopped at the newsstand on 23rd Street to pick up the latest issues of *Cosmopolitan* and *Bazaar* for Julie. Afterward, I went to our local Korean market at 25th and 8th Avenue to get a few more things I knew she would eventually need: a pack of More Lights, some Canada Dry Ginger Ale, and some Hubba Bubba chewing gum. These were the staples of everyday life for Julie, without which her earth was likely to stop rotating on its axis.

I discovered this fact firsthand when we found ourselves in Hana one day. Hana was a remote village on the island of Maui with only one general store, where, much to Julie's chagrin, there was no Hubba Bubba bubble gum to be had. "Well," she said, her face a mixture of suicidal anguish and despair, "what am I going to do now?"

I tactfully pointed out that there were other types of chewing gum available.

"I don't *want* any other kind of gum," she hissed.

As a practical matter, I mentioned that it was a good three-hour drive back to Kahului along the famous 620-curve, two-lane stretch of road known affectionately as "The Hana Highway," and that we were then in a place most would consider a damn good rival to paradise.

"You think I don't know that?" she shot back.

And so, for the next three days, Julie moped around Hana Heaven counting the hours until we could get back to Hubba Bubba Civilization.

When my little princess came home after the show that night, she sat down at our dining room table with a gigantic bowl of greens mixed with soupy ramen noodles; one of her favorite meals. "How did things go with Misha?" she asked. Julie had been well briefed on my impending chat and various talking points, and I went over every inch of it with her as she moved from slurping to smoking one of the handful of cigarettes that were her daily habit.

"You know," I said, "I'm really proud of myself for having had the courage to ask for a meeting with Misha and then to have expressed my feelings about the things I wanted."

What I didn't tell Julie was that not only was I not entirely certain what my arms looked like or should look like or how in the world I was supposed to begin improving them, I was now questioning what kind of dancer Misha truly appreciated. Did he really think that if I just watched Danny's arms they were somehow going to metastasize into my own? Maybe. Because the truth is, if Misha wanted to suddenly have a port de bras exactly like Danny's, he would.

Six months after my conversation with Misha, we were knee-deep in another United States tour when I found myself staring at the callboard outside the Windsor Ballroom in Chicago. Rehearsals for Antony Tudor's *Pillar of Fire* were just beginning, and my name wasn't on the call sheet. After company class, Richard Schafer, the dancer in charge of *Pillar,* approached me.

"Misha told me you'd like to learn *Pillar.* We're rehearsing 'Lovers-in-Innocence' today. Why don't you come?"

I laughed. "Really?"

"Yes, really."

Gelsey

ABT WAS NOT IN THE HABIT of performing in the summer, but in 1983 we began going to Philadelphia to perform for two weeks at the Mann Music Center, an outdoor amphitheater in Fairmount Park alongside the Schuykill River. There were three things about this engagement that made it memorable for me. I'd never been to Philadelphia. I'd never danced in the open air. And I'd never traveled on a bus with Gelsey Kirkland.

These were difficult times for Gelsey. She had been fired from the company for missing her dress rehearsal at the Kennedy Center in 1980, and thereafter spent a couple of years working around the fringes of the ballet world while trying to get a grip on her cocaine addiction.

Charles France had this to say about Gelsey's dismissal in 1980: "Well, somebody I knew at the time said to me, 'It's only a rehearsal.' And I said, 'Yes, it's a rehearsal. With orchestra and lights and sets and costumes and makeup. That so-called *rehearsal* Gelsey and Patrick missed probably cost us about $20,000.

"Gelsey was a very smart girl," Charles added. "I had her in my office during the first rehearsal period in 1980, and I said, 'You know, we just can't go on like this. You call every two or three days and say you have to go to the dentist. How many teeth do you have to have fixed? You're doing drugs. And you can't. Or you can't stay here.' She didn't say anything. She just got up and left. After that, she continued doing drugs, but it wasn't until about three or four years later that it got really bad, and she went into rehab in New York City. And then she just sort of disappeared."

The Gelsey Kirkland I knew was a continual source of amazement for me and frustration for Misha. He was driven nearly mad by her desire to repeat a phrase in rehearsals until she felt she'd gotten it right, but there was never really any "getting it right."

It was a commonplace in those days that if you were called to a rehearsal with Gelsey, you would never finish the ballet. This happened so consistently, I used to wonder how she ever developed the stamina to weather an entire performance, but somehow she did, always by the skin of her teeth, everyone on the edge of their seats wondering if she was going to fall flat on her face, collapse, or sail off into the orchestra pit.

Whatever Gelsey was, no one could deny she was a brilliant dancer and tireless in her investigation of movement. No one was as obsessed with trying to get at the energetic basis of ballet, and no dancer was as successful at illuminating the results of that investigation as Gelsey Kirkland. And it truly was an investigation, a scientific investigation.

Gelsey had been coached by Maggie Black while she was at New York City Ballet and later by David Howard. It was with David that she began doing much the same thing David's mentor, Jo Anna Kneeland, had done back at Harkness House. She slowed down films of dancers in order to see exactly where their bodies were positioned at certain moments.

"The first time Gelsey came to work with me," David said, "she came to Harkness House and took a boys' class. She'd just left Maggie. After class, she asked me if I'd like to work with her, and I said, 'Well, yes, but it won't be the same kind of experience, because I'm not Maggie.' Gelsey said, 'Well, what do you think about my work?' I said, 'Well, it looks all right to me.' She said, 'What do you mean it *looks all right to you?*' I said, 'You've got short arms and a big head.' We were on the corner of 79th Street and Broadway at the time. We ended up standing there talking about her dancing for the next two hours.

"She said, 'Well, there's nothing I can do about my head. How do I fix the arms?' And I said, 'You can't move that way. Remember, it's an illusion. You have to create *an illusion of here to there,* of length.' Gelsey didn't really like the word *illusion,* because to her it was all about the work. Later, when she was doing *Don Quixote,* we looked at everyone in the world who had done it, in slow motion. Gelsey would look at Plisetskaya and say, 'I want to look like that.' And I'd say, 'You can't, her arms are long.' Same thing with Natasha [Makarova]. I would say, 'You can't look like her either. Her arms are long.' She would say, 'What am I going to look like?' And I would say, 'You have to find a way to do it.' And in the end, she would."

So there I was on the bus with Gelsey in 1983, traveling to Philadelphia, when suddenly she appeared in the aisle in her dance clothes and started doing a barre.

This was one of those things that happen on a regular basis in a ballet company. Someone displays their eccentricity for all to see. And while they display this eccentricity, they know full well you will be watching them, but they can't help it, they have to do this thing, whatever it is, because some little voice in their head or their ambition or their coach or their career simply demands it.

Of course, the normal thing would have been for Gelsey to do a quick warm-up when we arrived at the theater in Philadelphia or, if she knew the bus was going to arrive too close to rehearsal time, take an earlier bus or a train or—call me crazy—fly. Surely, Gelsey wasn't that poor. Did she have to take the bus with all of us? Then again, if you're blowing all your salary up your nose, the bus might start to seem like a viable option.

I may not have known much about Gelsey's motivations, but I knew
one thing: Misha wouldn't have been caught dead on that bus. He rarely traveled with the company. He arrived on his magic carpet and disappeared just as mysteriously. How he got around I never knew. One
day he would show up and the next he would be gone, whisked away in
some mysterious car or plane.

Bus or no bus, there was Gelsey doing her fondues in the aisle as the
smell of diesel fuel mixed with the noxious blend of sanitizing cleanser
and urine wafted up from the toilet at the back of the bus. An occasional view of some trucker masturbating on the highway blended in my
mind's eye with visions of Gelsey's leg flying up towards the ceiling as
she did her grand battements.

Of course, I knew it was strange to be warming up for rehearsal on a
bus, but I also knew that in Gelsey's mind there was a routine to be followed, a certain amount of preparation she was accustomed to doing, and
she was going to do whatever it took to adhere to that routine. If people
stared or whispered or laughed or wrote stories long after the fact about
how crazy she was, well, so be it; that's the price you pay for being great.

True to form, once we got to Philadelphia and rehearsal began, I
spent the entire time sitting on my ass as Gelsey went over and over one
passage in Balanchine's *La Sonnambula*. And that evening, as usual,
she was both frightening and sublime. She bourréed around the stage
like she was possessed and on more than one occasion appeared to be
headed straight into the orchestra pit until Victor Barbee, dancing the
role of the Poet, arrived to stop her.

━━━━━━━━━━━━━━━━━

Later that fall, in October of 1983 to be exact, two events occurred in
the ballet world in New York, each a day apart, that were symbolic of

just how different American Ballet Theatre and New York City Ballet were at the time.

ABT held its Halloween Eve Ball at Xenon, a discothèque off of Times Square, on October 30. The next day, New York City Ballet held a memorial service for George Balanchine at the Cathedral of St. John the Divine.

ABT's Halloween party consisted of a series of spoofs in which members of the company and staff were caricatured with varying degrees of churlishness and adolescent glee. When the skits were complete, the partying began, and while I was up on stage dancing, I saw Gelsey wobbling around with her manager, Alex Dube. As Lionel Richie's latest hit, "All Night Long," began to play, Gelsey suddenly appeared before me, and the next thing I knew, she reached out and wrapped her arms around me. As secretly thrilled as I was to be that close to a dancer I so greatly admired, I sensed this girl hanging around my neck wasn't the Gelsey Kirkland I'd long idolized. This was the very antithesis of who she was meant to be, someone not in control of her body. I felt helpless to do anything but pretend I was enjoying myself. What I really wanted to do was slap her and tell her to pull herself together.

Whatever it was that was wrong with Gelsey, it always seemed to be hell-bent on killing her, and she never seemed to do much to stand in its way. She'd fallen in love with Misha when they first met, and he left her behind. He wasn't coming back. She had searched high and low for a replacement, but no one seemed to quite fit the bill. Was that what all this self-destructive drug drama was about? Or was there more to it? Hell if I knew. All I knew was that she hadn't really hit bottom yet. What she swallowed and drank and snorted over the years would have killed a horse, but somehow, with her wisp of a body, she endured. She was so incredibly strong and her will so tenacious, she couldn't completely destroy herself, no matter how hard she tried.

ABT Souvenir Program 1982. Gelsey Kirkland.
Photo credit: Gregory Heisler.

Balanchine's Memorial

THE DAY AFTER OUR HALLOWEEN PARTY, I awoke with a hang-
over. By the time Julie and I got off the train near Morningside
Park that evening, my headache was just beginning to subside. The Cathedral of St. John the Divine, where the Balanchine memorial service
would take place, is the largest Gothic Cathedral in the world, which
made this event a gathering of bunheads that won't likely be repeated
in anyone's lifetime. The dancers and administration of both American
Ballet Theatre and New York City Ballet were there, along with scores
of other well-wishers. Despite the throng, it was cold.

Julie and I were seated off to the side, far enough away from the
altar so there was virtually nothing to see but a few choir singers. Mozart's *Requiem* was going to be performed, and it set the tone perfectly.
As the voices of the choir meandered into and out of my consciousness,
I found myself gazing around at all the dancers I knew from the School
of American Ballet and New York City Ballet.

One image faded into another from that period in my life. I saw
myself standing in the downstage left wing at New York State Theater
on one of those rare occasions when I was a student at SAB and was
allowed backstage. It was 1977 or 1978, and dancing in the spotlight,
not ten feet away, were Peter Martins and Suzanne Farrell. Suzanne
was being Suzanne: hell bent for leather, possessed by supernatural

beings, throwing Vaganova as far as she could fling her. Meanwhile, Peter was there beside her, unflappable, never so much as a hair out of place, his partnering an astounding display of balance, beauty, and grace.

I never saw a dancer who could partner a woman as beautifully as Peter Martins. Watching him promenade Suzanne Farrell was something I'll never forget. He didn't shuffle or pad around like some coal miner, the way many men do it today. And he wasn't perpetually bracing himself on a completely turned-in leg. He was constantly aware of how he looked. He didn't "cheat" the classical positions. Whether that was simply his vanity talking or not, I couldn't say, but to control a mad genius like Suzanne Farrell and look as classical and debonair as Peter did was nothing short of its own mad genius.

And now, up there ahead of me at Balanchine's memorial service, mixed among the thousands of bunheads, was the man himself, Peter Martins. His promenading days were nearly over. Soon he would be taking the reigns at City Ballet and opening himself up to years of criticism for not having the good sense to realize that using George Balanchine's company so that you, yourself, can compete with him as choreographer is truly a fool's errand.

After daydreaming my way through most of Balanchine's memorial service, I came back to St. John the Divine. The Mozart was nearly finished. My ass hurt from sitting in the church pew. My feet were cold. I looked over at Julie. Beautiful as ever.

Our relationship, if I'd been able to characterize it at that point, was one of contradictions. I adored her and dreamed of having the kind of relationship where we shared absolutely everything with one another, good, bad, or indifferent, but I had to admit that I felt terribly inadequate in so many ways. As a dancer and a boyfriend, I often found myself wondering how on earth Julie managed to put up with me. And then, wouldn't you know it, in the midst of pondering my many short-comings, she looked at me as if there was no one else in the world she would rather have been with, took my hand in hers, and put both of them in her coat pocket.

American Ballet Theatre 890 Broadway New York, New York 10003-1278   (212) 477-3030   Cable: Ballethe, N.Y.

ABT

Mikhail Baryshnikov
Artistic Director

October 19, 1983

Dear Michael:

On Monday evening, October 31st, there will be a special com-memorative service at the Cathedral Church of St. John the Divine and a performance of the Mozart Requiem in memory of George Balanchine at 8:00 p.m.

Lincoln Kirstein has personally invited every dancer in American Ballet Theatre to join in this celebration of a man who has been so very important to all of us in the dance world.

This is a special evening, and we are the only Company that has been invited to sit with The New York City Ballet. I am very touched by this gesture, and I hope that each and every one of you will make every effort to attend.

Sincerely,

Mikhail Baryshnikov

MB:rl

P.S.   Even though there are 7,000 standing places in the Cathedral, there are actually only 1,200 seats. You will need a ticket to enter the seated section, so please let Florence know by Tuesday, October 25th if you intend to be there. The service will last from 8:00 to 9:15 p.m.

Invitation from Misha to Balanchine's Memorial. 1983. New York.

1984

PETER FONSECA AND I WERE LIVING separate lives by the time the rehearsal period for the 1983-84 season began. His star was ascendant; mine barely visible with the naked eye. Peter had been promoted to soloist at the end of 1981 and thereafter began accompanying Misha and a small group of select ABT dancers on Misha's annual sold-out summer tours of the U.S.

My life outside of ABT, meanwhile, was essentially an extension of my life inside ABT. Like most ballet dancers, Julie and I were most comfortable with our own. We saw outsiders or *pedestrians*, as we referred to them, as strange alien beings whose lives we didn't understand and, for the most part, had little knowledge of or interest in.

We lived in our own little ABT bubble, a place as full of mystery, intrigue, rumor-mongering, and backbiting as any high school. Our conversations revolved around what was happening inside the company; who was cheating on whom, who was getting what parts and why, who was an ass-kisser, who was garnering all of Misha's attention, who was getting fat, who was getting too thin, what overly ambitious girl or guy was faking an injury so they wouldn't have to dance some part they felt was beneath them, and so on and so forth. To those outside the company, it must have seemed awfully childish and deadly dull, but to us it was practically a drug. We couldn't get enough of it.

I still had no idea where I was going in the company, but suddenly I was cast as one of the two dancers who would share the role of the Cat in Misha and Peter Anastos's new production of *Cinderella*. Yes, I would be expected to wear a fake-fur suit and a gigantic cat head that would conceal my face, but I would get to dance with Cinderella and cavort about the stage garnering lots of attention—perhaps too much attention as it turned out, because one of the first things Misha would say to me about my interpretation was to tone it the hell down.

"Mikey," he said, after one of the first dress rehearsals at the Kennedy Center, "you moving too much. Every time you move, we see you. Cat take attention away from Cinderella. When you not dancing, just stay very still in your basket. Okeea?"

Gil Boggs was Top Cat, so to speak, and I could tell from the first rehearsal back in New York that he was less than thrilled about it. He had no interest in this tomfoolery. His star was burning holes in the repertoire, just as Peter Fonseca's was, and he'd already proven he could handle the pressure of being an ABT soloist. Dressing up in a cat suit was clearly not what he had in mind when he joined ABT.

I found Gil's attitude shocking, really, and wondered how it was that Misha couldn't see how little effort he was putting into it; but he didn't, apparently, and Gil sailed through rehearsals with nary an unkind word from Misha.

Unlike Gil, I had few standout opportunities, so I took the role very seriously, fake fur or no fake fur. I scrutinized everything Misha did when he was creating the part and tried to come up with my own nuances that would lend the Cat an air of individuality and greater believability. When the costume arrived, I put it on and worked by myself in the studio to further refine the movements.

It took some practice to figure out how to move the paws, where to place them so they accurately mimicked a cat's behavior. The actual surface of the Cat's face was a good five or six inches away from my own, so I would watch my movements in a mirror through the eye holes and memorize where my hand should be so it would look as if I were wiping a whisker or licking a paw and not inadvertently picking my nose.

And then one evening, after we'd been performing the ballet for a few months on tour, Misha came up to me as he was walking across the stage after the first act and said, "Nice job, Mikey. Cat is good."

What? Are you feeling okay? Are you sick? Have you been drinking again?

I was stunned, doubly so because Misha seemed to have said this almost as an afterthought. It was as if, in crossing the stage and seeing me there, the idea just suddenly popped into his Latvian head, and, rather than ignore it or keep it to himself as he normally did, he was overcome by angelic forces and just blurted it out.

"What Misha really had trouble doing," Charles France would confess, "was complimenting the dancers. He just *couldn't* do it. When he was prodded, he'd say, 'Oh, they know how good they are. What are you talking about?'"

Like most of what went on in the lives of the corps de ballet dancers at American Ballet Theatre, Misha had no idea what that brief, casual compliment meant to me or would come to mean to me in the ensuing years. So I'm going to tell him, and you:

It meant *everything*.

I cannot emphasize this enough. It was huge. It was, at long last, confirmation of the belief my parents had instilled in me that hard work would lead to something—wearing cat suits, compliments from Misha, who the hell knows? Anyway, hard work was supposed to lead to something, but up until that very moment, I wasn't sure it would lead anywhere, because it sure as hell didn't seem as if it were leading anywhere for me. (We'll overlook the fact that hard work had actually landed me a job with ABT.)

Misha's compliment was confirmation that there was something rational going on at ABT despite the many mind games I felt I was being subjected to. And last, but not least, it was confirmation that Misha had a few human qualities that were still vaguely recognizable.

What Misha didn't know was that, much like Gil, playing a cat was not exactly the type of thing I wanted to become noteworthy for at ABT. But it was too late. The Cat was out of the bag, so to speak. And then, before I knew what hit me, I was a "demi-caractère" dancer. Sancho Panza, here we come...do dah...do dah...

When all was said and done, here's the thing that really stuck in my craw: I actually enjoyed doing those parts. It was tremendous fun to dress up and transform myself with elaborate makeup and play a character onstage. I didn't feel as if I had to live up to some impossible technical standard, so I was more at ease and, as a result, enjoyed myself more.

As you might expect, I was skeptical of feeling too good about this new direction my career at ABT was taking and, at times, was even more miserable than I'd been before. Which just goes to show you there is some truth to the old saying that it's impossible to make a ballet dancer happy.

Style/Arts

PERFORMING ARTS

ABT's Beguiling 'Cinderella'

By George Jackson
Special to The Washington Post

The Cat is the audience's favorite character in "Cinderella," the fairy tale spectacle that American Ballet Theatre danced and mimed at the Kennedy Center for seven performances, from Wednesday through last night. Perhaps the Prince and Cinderella get the most applause at the end of a performance, but they take their curtain calls together. It is the Cat that steals scenes and that the kids will remember next year when it's time to buy tickets again or, perchance, turn on the tube.

Michael Langlois and Gil Boggs, who alternate in the role, are cats of somewhat different concept. Langlois is more mellow. The wise way in which he cocks his head suggests an old philosopher. It might well be that he's the only philosopher in all of ballet. Pleasures, like curling up in the laundry basket or being stroked, he consumes with relish. Last year, on New Year's Eve, he took the liberty of catching a Bluebird from the Spring divertissement and gobbled her up like a true Epicurean. This ad lib should have been kept.

Boggs is always daring. He'll grow up to be a Puss-in-Boots, the sort of cat about whom a whole ballet could be built. Watching him dance with Cinderella, one wishes the Fairy Godmother would change him into the Prince.

There was a brand new Prince and a new-

CYNTHIA GREGORY

to-Washington Cinderella in Saturday afternoon's cast. Johan Renvall's debut as the hero was one of the few chances this season to see this fine classicist in a major dance role. The Prince doesn't appear until Act 2, and when he does it is from an unexpected direction. This entrance is one of the ballet's best jokes. Once on stage, the Prince is overlooked by his court. Because Renvall was short compared with his honor guard, their initial neglect of him became quite plausible. His subsequent gruffness with his officers was not just mean but also funny because they towered over him. The scale of Renvall's dancing and deportment is far from small. His extraordinary clarity of movement was undiminished, though he seemed a little less pliant than

heretofore. In the Prince's variations, there is a deliberate asymmetry for the working leg. Renvall's penchant for perfect equilibrium actually diminished this interesting eccentricity.

Cheryl Yeager's Cinderella was one of her freshest performances in some time. She is a dancer who can make a change of speed or direction look like a delicious surprise. Her characterization, more than that of other interpreters of the role, showed a girl resigned to the lot of the drudge but one who bore no grudges. The acting was simple yet sure. Cynthia Gregory, Saturday night's Cinderella, played the part as if she were in scenes from realist plays. In the scullery, she is so harried that not only her steprelatives but even the viewers overlook her beauty. At the ball, she drips so much glamor that one wonders about her innocence. The Cinderella story is too slender a line on which to hang a lot of wet laundry. What made Gregory's performance worthwhile was the power of the dancing. The footwork could be lightning fast. Balances were developed slowly, luxuriously. She streamlined movement in ways other dancers, especially of her height, seldom risk.

Ross Stretton, Gregory's Prince, is more the standard tall dancer. He cuts a commanding figure on stage, but is at greater ease in steps that travel than in movement about a center. He's a very deft partner. Carla Stall ings' gentle Fairy Godmother and Deirdre Carberry's pert Springtime were noteworthy on Saturday evening. At the matinee, Peter Fonseca was new as the masochistic Step-Sister and Scott Schlexer was all nerves as the Step-Mother. Alan Barker conducted both performances. Boggs was the afternoon's Cat and Langlois the evening's.

Review of Cinderella. The Washington Post. 1984.

Rotten to the Corps

B ECOMING TOO COMFORTABLE IN THE CORPS de ballet at ABT was a slippery slope for many because it was, for all intents and purposes, comfortable, *really* comfortable. I felt respected simply because I was a member of American Ballet Theatre, a company whose name was synonymous with greatness. Attention was lavished, if not on me directly, then on those close enough to me for me to be able to see myself reflected in its mirror. I generally knew what to expect from one day to the next and one year to the next. I wasn't the center of attention, but I was close enough to the people who were to feel as if I was involved in something important, in something that mattered. Yes, there was pressure now and then, but by and large it was just enough responsibility spiced with the occasional genuine challenges so as not to lull me to sleep.

I could have had a great deal more fun in the corps de ballet if I hadn't felt this nagging sense that what I was doing really and truly wasn't enough. I also knew that, barring injury or unsightly weight gain or loss, I could have gone on like that for years. Dancers did. Amy Blaisdell danced in the corps de ballet at American Ballet Theatre for eighteen years, from 1963 to 1981. Scott Schlexer danced in the corps de ballet for nineteen years, from 1976 to 1995. There were many exceptions, of course, and I suppose the most glaring were those for whom being in the corps de ballet at American Ballet Theatre was, at times, its own private hell.

When a girl became so thin, for example, that Misha or Charles noticed and it was, ergo, potentially noticeable to an audience that believed we were all as skinny as sticks just because we worked hard, the usual remedy was for Charles to threaten the girl with being removed from certain ballets if she didn't gain some weight, or ask her to take a leave of absence to get some help. As the object of one of these chats, a girl in the corps de ballet told me about her run-in with Charles.

"Charles thought my arms looked too skinny onstage and it was distracting, so he threatened to fire me if I didn't gain weight. He said, 'You either go get help, or we can't use you.' So I got help. And that was the beginning of my therapy, which went on and on and on. It was odd, what happened with Charles. It was horrifying and embarrassing. Who wants to get a pink slip?

"From that moment on, I had to be weighed all the time. Peter Marshall, ABT's physical therapist, had a scale in his office, and I was supposed to maintain a weight of 110 pounds or something like that. But Peter wasn't interested in being Charles's little informer, so he would just lie about my weight. When you're expected to eat more, of course you can't eat more. Anorexia is about rebelling, not doing what you're told by Charles France, so that approach didn't really work with me.

"And now... I don't think a day goes by where I don't think about what I eat or my body. It's in me. You don't really recover from anorexia; you just learn to deal with it."

Apart from continually debating how much not to eat, or hating myself for not having a body like Fernando Bujones or a technique like Misha's, I was grappling with one major issue at ABT: did I really have what it was going to take to become a soloist? Sometimes I pushed through the difficult moments with more work and a constancy of purpose, but other times I was simply too tired or too despondent to make the effort because, deep down, I wasn't sure I was worth the effort. More importantly, I wasn't sure I could or wanted to handle the pressure that came along with performing soloist roles at American Ballet Theatre.

What I came to realize, because I saw so much of it around me every day, was that in a company like ABT, it is incredibly easy to become discouraged. It's easy to look around in company class and see people who are better than you are and find yourself thinking, I'm never going to have a body like _____. I'm never going to be able to turn like _____ or jump like _____ or move like _____. This is such a constant struggle. It's a battle, really it is. This class sucks. My foot hurts. I'm exhausted. What am I doing this for? I'm miserable. I just want to go home and go back to bed.

And while you're standing there coming up with a million different reasons as to why you won't make it or don't need to work harder, you're hardly aware of how you're sabotaging yourself. Maybe you're just having a weak moment. Maybe your foot really does hurt, or your knee or your hip just doesn't seem to get any better no matter how much physical therapy you do, and you feel like nothing is ever going to be right. It's hard enough to compete when you're completely healthy; how are you ever going to get anything going feeling like this?

━━━━━━━━━━━━━━━━━━━━━

By the time I got to the Met Season in the spring of 1984, I'd been in American Ballet Theatre for four years, and I was growing weary of the ABT callboard. From one hour to the next, between nearly every rehearsal, the dancers in the company stood in front of the callboard like sacrificial lambs ready to receive the silent news about where their day was going, where their week was going, where their year was going, and, finally, where their career at ABT was going.

Conversations with the callboard were entirely one-sided affairs. The board did the talking. You did the listening. When I looked up at the casting for a new ballet and didn't see my name, not even as an understudy, I knew that, in order to get an explanation, I would have to schedule an appointment with Susan or Charles. This was something I never did, because I knew Susan and Charles were incredibly busy and they were probably not the people who'd made the decision; that person was Misha, or the ballet's creator.

Speaking to Misha about such things was generally a dead end for all sorts of reasons. He didn't have the time. He didn't have the patience. He didn't deal with the day-to-day concerns of the corps de ballet. He didn't like dictating to a choreographer who they should choose, and much of the time he probably had no idea why some dancers were chosen and others not. Given all the hoops that had to be jumped through, I generally tried to reason these things out for myself.

I wasn't called to the rehearsal because:

(a) I wasn't right for the part.

(b) I wasn't good enough for the part.

(c) The ballet master or choreographer in charge thinks (a) or (b).

After ruminating on the many tragic possibilities for a day or so, during which time I would beat myself up for being too timid or too lacking in self-respect to speak with Susan or Charles, I would conclude that I didn't need to make an appointment to speak with Susan or Charles, because the answer was probably all of the above.

What was almost as discouraging as getting my career information from the callboard was getting my ABT company news from *The New York Times*. This happened with great regularity and was just another indication, in my mind, of the lack of concern ABT management had for us.

I wanted to hear about what my company was up to and where my career and my life was going from an actual person in my actual company, not Anna Kisselgoff of *The New York Times*. And I wanted that person to give me an explanation and some direction if I needed it. And I wanted that person to occasionally be the person who called himself my director. And if the staff was too busy or the director was stretched too thin or he was off making movies or chasing women, that wasn't my fault.

It came to a point at Ballet Theatre when I said to Julie one night, "Fuck it, if no one is going to put my name on the rehearsal list for the ballets I want to dance, then I'll just go to the rehearsals and start learning the ballets on my own."

What I eventually realized about this approach was that it's darn near impossible to really learn a ballet unless you get a chance to dance it, unless you have an opportunity to let the movement sink into your muscle memory. After standing around in the back of rehearsals for Paul Taylor's *Airs* for most of a year, Susan Jones, the ballet mistress in charge of this work, never once mentioned what I might do to improve my chances of getting into the ballet. This wasn't a surprise. Dancers in Ballet Theatre stood around for years waiting for a first cast dancer to hurt themselves, retire, leave the company, or get hit by a bus. I knew that. I also knew that this was how the old ABT operated under Lucia Chase. In Misha's ABT, this type of hierarchy fell by the wayside in favor of giving opportunities to dancers whenever and wherever Misha felt it necessary.

A part of me felt that my presence in *Airs* rehearsals was an unwelcome reminder that I didn't respect Susan's decision or Misha's decision or Paul Taylor's decision not to cast me in the ballet, even as an understudy. But the truth was I never knew for sure. Susan never told me how she felt, and I never asked. Years later, when I spoke to her about this, I realized she was completely unaware that I'd insinuated myself into *Airs* rehearsals, and this, I must say, made me laugh. The blind truly were leading the blind or, in my case, the half-blind.

What made me begin to see Susan Jones differently was that she was the ballet mistress in Spoleto, where, again, I had nothing to do and was given no opportunities or explanations as to why I wasn't doing anything. It was situations such as those that left a sour taste in my mouth, for it seemed at times as if Susan really didn't care how much initiative I showed or how hard I worked. And the more stagnant my repertoire became, the more convinced I became that she didn't really give a shit what I was doing in the back of the room because she probably had had thwarted ambitions of her own when she was in the corps de ballet at ABT and perhaps it was time I felt a little bit of her pain.

In spite of the many small humiliations that began to accumulate in my mind, some part of me was still determined to prove everyone wrong, and, as per Misha's suggestion, I began focusing more on my arms. I looked at how Danny was using his arms, but for the life of me I couldn't figure out what, exactly, it was that I was not doing relative to what it was he was doing, because as far as I could tell, Danny's arms operated like sticks. For a while, what I did was simply try to look more at my arms in the mirror instead of at my legs, but I had no idea if that attention was paying off, and Misha, no surprise, never said anything about whether I was making progress in this department or not.

And then, suddenly, I was asked to learn the first movement lead in Balanchine's *Bourree Fantasque*, a comedic part for a short man who's trying to impress a taller woman. The role was originally danced by Jerome Robbins in 1949.

I began learning *Bourree* from Johan Renvall, the Swedish soloist who would most often dance this role, and from the outset, he seemed intent on wanting me to dance the role as he did, but I didn't want to be Johan's clone. After a few unpleasant rehearsals wherein I kept waiting for Wendy Walker, the ballet mistress, to step in and act like a ballet mistress instead of letting Johan run my rehearsal, I was frustrated and angry. As rehearsals wore on, it became increasingly evident I was not measuring up, so I sat on the sidelines and watched Johan, Gil Boggs, and Danny Radojevic alternate dancing this part.

I was given more opportunities to prove myself at ABT, but those opportunities rarely translated in my mind to the fact that I was cared for or that Misha himself might be giving me those chances to see what I was capable of. I was called to rehearsals for Bronze Idol in *La Bayadère* and Russians in *Nutcracker,* and those experiences proved to be real eye-openers because there were technical aspects in both cases that I felt were beyond me.

What those thwarted chances demonstrated was that I could not have been more confused about what I wanted out of my career at ABT, and there was no greater evidence of that confusion than the relief I felt at knowing I wouldn't have to face the pressures involved with dancing those roles.

In order to get to the point where you are dancing a role like Bronze Idol at American Ballet Theatre, you have to be able perform that role in a rehearsal room in front of Misha, a ballet master, and all of the other dancers. This, in many respects, was more stressful than dancing the role onstage, because at least on stage the audience was relatively invisible. The second hurdle one had to overcome was the stress associated with dancing in front of three thousand people at the Metropolitan Opera House in New York. Both of those prospects scared me to death, but I managed to overlook the implications of that fear.

Many dancers are scared, and everyone gets nervous. From the time you are thrust out on stage, you learn to overlook those feelings, or you might be one of those dancers who is fortunate enough not to feel much trepidation. In my case, I think my fear was trying to tell me something.

It had been two years since the Spoleto Festival and the gala premiere of my eating disorder, and I'd made what I considered progress. I jettisoned the scale I once took on tour, but I was still deeply wedded to starving myself for long periods of time. As a result, I was fatigued so consistently I began to wonder if something more serious might be wrong with me. To that end, I made an appointment with Balanchine's physician, Dr. Edith Langner.

Dr. Langner was a charming older woman who was clearly accustomed to talking with dancers who ate next to nothing. She wanted to help me, God bless her, but she had nothing to go on, no idea what I was really up to, or how many hours of every day I spent not eating and waiting to reward myself at the end of the day with some treasured morsel. Had she known any of that, she might've mentioned that not eating for long periods of time actually slows the metabolism down considerably, thereby sabotaging one's efforts to not only stay thin, but to have any energy to dance.

After I gave Dr. Langner a run-down of my eating habits (my bran muffin or nothing for breakfast, my bunch of nothing for lunch, and my salad for dinner), she took a blood sample and said, in a soothing tone of voice that betrayed nary a shred of alarm, "You might be anemic. You should have some protein in the middle of the day."

What Dr. Langner didn't understand was that the middle of the day was a no man's land for me, a Saharan Desert of time I generally spent trying not to think about what I might be able to eat or not eat when I crawled back to my nightly oasis.

"Yoghurt, ice cream, cheese," she interjected, spoiling my reverie.

Ice cream? Clearly this woman was insane. A midday meal, if I had one, usually consisted of an apple, to which I might now contemplate adding a small piece of cheese.

With thoughts of ice cream cones dancing in my head, I left Dr. Langner's office wondering if Mr. Balanchine, when he was still alive, walked around eating an ice cream cone in the middle of the day and, if he had, what flavor a dance genius like himself would go for. Pistachio. Definitely pistachio.

━━━━━━━━━━

Why, one might obviously ask, are ballet dancers so good at being neurotic, at adopting strange and obsessive habits that cling to us like so much cat hair on a couch? Ballet class, I feel obligated to point out, is the ground into which we plant those seeds, so it is to ballet class we must look.

Virtually every ballet class in the entire world begins with the left hand on the barre and pliés in four different positions of the feet. From there, one turns to the other side and repeats the same exercise with the right hand on the barre. The exercises progress at the barre, becoming more difficult and complex, but they are repeated in more or less the same fashion from one teacher to another the world over. A dancer from New York can step off the plane in Tokyo and take a ballet class, and it will be completely understandable to them. The names of the steps will be the same because all of the steps have the same French derivation. The structure of the class, save a few idiosyncrasies, will be basically the same.

The barre will last thirty to forty-five minutes and consist of a series of short exercises. Once in the center of the room, the process begins anew with simple exercises leading to bigger, more complex movements that include turning and jumping, until one reaches grand allegro and combinations that move across the length of the studio. The center phase of class lasts about an hour, and when all is said and done, you are sweating, often profusely, and ninety minutes to two hours will have passed.

Because of the repetition involved in ballet and the discipline required to engage in that repetition, ballet dancers slip easily into habits that become open season for just about any obsession you can think of. And because a beautiful line is so essential in classical ballet and because most dancers believe that a thinner line is a more beautiful line, it stands to reason that the thinner you are, the more beautiful you are.

With respect to the issue of eating disorders within ABT, we all knew when we went out to dinner with certain dancers and it came time to order, it was only ever going to be a salad. And even though we knew there was a problem, there was little any of us felt we could do about it. The issue of thinness was a constant presence in our lives, for the women in particular. Admitting there was a problem was rarely contemplated because, for many of us, there simply wasn't one. This was the norm. This was what was expected of us: to be thin and beautiful. This was how we lived our lives.

Man's Best Friend

A T SEVEN O'CLOCK IN THE EVENING, a few weeks before the end of the Met season in 1984, I found myself sitting down with Misha again in a dark, empty principal dressing room at the theater. I looked around at the luxurious amount of space I felt certain I would never inhabit, then turned to look into a face that said, "Shoot me now, please."

I was just guessing this was what he was thinking, mind you. Just guessing based on the fact that Misha was one of the most accomplished conveyers of emotion to ever set foot on stage, and the slightest thought that entered his head was instantly telegraphed to the nose-bleed section of just about any theater you could mention.

Oddly enough, I used to think Misha's uneasiness with people was because he was self-conscious about his English-speaking abilities, but Charles France assured me this wasn't the case. Although Misha's English was far from perfect, he certainly could express himself when he wanted to, especially if it was something negative.

"You tink dis funny?" he said to us one day in rehearsal when someone made some sort of gaff and we all burst out laughing. "Vell, let me tell you," he added, "dis not comedy, dis tragedy."

We got a lot of mileage out of that little phrase.

Sitting across from Misha every spring was hard for me, and it was hard for him. I knew that. I knew Misha's life was overflowing with obligations, so I tried not to create a problem or a distraction. No matter what I did, however, nothing seemed to make him happy. At a certain point, I came to accept the fact that there was very little, in fact, that could make him happy, except a dog.

Strange as it may sound, dogs became an increasing part of everyday life at ABT, and that was not entirely an accident. Whenever one person did something in a ballet company, you could pretty much bank on the fact that ten other people were soon going to be buying it, visiting it, wearing it, investing in it, eating its food, or taking its class.

In ABT in the 1980s, this faddishness began to revolve around dogs. More and more dancers adopted them and began bringing them to the studio or on tour, and in each and every case, when Misha encountered one of these animals, I saw a side of him that was so joyful it was startling. If it weren't for the presence of dogs, I'm not sure I would have ever seen that joy. All of which begged the question: What the hell did he want out of this directorship job? It certainly wasn't brightening his mood.

Virtually the only other time I saw the human side of Misha was when he occasionally sat down and played the piano. His repertoire and his technique may have had been limited, but he played a beautiful, melancholic kind of jazz that he appeared to improvise. And while he played, which was generally while we were waiting for class or rehearsal to start, most of us would be sitting around stretching on the floor or at the barre. Some conversations would cease, but most continued doing what they were doing. We were accustomed to such things. I was always attentive to Misha's playing, however. It made me wistful, and somehow that seemed right. Wistfulness was a mood that suited him.

But back in that darkened dressing room at the Met, it was, for a few minutes a year, just the two of us. No dogs. No pianos. No groupies. No pretty girls. No one watching. Misha didn't have to look at my awful arms or my less-than-stellar dancing, and for a moment I sensed he didn't want to hurt my feelings, didn't ever want to tell me what I suspected might be true, i.e., that I simply wasn't good enough. What person, after all, could say that to a dancer? Well, some could obviously, but most people are aware of how hurtful that might be, so they pussy-foot around the issue by saying things like, gee, maybe you'd be better suited for a different company.

In my case, I think Misha and I both knew after my anthropomorphic talents were unveiled as the Cat in *Cinderella* that I had turned a corner and my future at ABT was cloudy. What I didn't tell Misha was that I'd fallen in love with the Nederlands Dans Theater after seeing them perform at the Met in July of 1981, and, while ABT was in Washington, I had flown back to New York to audition for Jiří Kylián, the choreographer and director of NDT.

Much to my surprise, what Jiří said to me when the audition was over was that I was too *classical*; that I belonged in a company like…er… American Ballet Theatre. As a consolation prize, he said, "If you'd like to join our second company, I could offer you a contract there. Many of the regular NDT dancers come up from NDT II."

"Let me think about it," I replied.

On the plane back to Washington, I thought, I'm too good to move down into a preparatory company. I'm already in ABT. Why would I want to go backwards? Little did I realize how much I would come to regret that decision.

I never told Misha or anyone at ABT about this audition, but Misha wasn't stupid. He was aware that I hadn't handled the more demanding roles I'd been offered. At the same time, he saw that I still had ambition and that I was willing to work hard. The only logical conclusion he could come to was that I would be better off somewhere else, somewhere where the standard was such that I could get opportunities. And because he knew this, this is what he said to me toward the end of our discussion: "I vill talk to Baub."

Translation: Robert Joffrey. He would talk to Bob Joffrey about how good I'd be in his company because, obviously, I was not quite up to the ABT soloist standard, which was the first step out of the corps de ballet valley I was in.

Yes, the Joffrey wasn't much of a step down, and I would've been the first to admit they had a fantastic repertoire and an eclectic group of dancers, but I didn't want to dance in the Joffrey. I'd heard too many horror stories about their sadistic ballet master to contemplate subjecting myself to any more abuse than I was already inflicting on myself.

After mentioning Bob Joffrey, Misha said, "I tink, maybe...you vould be happier in smaller company. Different company vair you can dance more."

"Maybe you're right," I said, staring down at the dark, carpeted floor where a mini version of myself was running around screaming, "I won't give up! I won't give up!"

We both stood and shook hands, leaving the Joffrey idea lying on the ground. I never mentioned it again. Neither did Misha.

━━━━━━━━━━

In August of 1984, Taylor Hackford began filming *White Nights*. Misha had a starring role in the film alongside Gregory Hines and the woman Hackford would eventually marry, Helen Mirren. While the film was being shot, Misha periodically disappeared for weeks at a time. No one ever told us when he was leaving, when he would be back, or how long he would be gone. One day he was there and the next he wasn't.

We rarely, if ever, knew where Misha went when he wasn't around, but in this case his absences lasted far longer than they had before. We were all left to assume what we usually assumed, that he or "the company" thought it unimportant for us to know his whereabouts. Like so much that went on at ABT, I couldn't help but wonder what the administration was thinking. Did they think we didn't care? Did they think we might not be curious? That we might not be insulted or hurt or left to conclude that, in Misha's mind or their minds, we just weren't worth telling?

If Lucia Chase acted like a mother to the dancers of ABT for thirty-five years, Mikhail Baryshnikov acted the distant, disapproving father who worked long hours and rarely saw his children. He must have realized after four years that juggling a career as a dancer with the huge responsibilities of being the director of ABT was more than he'd bargained for, which was why he decided to go off and make a movie called *White Nights*, hire Kenneth MacMillan as "Artistic Associate," and John Taras as "Associate Director."

As usual, there were many things going on behind the scenes at ABT, things the dancers were never apprised of, and one of those things, according to none other Anna Kisselgoff in *The New York Times*, was that "in September 1983, he [Misha] threatened to resign after a dispute with the company's board, which had asked him to dance at certain galas to raise money. Mr. Baryshnikov took the position that the company should be promoted as an entity and should not depend upon any star or individual, including himself. He won his battle and soon after hammered out the agreement that would give him the freedom to be involved in other projects [like *White Nights*]."

Yes, Kenneth MacMillan and John Taras suddenly did appear simultaneously on the scene in 1984 with confoundingly similar job titles, but as far as I was concerned, nothing had changed. The dancers, as usual, were left in the dark and never told whether, in fact, anything *had* changed. I still looked to Misha for the many microscopic clues I was always on the lookout for as to how I was doing, and I looked at John and Kenneth as I looked at all the other ballet masters, as people who took charge of certain ballets and ran rehearsals. I don't think any of us felt—I know I certainly didn't—that John or Kenneth had any real power to make decisions about who was going to dance what. That was Misha's job.

The irony of Misha's absences during the 1984-85 season was that, while he was away, I was a great deal more at ease. The long shadow he cast over my life in the company was gone. I didn't have to worry about what he was thinking of me in company class or in rehearsals or onstage, and as a result, I was actually a lot happier.

The Fall of Fernando

THE FALL REHEARSAL PERIOD IN 1984 was a strange juxtaposition of old and new at Ballet Theatre. Fernando Bujones, after pestering Misha for a long time, was finally given the green light to create a ballet, *Grand Pas Romantique,* to music by Adolphe Adam, the composer of *Giselle* and *O Holy Night.*

Fernando was well-liked by the dancers in the company and the men in the corps de ballet in particular, several of whom were very adept at imitating his somewhat high-pitched Spanish lisp and his habit of joking about how fabulous he was.

We could all see what a huge talent Fernando was. We could also see that his desire to usurp Misha in terms of fame and fortune had been continually sabotaged by circumstances that were not always within his control.

At nineteen, Fernando became the youngest principal dancer in American Ballet Theatre history. That same year, 1974, he won the prestigious Gold Medal at the ballet competition in Varna, Bulgaria. Three days later, Mikhail Baryshnikov, after defecting in Toronto, made his debut in New York, dancing *Giselle* with Natasha Makarova, and nobody paid much attention to what Fernando Bujones had done.

Despite his enormous ego and the obvious chip he carried on his shoulder where Misha was concerned, Fernando was a down-to-earth guy who would talk with anyone in the company. He was a sweet man in many ways, and a testament to this sweetness was the champagne he brought in for all of us to drink after we'd finished creating his first ballet for ABT.

Champagne or no champagne, Fernando's choreography was an unoriginal testament to his love of classical ballet. It got a polite response from audiences and critics before it quietly left the repertoire, proving once again to all concerned that Misha was not only a superior artist, but a much shrewder judge of his own lack of talent for choreography than Fernando ever would be.

═══════════════

When Kenneth MacMillan joined ABT as Artistic Associate in the fall of 1984, he immediately began setting his famous *Romeo and Juliet* on the company, a ballet I could not fully participate in because of the potential danger of the swordplay and the one good eye that I had left.

On the choreographic front, David Gordon, one of the original members of the Judson Dance Theater, came up from the downtown dance scene to create a ballet using folding chairs set to the music of John Field. Appropriately enough, it was called *Field, Chair, Mountain*. In addition to David's ballet, there were restagings of *Coppélia*, Balanchine's *Donizetti Variations*, and Tudor's *Dim Lustre*.

I was cast in David Gordon's new ballet, as well as in *Coppélia*, where I had some actual classical dancing to do, so I was as content as I could be, I suppose. I mention classical dancing in *Coppélia* because, despite the fact that American Ballet Theatre was considered a classical ballet company and everyone therefore assumed you were bouncing around on stage night after night in white tights perfecting your Vaganova technique, the actual opportunities for the men in the corps de ballet to use their classical training were few and far between.

Apart from *Coppélia*, the only other ballets where I put on white tights and was expected to dance in a purely classical fashion were *Theme and Variations*, *Cinderella*, and, to a lesser extent, *La Sonnambula*. Three ballets out of thirty—that's not a lot of classical dancing.

Coppélia then, albeit a lite classic, was a happy exception to the rule, and perhaps this was why Misha brought it into the repertoire, to keep the men on their toes, so to speak. Whatever the reasons, I was happy to get an opportunity to do double tours en l'air alongside John Gardner in the third act. This opportunity gave me, and all of the men involved, something to work on, and we collectively puffed out our chests and set about the task at hand, much as we did in *Les Noces*.

As exciting as it was to see what another year might have in store in terms of new ballets, the three weeks we were going to be spending in Japan in October loomed large in everyone's mind. This was, after all, our first trip abroad with ABT and, for most, their first visit to Japan. At the conclusion of three weeks of performances, the company was not due back in New York for another week to ten days—time enough for many of us to travel around and take in the sites.

I Think I'm Speaking Japanese.
I Really Think So...

THERE REALLY IS NO EASY WAY to describe Japan or its rampant fanaticism. Things I'd taken for granted as having a casual place in everyday life were blown all out of proportion there or, perhaps, into just the proper proportion, depending on your point of view. From gardening to making tea to wrapping a simple purchase at Mitsukoshi, a big Japanese department store, everything warranted a kind of obsessiveness that transformed the seemingly mundane into art.

Like most of the dancers in Ballet Theatre, I used to wonder what being Misha would be like. I finally got a taste of it after our first performance at the Nippon Hoso Kyokai Theater in Tokyo in October of 1984.

What at first glance might seem thrilling or incredibly flattering about being mobbed by scores of young Japanese girls soon wears quite thin, however, when you realize that those girls have no idea who you are, nor do they much care. In their minds, you might be a famous American dancer and bosom buddy of the most famous dancer in the world, Mikhail Baryshnikov, but in your mind you know you are none of those things. As a result, all that adulation seems misplaced.

Yes, I was happy to be signing autographs because I was rarely asked for an autograph back home, but after several nights and hundreds of signatures, I tired of the charade and wanted to just get the hell back to the hotel and drink myself silly with sake, which is what most of the Japanese in Tokyo seem to be doing every night of the week.

Being in Japan with Misha was like being on tour with The Beatles. Everywhere we performed, there were mobs of people crowding the stage door. Everywhere I went, even when I was just casually strolling though a museum in Tokyo, I attracted scores of young Japanese girls who began following me and whispering at a distance, their hands cupped over their mouths to show politeness or embarrassment or to simply hide their often unruly teeth—who the hell knew?

The company was booked into the New Otani Hotel in Tokyo, and, apparently, we were not alone. Some outer-space version of the Baltimore Orioles was also inhabiting the hotel, and they were being treated to the kind of scrutiny I was beginning to grow accustomed to outside the theater every night.

The lobby of the New Otani was more or less one gigantic hallway, and it was along this carpeted expanse that I encountered (morning, noon, and night) the many baseball fanatics I never knew existed outside the United States. There was a continual sentry of these Japanese baseball fans milling about for hours at a clip, waiting for a glimpse of some minor-league hero or Major-League has-been who'd been seduced by the money of the Far East.

My dancing responsibilities in Japan were relatively few. Among the ballets we brought, I was in but three: *Raymonda, Gottschalk,* and *Don Quixote.* As a result, I had a number of nights off and very few rehearsals. My four years of touring with ABT had served me well in this regard, and I took advantage of my free time in much the same way I did on our U.S. tours. I visited museums, went shopping, made con-

.The
Orient

ABT
Tours japan

...and the Friends do, too!

The Orient Express or Extremely Disoriented.

tact with some Japanese who wanted to practice their English, saw the Kabuki theater, and went to the famous Tsukiji fish market at the crack of dawn with Julie.

After a week in Tokyo, the company traveled to Osaka and then Nagoya, and in no time at all, our three-week tour was over. I said good-bye to Julie, who was heading back to Honolulu to visit her parents, then headed out to see a bit more of the country.

It was November, and, after a few days in Kyoto to visit its many temples, I headed south to the Izu Peninsula to a small surfing village called Shimoda. At that time of the year, the place was deserted. The tiny ryokan where I was staying had no heat, but I managed to stay relatively warm in my old, tatami-matted room, wrapping myself in a huge coverlet atop a futon on the floor. Every morning, I was awakened at the crack of dawn by roosters and an old woman who brought me a tray of cold fish, rice, and hot tea.

It was all terribly austere—very few people in Shimoda could speak English—and I felt as if I were continually staring at a bunch of exotic fish in a gigantic aquarium and they were staring back at me. I could put my hand up to the glass and tap on it, scaring the hell out of the imprisoned masses, but that was about the extent of our interaction.

When the company returned to New York, the dust of Japan remained embedded in our collective psyches. Julie and I frequented our favorite Japanese restaurant with newfound chips on our shoulders, using the few phrases of Japanese we'd learned so that everyone would know we'd been to Japan and acknowledge us as superior beings. We bought sushi-making equipment and held sushi parties at our apartment, but by the time December rolled around, the chopsticks were put away, and we headed out on the road once again.

And the Beat Goes On

B ECAUSE OF BALLETS SUCH AS *Coppélia; Field, Chair, Mountain;* and *Graduation Ball,* I got through the tour and the Met Season without feeling entirely forgotten. And while she rarely got opportunities to step outside the corps de ballet, Julie didn't seem terribly troubled by this. She was, like all of the girls Misha selected, possessed with beautiful legs and feet. What she might have lacked in strength and technical wizardry, she made up for with her looks.

Over the previous four years, Julie had, like most of the girls in ABT's corps de ballet, worked her ass off. While I was often wondering what to do with all my free time, she was habitually dancing two to three ballets a night. When she did have a rare night off, she often spent that time sewing pointe shoes or nursing injuries, injuries that were, at times, serious enough to warrant an ambulance.

I spent a good many hours of our relationship holding Julie's hand while she waited for a doctor, a chiropractor, a physical therapist, or an acupuncturist to put her back to together again; and while I was waiting, I came to the conclusion that her injuries were indicative of more than mere physical weaknesses or exhaustion—though she certainly was exhausted much of the time. Julie may have had different reasons for dancing through all that pain, but I think she had the same sort of love/hate relationship with ballet that I had.

Given the fact that we worked in the same company day in and day out, it always struck me as odd how different our professional lives truly were, and how unfair. I wanted to be working as hard as Julie. I wanted to feel real, genuine fatigue at the end of the day, but the opportunity rarely, if ever, presented itself. In fact, during the entire time I was in American Ballet Theatre, there was but one single solitary occasion when I danced all three ballets in a repertoire program. That evening, as Julie and I boarded the downtown number 1 train at Lincoln Center after the performance, I turned to her and said, "Wow, now I know what being you feels like. It's awesome."

She looked down her nose at me, her eyeliner smudged, her shoulders drooping from exhaustion and the weight of her dance bag. "Yeah, right," she said, patting me on the knee. "Get back to me when you've done that eight times a week for about seven months. See how awesome you feel then."

I was about to finish my fifth season with the company, and, after that brief taste of satisfaction, I was beginning to realize that inspiring the envy of others might not be a compelling enough reason to overcome the ennui of my life in American Ballet Theatre. To add insult to injury, Misha was still calling me Mikey, and I was still playing a child in the party scene of *Nutcracker*.

In the midst of discussing my career frustrations with Julie, we began to consider the possibility of separating. As much as we still loved one another, we both wondered if the relationship we had was ideal. (Surely, we thought, you couldn't hit three cherries on the first pull of the one-armed love bandit.)

As patently ludicrous as this idea seems to me now, it gained an insane amount of traction in our minds, and we both began imagining all the fun we could be having fooling around with other people before happily reconnecting and riding off into the sunset, convinced that our love, if it was as pure as a Russell Hitchcock vocal in an *Air Supply* song, could withstand anything.

"I'm going to Greece this summer with Deannie and Kathy," Julie told me, apropos of our grand plan.

"That sounds great," I responded. "I'll look for another apartment while you're gone."

With my relationship up in the air and my career at ABT still solidly on the ground, I met with Misha again at the end of the 1985 Met Season. By then, Flo, Misha's secretary, had come to rely on the fact that I wanted to speak with Misha every year, and before I had a chance to ask her about it, she hollered at me as I was passing by the Green Room one day, "Mikey, we need to schedule your meeting with Misha!"

As in previous years, Misha and I found an empty principal dressing room and sat down opposite one another to discuss the difference between the dancer I thought I was and the dancer he knew me to be. We didn't speak of my missed opportunities. We didn't speak of my fears, or my confusion over what I really wanted, or anything, for that matter, that might have shed some light on what was truly at the core of my relationship with dance or my place in American Ballet Theatre. And in that respect, what was happening was what happens in most ballet companies.

You are the dancer. Your expression is a silent one. Talking is not on the menu. You are given roles to test your abilities, and if you prove yourself capable, you might be given more important roles; if not, the roles are taken away and your career path is reevaluated in ways that are often unknown to you. To the director who watches you dance, it is always obvious what you are a capable of. To you, it rarely is.

Misha mentioned in our discussion that there would be some new ballets on the horizon the next year: another new David Gordon ballet, *Murder*, and another by John Taras, *Francesca da Rimini*. Perhaps there would be opportunities there. He couldn't guarantee anything, of course, just as he couldn't guarantee that Tudor would ever cast me in one of his ballets. Those weren't Misha's decisions to make.

As we stood to shake hands, I rallied every ounce of courage I had and said what had been on my mind for the past few years, most of the previous week, and nearly every second of the entire ten minutes we'd been sitting there. "Oh, Misha, there's one last thing."

"Yes, Mikey?"

"Do you think you could call me Michael?"

Oh shit. I've caught him off guard. He smiled, almost laughed. I leapt in. "After five years, the 'Mikey' thing is a getting a bit old, if you know what I mean?"

"Yes. Okeea," he said. "Mike...ill."

In Misha's defense, the Mikey stuff never would have happened if it hadn't been for that damn Life Cereal commercial. Of course, in Misha's mind, turning Michael into Mikey must've been akin to turning Mikhail into Misha or Alexander into Sasha or Natalia into Natasha. It was nothing. It was a term of endearment. It was sweet. I knew this. I knew there was a cultural divide and that he wasn't trying to be demeaning, which was also why he needed to be reminded that I wasn't

Russian and going from Michael to Mikey in America was not really
akin to turning Mikhail into Misha.

I will say this for Misha: he never called me Mikey again. He stammered. He hesitated. He almost let it slip out of his mouth any number
of times, but he always caught himself somewhere between *Mike* and
eee, and in that brief pause, he would remember. Mike-ill.

ABT Souvenir Program. 1985. Julie and I.
Photo credit: Gilles Larrain

A Grecian Holiday

W HILE JULIE SPENT THE SUMMER OF '85 gallivanting around the Greek Isles doing God knows what with God knows who, I spent the sweltering month of August looking at squalid, overpriced, shoe-boxed-sized apartments in Manhattan with my mother. To be fair, most New Yorkers are well acquainted with this kind of abuse. I, however, was not, and after about a week, I was so depressed by the entire prospect that I said to my mom, "I can't do this. I can't live in some crappy apartment by myself. What was I thinking?" My mother, as was her habit, tried to boost my spirits by saying, "Why on earth you were thinking of leaving the nicest girl I've ever met in my life, I sure as hell don't know."

Before Julie landed at Kennedy Airport in late August, I filled our apartment with flowers and candles and headed to the airport in a limousine to surprise her. She, of course, was shocked, partly because virtually no self-respecting New Yorker ever goes out to the airport to meet a visitor (that's what cabs are for), but mostly because she assumed she was coming home as a single woman.

Over the course of the next few days, we talked about our future together. I ignored the nagging feeling I had, as Julie showed me her photos, that she'd had an affair in Greece. She spoke vaguely about a group of English friends, one of whom might come to visit. There were a few mysterious phone calls. Neither one of us knew exactly what to say or do, so we did what we typically did: we went back to class and got on with our lives at American Ballet Theatre.

ABT was scheduled to perform at Wolf Trap, an outdoor amphitheater near Washington, D.C., and during my first class back after our holiday, I severely sprained my ankle in class and was forced to stay home. Having never been the type of dancer who was injured, this was something of a novelty for me.

It was early September, and the weather in New York was glorious. The sun poured in through our open apartment windows as I lay on the couch day after day with my foot iced and elevated. My forays to the grocery store just around the corner were hour-long escapades defined by hundreds of miniscule steps.

As sad as this might have seemed, it was a revelation for me. I learned to appreciate something as mundane as walking. That simple act, which I'd always taken for granted, suddenly seemed as physically miraculous as I then understood it to be, and I finally understood how truly blessed I was to be able to dance.

The revelations didn't end there. Even New York City, that filthy repository of human desperation I generally passed through at a whirlwind clip, became a marvel of riches when observed at speeds most turtles would appreciate. It took me twenty-five minutes to walk a block I normally covered in less than one. You see a hell of a lot of detail at that speed, and what I finally saw was just how complex and beautiful the world was around me. And just how much of it I'd been missing.

Of course, the other thing I had a lot of time to think about while I was lying on Julie's couch was Julie herself. I knew she was still ambivalent about our relationship and that she'd developed feelings for someone else that were going to take her some time to get over. But I also knew that I loved her and she still loved me and that whatever we had built together over the previous four years had to be more meaningful than a summer love affair in Greece. It just had to be.

Misha

AFTER FIVE YEARS, one might reasonably assume, given how much *The New York Times* mentioned Misha's positive affect on the quality of the dancing and the morale of the corps de ballet at American Ballet Theatre, that I would have a lot to say about this particular subject, but for the life of me I can't remember learning anything from Misha in the classroom, and I learned next to nothing from him in rehearsals.

Yes, he taught me how to kick my Mazurka up a notch my first year in the company, but if you put a gun to my head, I couldn't tell you what his teaching philosophy was, and that had nothing to do with the fact that he rarely taught class and seemed to dislike it whenever he did. What I never knew was that Misha preferred being a student.

"Misha didn't see himself as a teacher," Cynthia Harvey would tell me. "He was self-conscious about doing it and preferred being a student. He devoured learning and was a voracious reader. Of course he had a lot to offer as a teacher, but even on the summer tours I did with him, he didn't like to teach very much, so the other dancers would take turns teaching class.

"When I was injured once, he said it needn't be a waste of time. He suggested I sit on the bed in front of a mirror and go through an entire ballet working solely on the port de bras movements to improve the way

I worked with my arms. And I did just that. And you know what? That became one of my signatures, my arms."

Misha suggested I work on my arms as well, but watching Danny Radojevic was as far as that suggestion went. No, in order for me to learn anything from Misha, I had to go about it more indirectly.

I saw virtually every one of Misha's performances of *Giselle* while I was in American Ballet Theatre; that's a lot of *Giselle*'s. After my earth-shattering peasant portrayal in the first act, I would shower and go out front to watch the second act. I had two motives. I was waiting for Julie so we could go home or back to our hotel together, and I genuinely wanted to see Misha dance Albrecht again.

I often thought that the rest of the boys in the corps de ballet would have wanted to stick around and watch Misha dance whenever the opportunity arose, but few did. They headed out as quickly as they could after the first act to dinner, a bar, back home, wherever. They seemed to take for granted something I didn't. I knew Misha wasn't going to dance Albrecht forever. I knew he had only so many performances of *Giselle* left in those knees of his, only so many years his body could do what he then demanded of it. I also knew what he meant to the history of ballet and how jealous future generations of dancers would be of the opportunity I'd been granted. I knew that even if I wasn't doing the things in ABT that I hoped to do and was, as a result, often frustrated and angry, my getting to see Misha dance was a kind of payback. It was a gift I gave to myself and, unbeknownst to Misha, a gift he gave to me.

Watching Misha dance *Giselle* over and over again led me to conclude that this really was his signature role. Albrecht was for Misha what Hamlet was for Olivier. Furthermore, it was a role that symbolized, for me, a great deal about who he was at the time.

The story of *Giselle* revolves around a duke, Albrecht, who falls for a young peasant girl, Giselle. Albrecht, however, is betrothed to Bathilde, a woman of his own station. Ignoring any possible consequences, Albrecht decides to take a small cottage in Giselle's village and dress up as a peasant in order to woo her. Giselle falls in love with him, but Albrecht's true identity is revealed when Bathilde is called to the village by Hilarion, a peasant who is in love with Giselle. Giselle then realizes she's been duped, goes completely mad, and dies of a broken heart. End of act one.

In act two, Giselle, though theoretically dead, becomes a Wili. Wilis were supernatural beings, women who died as virgins before their wedding day. For a Wili, dance and revenge were both paramount to their existence, and every man they encountered during the night came under their power and was danced to death. Hilarion suffers this fate in act two. But Albrecht somehow endures the wrath of the Wilis. We don't know for certain why he survives, but it could be assumed that it is via a combination of his strength, his true love for Giselle and hers for him, his remorse, or Giselle's willingness to forgive him (all of which is played out in various dance interludes over the course of act two). Once Albrecht's survival is assured, Giselle returns to her ethereal home at daybreak, and Albrecht is left alone at the end of the ballet, a broken man with a deep sense of regret over what he's done.

In real life, Misha, much like Albrecht, was a man who had acquired royal attributes. He had fame, fortune, men, women, everyone throwing themselves at his feet, everyone clamoring for a piece of him. And because of the many responsibilities that came along with being famous, I suspected there were aspects of his life he wished he could change in much the same way Albrecht pretended to be a peasant so he could experience something different.

And like Albrecht, Misha was a ladies' man. He left a lot of heartache in his wake, and much of that heartache endured. One could understand why he might cut a wide swath through the stunningly beautiful female ranks of a ballet company, but I suspected that, underneath all of his dalliances, he was looking for a more enduring love and needed some kind of anchor in his life. He needed a Bathilde-like mooring he could return to when he tired of the pleasures of silly little peasant girls, and, ironically, that's exactly what he got.

From the moment he arrived at ABT and laid eyes on Lisa Rinehart, Misha was smitten with her. The fact that she played Bathilde to his Albrecht and they eventually married and had three children together was ironic, to say the least.

One of the most telling moments in Misha's interpretation of Albrecht, for me, took place in the first act, after he had already won the frail heart of the peasant girl, Giselle. It surrounded the brief, pantomimed explanation he gave to his fiancé, Bathilde, for his presence in the peasant village and his association with Giselle.

Stepping forward in front of Bathilde and the royal retinue, Misha circled his hand in the air beside his face and shrugged his shoulders ever so slightly, as if to say, silly me, I wasn't really thinking. In this respect, Misha's explanation was brilliant. The message was conveyed, and our collective confusion about Albrecht's true motivation was established. Quite often, it was at this very moment that the audience actually laughed or chuckled at what was so obviously a lame excuse for why he was running around behind Bathilde's back. It was bizarre. It was awkward. And in some perfect artistic vortex, the uncomfortable feeling I had due to the audience's reaction was exactly the same uncomfortable feeling Albrecht, Bathilde, Giselle, and the royals must have had as well.

I used to wonder if the audience's laughter wasn't the mark of some mistake on Misha's part, but I knew it was not a mistake. Misha had given this moment a great deal of thought, for it was perhaps the most important moment in the entire ballet for his character. It was the moment when we come face to face with who Albrecht might be, and this was difficult to figure out, and open to debate, which was what made the character and the story so compelling.

I sometimes thought to myself as I stood there on stage and watched Misha toss off this devil-may-care excuse when confronted by Bathilde that the audience laughed because they saw right through Misha/Albrecht's excuse, but didn't want to necessarily separate this liar, Albrecht, from the lovable lothario they knew from the movie that made Misha famous: *The Turning Point.*

In *Baryshnikov at Work,* Misha was quoted as saying, "For me, Albrecht is so in love with Giselle that his love is his undoing. The love is so true, so perfect, that he does not want to jeopardize it by revealing his true identity. If Giselle knew who he really was, his passion could all too easily be taken to be a kind of *droit du seigneur* [right of the master]...It is the honesty of his feelings that leads him to his dishonesty. I want the audience to know that Albrecht is innocent; not that he is not responsible for what occurs, but that his motives are pure."

Whether or not you are able to grasp Misha/Albrecht's motives, the fact of the matter is that Albrecht plays with Giselle's emotions to a fatal degree. He was a Duke pretending to be someone he was not. The only person in the ballet he was honest with was Wilfred, his attendant, a man he clearly didn't respect and didn't listen to despite Wilfred's assessment that none of what he was up to could lead to anything but disaster. The "droit du seigneur" behavior Misha referred to was actually the perfect description of how Misha acted with many of the girls in Ballet Theatre, some of whom were more than a bit uncomfortable with his public displays of affection toward them.

And then in act two, Giselle comes back from the dead and forgives Albrecht because, well, he didn't know what he was doing, did he? He was young. It was all a big mistake, some innocent fun that went awry.

In the end, as with most of the old warhorses, there is a kind of morbid closure. Giselle returns to a happier death as a Wili, and Albrecht, having displayed remorse, is left alone to stumble quietly backward into the forest, dropping a bouquet of white lilies in his wake.

It was this moment in the ballet that I always watched closely because, in Misha's case, there appeared to be a degree of luck involved in that final moment, and this luck colored very much how I viewed Albrecht.

Every time Misha performed the ending, he began walking backward, upstage, on a diagonal, with a bouquet of large white lilies pressed to his body. He dropped the flowers as he walked. Sometimes he dropped them one by one; sometimes he dropped them in bunches, almost absent-mindedly, because at that point in the ballet, Albrecht had been up all night dancing, and he was delirious.

No matter how tired he was, however, Misha always timed the dropping of the flowers perfectly. What he did not seem to plan from one performance to the next, however, was whether or not he would be left with one flower in his hand or none. It appeared to be happenstance, this last bit; whether it was or not, I never knew. I never asked him. What I noticed was that one of the lilies often got caught between his hand and his body, just so, and he was able to get some purchase on it. When this happened, he held it there, tenderly, his face wrought with pain as the curtain descended.

With this ending, I felt something more for Misha and for Albrecht. I felt a greater sense of his actual love for Giselle, as represented by this single flower and how deeply saddened he was by what he'd done. I felt as if I might have judged Albrecht too harshly and was more apt to forgive him, as Giselle had done.

When all the flowers tumbled to the ground and he was left with nothing, I felt as if God had rendered his judgment: guilty. Even Albrecht's love, if he really ever felt it, was shattered. The emptiness of this ending conjured up something of the Old Testament God, a creature who spared no one and forgave nothing.

———————————

I read Gennady Smakov's 1981 biography, *Baryshnikov*, the moment it came out, hoping to learn something more about the man I worked with every day, but it was, in point of fact, a misleading account of Misha's traumatic early life.

Misha's mother didn't "abandon" the family when Misha was twelve, as Smakov wrote. She committed suicide by hanging herself in their communal apartment. This tragedy left Misha to a father who disapproved of his dancing and was indifferent to him. After leaving home to attend the Kirov school in Leningrad at age sixteen, Misha's beloved teacher, Alexander Pushkin, died prematurely of a heart attack. And, finally, Misha abandoned his ballet company, his friends, and his country when he defected in Toronto in 1974.

I might not have known about Misha's mother's suicide at the time, but I was always aware that something was terribly amiss in his life. I sensed that he had been profoundly hurt in some way, and as a result, I always had a kind of sympathy for him that made it difficult, if not impossible, to ever truly be angry with him no matter how ornery he was at times or how few compliments he handed out or how often he deserted the company.

What I learned from watching Misha dance *Giselle* year after year was that, in spite of all the fireworks people associated with his dancing, he was a dancer for whom bravura and nuance operated at equal measure. He was not vulgar. He was not, unless called upon to do so, a showoff. He danced in service to the choreography, the music, the character, the art form, and all that he knew about the art form and could bring to it.

It appeared to me when I watched him that, like Gelsey, he was trying to get at the heart of the matter, to the experience or the ballet as a whole, and in the midst of that intense investigation, his interplay with the music was staggering.

I sensed something incredibly obvious by watching Misha, and it was this obviousness that made him the artist he was. It is music that inspires us to dance. Music is the impetus for everything, and our fame, our talent, our ego, our wish to do eight pirouettes because we *can* do eight pirouettes should never take precedence. If it does, we might as well join the circus or try out for *So You Think You Can Dance*.

There was always a larger purpose at work with Misha, and while for many of those who watched him it seemed to be all about him, I never felt it was about him at all. He humbled himself in service to every ballet he danced, and that was why, in spite of everything, I respected and admired him. It was why he didn't pretend to be a choreographer or a teacher. He was as honest an appraiser of his artistry as one can be, and that is not an easy thing to accomplish when you're talented and famous and surrounded by people who are afraid to criticize you. Misha knew what he did well. He didn't let his ego delude him into believing he could dance Albrecht until he was sixty (see Nureyev) or choreograph like Balanchine (see Peter Martins).

As much as I respected Misha as an artist, it took me a long time to learn to accept the fact that the artist and the man were not one and the same. When I watched Misha dance, I was almost always enthralled.

He seemed like a God to me. When we were working together in class or in rehearsal, however, I couldn't entirely marry the handsome man at the front of the room with the deep-set eyes and aura of sadness about him with the creature I saw dancing Albrecht the night before.

I needed to keep those two Mishas separate for my own sanity; otherwise, there was simply too much disappointment, too much pain at having my impossible, childish illusions continually shattered by the day-to-day reality that Misha, my world-famous boss, was a man like many others. He wasn't a God. He wasn't perfect. He didn't have all the answers. He made mistakes. He could be an asshole.

As much as those of us in the corps de ballet might have appreciated the brilliance of his dancing, Misha was not someone most of us spoke very fondly of. To varying degrees, we respected his artistic decisions and his eye, but as a person, we couldn't figure him out. We had no idea who he really was underneath his cloud of melancholy, so we resorted to mocking him, criticizing him, and joking about him, much as he criticized and mocked us. We called him *The Troll*. And we called him *The Troll* because he often came across as a gigantic killjoy, an ornery old goat who lived under his bridge and accosted every passerby, hoping to make them feel as miserable as he did.

Home Stretch

After years of going through the motions at ABT and being relatively content with those motions, Julie decided she was just bored enough to warrant an audition tour to Europe. We both understood what the ramifications of this trip might be (an end to our relationship), but I encouraged her in this effort because I knew what every dancer knew: the clock was ticking and her career deserved everything she had to give it.

Julie made a list of companies she was interested in (Ballet Rambert in London, London Festival Ballet, Frankfurt, Zurich, The Netherlands Dance Theater) and set off on her own. These types of audition tours to Europe were commonplace in those days. For dancers in an established company like American Ballet Theatre, it was relatively easy to make a phone call or write a letter and be given permission to take a company class wherever you fancied. This was one of those professional courtesies extended to dancers in major ballet companies.

Strange dancers were forever appearing in ABT company class. We had no idea who most of them were, unless they were Nureyev or some other superstar. They came and went with regularity, and we rarely remarked on their capabilities or considered them competition because we were already where they wanted to be. We weren't going anywhere unless there was a damn good reason to go somewhere.

Julie wrote me a number of letters during her weeks abroad, and I could tell from the tone of those letters that while she might not have been offered a contract on the spot, she'd made a favorable impression on every director she met and, more importantly, she'd gained a degree of confidence in herself and in her dancing that could only come from doing something like that on your own.

In this respect, our professional lives were developing along similar tangents. While Julie was off broadening her horizons in Europe, I went to Pittsburgh with a small group of ABT dancers to perform "The Dying Poet," a featured pas de deux from Lynn Taylor-Corbett's *The Great Galloping Gottschalk*.

Dancing this pas de deux was something I'd likely never have been given the opportunity to do at ABT, but I knew I was capable of dancing the role, and, more importantly, Lynn Taylor-Corbett thought I was capable of dancing the role, so she gave me permission do it.

The performance took place at Heinz Hall (of tomato ketchup fame), and my partner was Lisa Lockwood, a dancer from ABT's corps de ballet. I was unaccustomed to being in the spotlight, but I have say, the spotlight at Heinz Hall in Pittsburgh was practically nuclear-powered. Despite being unable to see whenever I was facing the audience, I managed to get through the turning sequences in the pas de deux without falling on my ass, and when it was all over, I went back to New York and my miniscule parts at ABT with a secret confidence that helped me endure playing a peasant in *Giselle* for the ninety-fifth time in a row.

In spite of Misha's hopes that I might get something worthwhile to dance that I was actually capable of dancing, the fall rehearsal period of 1985 didn't offer me much. The most memorable event was that Fernando Bujones was fired.

Charles France: "To tell you the truth, Fernando and his cousin Zeida, who was also his coach, were out of control. Fernando would say things like, 'I'm not going to sign this contract unless you do this, that, and the other thing.'

"And we'd say, 'Sorry, we can't do those things.'

"And then he'd get upset. He wanted to choreograph, for example, and we let him. But then there came a day when Fernando and Marianna Tcherkassky had been cast for the opening night of *Romeo and Juliet* in our fall Met Season, and Marianna injured herself while we were on tour. Kenneth MacMillan suggested Amanda McKerrow would be the easiest replacement. And I said, 'Yes, we'll send them to New York. They can rehearse over the weekend and be ready for opening night the following week.'

"So I called Fernando and told him, and he said, 'I don't know. I'll have to get back to you.'

"Well, when I got back to my hotel, his cousin Zeida called and said, 'He's not going to rehearse unless Misha does this new ballet.'

"And I said, 'You know what? We just don't operate on the blackmail system. Either Fernando goes to the rehearsal or there are going to be consequences.'

"So I told Misha what had happened, and Misha said, 'He's fired.'"

Once Fernando was out of the picture, Misha once again did what came naturally: he completely upstaged him. The film *White Nights* opened in November, and, much like *The Turning Point*, it put Misha in a spotlight Fernando could never step into.

I went to see the film with Julie, and like most of those in the audience, I was entertained by the dancing, some of which (the pirouette sequences) seemed dubiously edited in order to make them look more spectacular than they otherwise might have been. No matter, the film was a popular success, and Misha proved once again that his acting skills could translate to the big screen.

That fall, I was cast in the corps de ballet of John Taras's *Francesca da Rimini*, an instantly forgettable vehicle for Patrick Bissell and Cynthia Gregory. I would not appear in Tudor's *Dark Elegies* or *Dim Lustre* or *Pillar of Fire* or *The Leaves Are Fading* or *Jardin Au Lilas*. In fact, I would never dance in a Tudor ballet. I did not dance in MacMillan's *Requiem* or David Gordon's new ballet, *Murder*, or Karole Armitage's *The Molino Room*. Instead, I spent most of the year watching the person I once considered my closest friend struggle to dance again.

During the summer layoff in 1985, Peter Fonseca underwent a routine foot surgery for some bone spurs in his heels. After his promotion to soloist in December of 1981, he had become one of Misha's favorites, dancing a host of principal parts during the regular season as well as on the summer tours Misha organized in those days.

What I found a bit startling was that in spite of his tremendous talent and his obvious success, Peter still had his frustrations. On occasion, the two of us would talk about the roles he wanted to dance and certainly seemed capable of dancing (Albrecht, Basilio in *Don Quixote*, Romeo).

Misha obviously didn't think Peter was right for those roles, or perhaps he felt Peter just wasn't ready. I never knew what to say. Was it Peter's boyish femininity? His weaknesses as a partner? His less-than-stellar jump? It might have been any one or a combination of those things, but only Misha could answer those questions, and Peter was certainly close enough to Misha to be able to ask.

When the freight elevator arrived at Peter's loft during a hot summer day in 1985, he greeted me on crutches, both feet in casts.

"How the hell do you get around like that?" I asked.

"I manage."

"You're so goddamn thin," I said, gazing at his protruding collar-bones. "Thinner than I've ever seen you before."

"I know. Don't I look good?"

I stared at his bony arms and the deep hollows in his cheeks.

"You're certainly skinny," I confessed, thinking back to the worst days of my anorexia and how great I thought I looked.

It had been a while since Peter and I had spent any time togeth-er at his loft. Over the previous few years, his coolness towards Julie had thawed and we had regained some of our earlier rapport, though it would never be quite the same. I found myself looking around at all the progress he'd made, the curved walls he'd built, the summer sun streaming in through some of the new windows he'd recently installed.

"When do you think you'll be back?" I asked.

"Dr. Hamilton [the orthopedic surgeon who treated most of the professional dancers in New York] seems to think I should be able to start doing barres in four to six weeks. We'll just have to see how it goes."

"Jesus," I said, looking once more at Peter's gaunt face, "you really have lost a lot of weight."

He beamed, proud as peacock.

Peter rejoined the company later that fall and was nearly as thin as I'd seen him just after his surgery. We all expected him to pick up where he left off, dancing leads in Balanchine's *Theme and Variations, La Sylphide, Les Rendezvous,* and *Flower Festival,* but his return to form was inexplicably slow. When he was finally capable of perform-ing again, what little jump he formerly possessed was gone. He had no stamina, and no one could really explain why.

It was painful to watch him struggle to do things he once sailed through with ease, and I began to wonder if there wasn't something more serious going on. He was working hard, but he just couldn't get over the hump. The only explanation I could come up with was that something had happened to him in the hospital. It would be months before any of us truly understood what was wrong with Peter.

———————————————

The First Annual ABT Choreographic Workshop took place in the spring of 1986, toward the conclusion of the Met season. It was, as its title suggests, Misha's first attempt to ferret out potential choreographers from within the company.

I was itching to do something that might shed some light on the many injustices I felt I'd suffered in the company, but the more I thought about how I might make a ballet about Rambo, the more I realized this idea just wasn't going to fly, or, more accurately, I didn't know how to make it fly. So I went in a completely different direction: camp.

I would do a little narrative piece inspired by my idol, Antony Tudor. To that end, I concocted a silly love story. A girl sits in a frame as the piece opens. A boy wakes up in his bedroom, and, as Keith Jarrett improvises on his piano, the boy sees his sweetheart and starts dancing around in a pair of red polka-dot pajamas. When he's done, the girl springs to life and jumps out of the frame dressed in a white baby-doll skirt as Aretha Franklin begins singing "Baby I Love You." The audience gasps at the audacity and sheer originality of it all as the two dance a duet together before riding off into the sunset and everlasting love.

Original? Yes!

Controversial? Yes!

But will it sell?

My piece was first on the docket that day, and, rightfully so, I was sweating bullets. Fortunately, I'd selected two wonderful corps de ballet dancers to portray my Romeo and Juliet, and they managed to get through the embarrassment with aplomb. When I saw how awful my ballet was, however, I felt terrible for them and secretly wondered if I hadn't completely ruined their careers. Thankfully, they managed to take it all in stride.

What was truly humiliating was that I had laid myself open with this silly travesty in front of the likes of Misha, Kenneth MacMillan, John Taras, and most of the staff and dancers in the company, all of whom must have been wondering if I'd forgotten to take my medication. After eight or so presentations, the finalists were announced, and I was, much to my surprise, not among them.

John Taras, who'd been asked to present the winners, had this to say to all of us about our efforts: "Well, I just hope that in the...the...the... future, all of you think about se...se...se...lecting better music."

Better music? Just what the hell is wrong with Aretha Franklin?

Finale

D URING THAT SAME 1986 MET SEASON, the restlessness I'd
felt throughout the entire year reached a fever pitch, and once
again I tried to take matters into my own hands, this time by learning
the Peasant Pas de Trois from Act 1 of *Swan Lake*. I was convinced
this was something I was capable of doing, so I spent a couple of weeks
alone in the basement of the Met in studio C-3, practicing the short
male variation. I asked a couple of friends in the company to look at
what I'd done, and they seemed impressed, so I took the next step and
asked John Taras and one of our ballet mistresses, Wendy Walker, to
come observe the results of my labor.

When the variation was over, I stood in front of them huffing and
puffing and awaiting their reaction—a reaction which, I hoped, was going to be one of dismay at why they'd overlooked me all this time and
how, yes, I was more than capable of dancing Pas de Trois. How would
next week be?

"Wuh...wuh...well..." John stammered, as he often did, "eh...eh...
eh...it nee...nee...needs a little more work." Wendy nodded her cute little English head amiably and smiled.

There were no offers to help me, coach me, or try to get me over the
hump I so obviously wanted to surmount but seemingly never could.
There were no congratulations for giving this a go on my own, no 'How

about we get someone to work with you on it, then see how you do.' It was, er...not quite good enough. Next!

Whatever John Taras or Wendy Walker thought about my variation, I had a sneaking suspicion there might not be a next year at American Ballet Theatre for me. Alfonso Cata was in town, and I ran into him at Steps, a popular dance studio on New York's Upper West Side. Alfonso was then directing the Ballet du Nord in France. We'd known one another for years, since the time I was a nineteen-year-old student at Melissa Hayden's studio and he was on the teaching staff there. He'd given me some of my first professional opportunities when he was working with the Puerto Rican Dance Theatre in the late 1970s, and I'd always been grateful to him for that. He was a brilliant man, a clever choreographer who worked quickly and made dances that were flattering to his dancers, fun to dance, and enjoyable to watch.

When I saw him after Willy Burmann's class that day at Steps, I made it known that I was frustrated by how little I was getting to do at Ballet Theatre, and he said, "Well, I'm losing a principal dancer. Maybe you'd like to replace him?"

"A principal dancer?"

"Yes. Why don't you learn the pas de deux and variation from *Theme* [*and Variations*] and show it to me in a couple of weeks?"

"Okay," I replied, "sure."

After countless hours working in what had seemingly become my own private cave (studio C-3 in the basement of the Met), I showed up at City Center two weeks later. The pas de deux from *Theme* went fine, but following directly on the heels of the pas de deux is a famous male variation created by Balanchine in 1947 for Igor Youskevitch. This variation is fairly straightforward, but it is relentless and requires more strength and stamina that it might appear. It builds from the very first diagonal to its conclusion, with no opportunities to catch your breath. At the end, just when your heart rate is being pushed to the limit by the jumps you've just completed, comes a series of seven double tours en l'air interspersed with an equal set of pirouettes in place. It's essentially the male version of Odette/Odile's famous thirty-two fouettés from the Black Swan variation in *Swan Lake.*

I had yet to get through this section cleanly on my own, and, at that moment, in front of Alfonso, after about the fifth double tour, I lost my focus as I often did during a long series of turns. I wanted to continue, but realized I had to stop before I fell flat on my face. Standing there, embarrassed and exhausted, my focus blurred, I tried to get my bearings.

"I'm sorry, Alfonso. Let me try that section again. I can do it."

"No, no, no. It's fine. It's fine. I've seen what I need to see."

And with that, I assumed my move to France had become as likely as a dinner invitation from Misha.

After I got dressed, Alfonso approached and said to me, "Michael, do you think you could make it to Roubaix by the beginning of August?"

"You want me to come?"

"Of course I want you to come."

"But I screwed up that double tour section."

"Don't worry about that. You'll be fine."

"But what about Julie?"

"She can come, too. I'm sure we can find a place for her."

When I arrived at the Met the next day, I entered the stage door and walked down the long, red-carpeted hallway much as I'd done over the previous six years. Turning left, I found the door to the Green Room, ABT's makeshift inner sanctum, wide open. The Green Room was a moderately sized office space where Misha's secretary, Florence

Pettan, could generally be found working alongside Charles France or Misha, if he was around.

Flo hardly batted an eyelash when I told her Julie and I were leaving the company. She seemed accustomed to such news. Dancers did, after all, leave ABT every year (willingly or unwillingly), and the Met season was the time when most of these leave-takings took place. And while it was true I might have appreciated a little more shock and awe or some sadness after six years, I knew that wasn't Flo's style. I think she was offended, actually. She had, after all, devoted her life to American Ballet Theatre, and there I was, throwing that life away. As we stood there together, I thought about how she had reacted in 1982 during the lockout.

"How could you do this to us?" she said to me at the time, her voice a mixture of anguish and bewilderment.

I had nothing to say to her then, and I had nothing to say to her now as she flitted about, attending to the million and one things she always had on her plate. "Well, do you want to talk to Misha about it?" she said, a note of exasperation in her voice that let me know I was somehow in the way, one of a mass of flies in her lifetime supply of ointment.

"No, there's nothing to talk about, really. I got an offer from a company in France, and I want to take advantage of it. And anyway, Misha and I have spoken about the possibility of me dancing elsewhere. I don't think he'll be upset or surprised."

"Okay, *Mikey*, well, good luck with that," she replied, her gaze fixed on a pile of papers on her desk.

Had things been different, I'm sure I would have been more circumspect about what leaving American Ballet Theatre symbolized (a gigantic failure), but I could not deny I was happy. I would be missing the upcoming filming of *Dancers* that was due to begin shooting in Bari,

Italy over the summer, but I knew enough about filming, having done a handful of shoots with Ballet Theatre, to know what tedious torture that was going to be. I also knew that six years was long enough to know if I was going to get out of the corps de ballet. I wasn't going to walk away wondering what might have happened if I stuck around. I knew what would have happened: it would have been more of the same.

Charles France: "Most of the people in the company who were really talented got opportunities. We were always looking into the corps de ballet to see who should start doing some soloist work or even some principal work. I think our corps de ballet dancers got more attention than any dancer in the corps de ballet ever got from Mr. Balanchine."

What Charles said was undoubtedly true, but no one in the corps de ballet at American Ballet Theatre ever knew this because no one ever told us these things. In addition to the deafening silence from above, here's the thing that drives ballet dancers nuts: there's a Charles France in almost every ballet company. Someone who, for whatever reason, is friendly with the director or sleeping with the director or married to the director or the son or daughter of the director, and it is at the feet of this person that dancers lay bouquets of blame for their professional frustrations. This perspective, the one that says "it's them, not me," is locked in a continual battle with every dancer's belief in the integrity of the art form, the control they've had thus far over their own destinies, and the unassailable reality that, as Misha used to say, "You cannot hide talent up your sleeve." The result of all this is that ballet dancers tend to think they are entirely responsible for everything good that happens to them and probably not to blame for everything that isn't happening exactly the way they would like it.

When the special joint performances between American Ballet Theatre and the Paris Opera Ballet had come and gone during the 1986 season at the Metropolitan Opera House, I had appeared in *Giselle* alongside the greatest male dancer of his generation, Rudolf Nureyev, and the greatest male dancer of my generation, Mikhail Baryshnikov. I had taken class with one of the hottest ballerinas on the planet, Sylvie Guillem, and watched as she stuck her foot behind her ear while bringing down the house during a performance of *Le Corsaire* with Patrick Dupond. It seemed only fitting that things should end this way. The French were invading New York. I was defecting to France. And there, across the pond, I would get to do what I never could have done at American Ballet Theatre.

Before Julie and I left New York, we took the train down to Washington, D.C. to see Peter Fonseca. He was convalescing at home. The talk around ABT by then had begun to include an acronym that most of us had only recently added to our vocabularies: AIDS.

Over the previous couple of years, we had begun hearing about this mysterious illness, and while I was never certain how promiscuous Peter had been, it seemed an obvious explanation for his troubles. Because few of us in the company had gone down to Washington to see him, the severity of his situation remained a bit of a mystery, but from the moment his mother opened the door to his bedroom and I saw him lying in bed, I knew he was dying.

"He can't speak," his mother said, propping up his pillows and stroking his hair, "but he understands what you're saying. Look who's here, mi amor," she continued, standing off to the side. "Michael and Julie."

Peter nodded his head and widened his deep-set eyes.

"The doctors say he has some rare brain disorder," his mother said. "That is why he cannot speak."

I smiled and tried to appear buoyant because I didn't want Peter to feel anything but optimistic about his future, but he looked terribly frightened by what was happening to him and seemed baffled by his inability to speak. I knew he wanted to speak and was spitting out words in his head, but nothing would come out. As I looked into his eyes, his mother said, "He is so thin. You must keep eating, mi amor, and everything will be fine. You must keep eating."

I didn't know much about AIDS, but I knew things were pretty far from fine. I also knew Peter's mother was dying inside. He was her baby, the youngest of five boys, and because she herself was a very gifted ballet teacher, Peter's accomplishments at ABT were that much closer to her heart.

I didn't have the presence of mind or the maturity, however, to comfort her. I had known Peter's mom for six years, had stayed in her home when I first arrived in the company, but I never knew what she really thought of my friendship with Peter. I don't think they ever spoke openly about his homosexuality. His parents were old-fashioned Costa Ricans who may not have wanted to have this kind of thing spelled out for them, and that was fine. Peter knew he was loved, and I could see that. His mother and father were wonderful people who treated me like family. I'm sure Peter's mother, without any evidence to the contrary, assumed what everyone else did: that we were lovers. I never bothered to disabuse her or anyone else of that notion. Everyone makes assumptions. I didn't think it was my job to figure out if they'd made the wrong ones. It didn't seem important, not in light of what was happening.

I sat on the edge of Peter's bed that bright summer day and held his hand as Julie sat in a chair nearby. I had no idea what to say. I felt awkward, like this whole thing was an act that all of us were orchestrating. The only one who wasn't acting was Peter. All he could do was lie there, his eyes sunk deep into his skull as his mother fed him liquidy tuna fish like a baby. It dripped repeatedly down his chin, where she collected it with a spoon and put it back in his mouth. It was at once touching and so awful I almost couldn't bear it.

I tried to fill the void by telling Peter what was going on in the company—that Julie and I were leaving soon to dance in Ballet du Nord. He nodded his head as if to say, I understand, it's okay, you do what you have to do. I looked hesitantly into his eyes and said that as soon as we had a break in France we would come back and see him again. I knew, however, that when I walked out of his bedroom that day that I would never see him again.

Act III

1986. Ex-Pats.

IT's THE MIDDLE OF AUGUST, 1986, and at five in the morning
a faint light begins to fill our room at the Hotel de France in the
center of Roubaix. Julie lies beside me, fast asleep. I have been awake
for most of the night. Two weeks have passed since we landed in Lux-
embourg and drove our rental car to France to begin a new life in a
new company in a new country. And every night since our arrival it
has been like this.

As soon as the coffee shop opens downstairs, I head down for a bit-
ter cup of café au lait and a croissant. I sit there and peruse the local
newspaper, *La Voix du Nord*, and watch the locals spike their morning
coffee with shots of cognac and whiskey. And who can blame them, really, when the coffee is so uniformly shitty? I pretend it is good, though,
because I'm convinced that everything is better in France.

Only fourteen days have gone by, but I've learned three new ballets
and have lost five pounds from what was already a lean, fat-free body. I
haven't slept more than an hour a night, but for some reason I'm not the
least bit tired. I'm up at the crack of dawn, and after breakfast I head out
to look at apartments or cars or to visit some government office for the
million and one pieces of paper that will allow Julie and I to insinuate
ourselves into La République and keep the massive wheels of French
bureaucracy inching forward into file-cabinet nirvana. I do more before

a ten o'clock class in Roubaix than I used to do in an entire day in New York.

After six years of waiting and and wondering when I would get a chance to do something meaningful, ten minutes after my first company class with Ballet du Nord, the wait was over, and I was moving to the center of the room to learn the lead in George Balanchine's 1957 classic, *Square Dance* (a role originally danced by Michael Lland, our ballet master at ABT).

None of the other dancers in Ballet du Nord questioned my add-water-and-stir promotion, so I went about my business as if I belonged there. I came from one of the finest ballet companies in the world, let's not forget, and I was good at pretending, so I pretended this was an everyday thing for me. But, obviously, some part of me was wondering what the hell was going on, because after two weeks my nervous system was still on Red Alert. I couldn't relax. Couldn't sleep. Couldn't eat. I had dropped a lot of weight and looked more emaciated than I'd ever looked in my life—so I was happy. I thought I looked fabulous.

In the midst of learning *Square Dance*, John Clifford, a former dancer with New York City Ballet and director of Los Angeles Ballet, came to Roubaix to teach class and set his ballet, *Glenn Miller Time*, on the company. I was given the lead and had just finished learning the role when I suddenly found myself getting undressed in the mountains of Italy, twenty miles north of Napoli.

Ballet du Nord had been asked to appear as a last-minute replacement at a summer festival in Casertavecchia, and the theatrical conditions, while outdoors and primitive, were absolutely glorious. The sound of cicadas filled the warm summer air as I picked at a late afternoon lunch of perfect pasta topped off by sweet, fresh figs. I was preoccupied by the upcoming performance, but sober enough to recognize I was back in Italy for the third time in my performing life, and the food and the scenery were out of this world.

As the sun was setting, the company retired to a dressing area behind the open-air stage. The men and women were all jammed in together, applying makeup, undressing, smoking, and giving barely a thought to warming up, a ritual I never knew was optional until I arrived in France and noticed that virtually none of the European dancers did a barre before a performance. Mon dieu!

When the show finally got under way and I was out on stage in *Square Dance*, I felt strong and confident and tried to exude that seasoned, aloof air I came to know so well from watching Misha all those years. My performance, in my opinion, went off without a hitch, and afterwards I was feeling rather proud of myself.

I can do this. I can handle this. This is great. Dancing Balanchine is fun and easy. I'm so happy I made this decision. I love Italy. I love Alfonso. I love Julie. I love my life!

When I approached Alfonso after the show and asked what he thought, he said, "It could use a little more work."

In keeping with most of my dance career thus far, I would be left to figure out for myself what needed a little more work, which, when you happen to be me and find yourself in northern France without a coach or a video camera or a decent teacher, isn't easy. Fortunately, Alfonso didn't seem to mind that, as a freshly minted principal dancer, I was still a work in progress. He was a pretty easy-going guy, obviously, and while I did not impress him greatly with my performance of *Square Dance*, I knew he was not going to fire me.

I had a tiny, scintillating partner by the name of Ena Naranjo who'd come to France from Tulsa Ballet Theater, and she and I were a perfect match for one another. Given the minor status afforded most of the male roles in the Balanchine repertoire, I knew my deficiencies would be less of a concern to Alfonso than what Ena brought to the table. But even an easy-going guy like Alfonso had a certain standard, and I had to believe I was close to that standard. Everyone at Ballet Du Nord was an employee of the French government, after all. Alfonso couldn't easily justify paying an American to do something twenty other French dancers could have done just as well, if not better—could he?

Michael Langlois. Rubies. 1986. Ballet du Nord.
Photo credit: P. Perazio.

Alfonso and Ballet du Nord

Fifty years old when I joined him in Roubaix, Alfonso Cata was born in Cuba and danced professionally with New York City Ballet, Stuttgart, Roland Petit's Ballet de Paris, the Joffrey Ballet, and Marquis de Cuevas. After leaving City Ballet in 1967, he opened a boutique in New York where he designed and sold dresses. Two years later, at Balanchine's suggestion, he became the director of a company in Geneva devoted primarily to promoting the works of Balanchine abroad. After a brief stint as director in Frankfurt, he took over Ballet du Nord in 1983.

I knew very little about Alfonso. I knew he'd been in City Ballet, and I knew he'd not been a terribly gifted dancer. He was a decent teacher from what I remembered of his classes at Melissa Hayden's studio. He was smart. He made well-crafted ballets in the Balanchine mold and spoke a multitude of languages. He seemed, from my youthful perspective, to be someone with a breadth of knowledge and a quickness of mind far beyond the norm.

If he was teaching class in Roubaix, he was never at a loss. He could choreograph a twenty-minute ballet in no time at all and loved to hang out and gossip with the dancers. He had a solution for every problem and turned out to be the perfect director for me at the time because he wasn't the least bit intimidating. He didn't pressure me to be something I wasn't. He seemed to understand and accept that there would be growing pains, and if, in fact, he was concerned about how I would develop, he never mentioned those concerns to me. He left me alone, a place I was quite familiar with.

While I was I basking in my qualified glories as a principal dancer, Julie, who spoke no French whatsoever (I'd been studying it since seventh grade), was struggling to make a friend among the bitchy girls of Ballet du Nord. Only a few of them spoke English, and they were perpetually pissed off by the Americans Alfonso brought in to dance the soloist and principal parts they undoubtedly felt they deserved.

Julie had been ready to retire when we left ABT, so she didn't care too deeply about her status in Ballet du Nord, but the fact that she was moving down a few notches to a relatively obscure company in France, combined with the coldness of these provincial bunheads, was almost too much for her to bear.

As the weeks in Roubaix piled up, we went from being American arrivistes to parts of the daily scenery. We found a brand-new one-bedroom apartment in an HLM, one of the millions of subsidized housing projects that populate France. We bought a Volkswagen Golf that we drove ninety miles an hour on the Autoroute because even though there were, technically speaking, speed limits in France, no one paid the slightest bit of attention to them. We became regulars at the weekly flea market, the Marche Aux Puces, where we bought a whole apartment's worth of beautiful Art Deco furniture for peanuts because no one in France considered anything from the twentieth century worth collecting in those days. My use of the subjunctive, my ability to sleep, and my repertoire of new ballets grew and grew as the weeks turned into months and the long French winter set in.

Not long after we arrived in Roubaix, Julie's parents came to see us. As was their globetrotting habit, they had moved to Amsterdam for a while so Julie's father could engage is some linguistic research. Over the previous six years, we had traveled all over the world with them and spent enough time with one another to think of ourselves as a family, or, more accurately, I thought of them as family.

It was a cold, rainy night in Roubaix when they arrived. The restaurant we'd chosen for dinner was virtually empty. Once the wine had been poured and we'd covered the basics of our first few months in Roubaix, Julie began discussing some ancient family history. The more she talked about her middle brother, the deeper she fell into the long-simmering resentment she harbored towards her parents, and her mom in particular, for not protecting her from him.

By the time we finished eating, Julie was having a serious emotional breakdown. Between her tears and her increasingly hateful recriminations, her father stood up. "Come on, Vonny," he said to Julie's mother. "We're leaving. I didn't come all this way to listen to her berate you all night for what she thinks you didn't do for her."

I was dumbfounded. Of course I was familiar with this aspect of Julie's life, but I'd never seen her lay it out quite like that in front of her parents, and in public no less. As the proprietors of the restaurant cowered in the corner waiting for us to leave, I tried to be sympathetic to both Julie and her parents, but in doing so, I ended up feeling as if they all hated me.

Happily, I was wrong to conclude that her parents might never forgive her for the scene she caused in the restaurant, and Julie, as was her style, vomited up her emotions and moved on, seemingly oblivious to the wreckage she left behind. Perhaps some good came of all that emotional purging, I don't know. At the very least, her parents could no longer confess they were unaware of Julie's actual feelings about them or what happened with her brother. Thankfully, she and her mom patched things up over the phone, and a few weeks later we drove up to Amsterdam and spent a delightfully uneventful couple of days drinking tea, munching on toast and Marmite, and listening to the BBC with them every morning.

———————————

After my debut in *Square Dance*, I went on to learn the leads in Balanchine's *Scotch Symphony, Rubies, Concerto Barocco,* and *Tarantella*. There would be major roles in *Coppélia*, a number of Alfonso's ballets, and works by Jean-Pierre Bonnefoux, Jean-Paul Comelin, and Vicente Nebrada to add to my repertoire as time went on.

Lurking beneath my excitement over dancing principal parts in every ballet, however, was a nagging concern that my technical level was diminishing daily. Fearful that I might be seen as undeserving of my new status, I had prepared feverishly in New York before coming to Roubaix and was in the best shape of my life when I arrived, but I could see that Alfonso's casual stabs at teaching company class and my rehearsals in and of themselves weren't really going to be enough to sustain me. Unfortunately, there was nowhere else to turn. There were no other ballet studios in Roubaix, no coaches, no Pilates or Gyrotonics studios. It was Ballet du Nord or bust.

And then one day, prior to leaving for a three-week engagement in Barcelona, I got a phone call in Roubaix. It was Elaine, a friend of ours from Ballet Theatre. "I don't know if anyone has called you, Michael, but I just thought you should know. Peter Fonseca has passed away."

I sat in the wooden chair we'd bought on one of our many trips to the flea market and stared at our strange French phone. It was orange, with an extra listening earpiece hooked onto the back. Julie was listening in on that earpiece. She nodded her head and put her hand on my shoulder. I felt nothing, not sadness, nothing. The whole thing just seemed like such a waste. A waste of a life, a waste of a friendship that at one time meant so much to me.

Peter Fonseca's death was just the beginning of the damage AIDS would exact on the dancers of American Ballet Theatre: David Cuevas, August 16, 1988. Age 33/ Clark Tippet, January 20, 1992. Age 37/ Gary Cordial, June 15, 1992. Age 39/ Greg Osborne, January 8, 1994. Age 39.

The Socialist Agenda

FOR A BALLET COMPANY SUPPORTED LARGELY by the government of France, Ballet du Nord not only had quite a few non-French dancers, it also did a surprising amount of touring outside of Roubaix and the country. We visited most of the cities of northern France, but more often than not, we found ourselves in the smaller cities of Belgium, England, Italy, or Spain.

Our weekly schedule was Monday through Friday with a half day of work on Saturday or sometimes no work on Saturday if Alfonso didn't feel we needed it. We generally performed every four to six weeks, and these performances might be as short as one evening or encompass an entire weekend. We had no union, but Alfonso was very reasonable with how he worked us. He liked to enjoy himself, so unless there was some dire need—and there rarely was—he could be counted on to give us extra days off and little holidays here and there, all of which the French taxpayers paid for, of course.

One of the many perks of living and dancing in France was a constant paycheck, fifty-two weeks a year, deposited directly into my bank account. (Ballet Theatre contracts were usually forty-two weeks a year. The remaining ten weeks were filled with unemployment checks and our own Supplementary Unemployment Benefits.) The first time I came back from vacation in France and checked my bank balance at the Banque Nationale de Paris, I was stunned to discover I actually had quite a bit more money in it than before I left. Vive La France!

Needless to say, I rather liked living in France, and it wasn't simply the total disregard for speed limits or the largesse of the government that appealed. Because of our weekly work schedule, it was possible for Julie and I to hop in our car on Friday night or Saturday afternoon and spend the remainder of the weekend in Paris. It was only about a two-hour drive on the Autoroute. Why not? We would stay in some inexpensive Left Bank hotel, have a nice dinner in the Latin Quarter, take in some museums or a movie, and walk around the city, before heading back to Roubaix on Sunday evening. If it wasn't Paris, we might drive an hour to Brussels to have dinner, or the ten minutes it took to drive to Lille, where there was an old theater called the Metropole that showed classic American films in English. If there was a bit more time, we drove a few hours to Amsterdam to see Julie's parents.

Despite the many upsides of living in France, less than a year into our stay, Julie and I began discussing the possibility of leaving. She was becoming increasingly intent on getting away from Alfonso, and while I had to agree he wasn't much of a mentor, coach, or teacher, he was easygoing and always a pleasure to work with. Our relationship had been wonderful thus far, but that was about to change.

Ballet du Nord was scheduled to spend three months in Torino, Italy, and I assumed, without asking Alfonso about it, that it would be all right for Julie and I to drive down so we could have our car there. A couple of weeks before we were scheduled to depart, I approached Alfonso in the theater in Roubaix. He was with his longstanding boyfriend, Willy Burmann, who was making one of his regular visits. When I mentioned driving down to Torino, Alfonso, much to my surprise, said,

"Absolutely not. I don't want you driving to Italy. I want you to come on the plane with the company."

I was stunned. "Why?" I asked, having assumed he would treat it as casually as he treated most things.

"Michael, I don't want to discuss this. It is not a negotiation. You will come on the plane. With the company. And that's the end of it."

I asked again what possible reason there could be for us not to drive. It seemed so innocent. If he could give me a logical explanation, I would accept it. We had, after all, met the company in Barcelona after a holiday in Portugal. And in this instance, two other dancers were not traveling on the flight to Torino with the company, so it struck me as completely reasonable that I could make my own way there as well. And besides, it would save the company money on two plane tickets, and we would have the convenience of a vehicle for several months.

"I don't have to give you a reason," Alfonso said, his irritation beginning to show.

"But I would like a reason," I replied, realizing as soon as I said this that I'd gone too far. Apparently, it wasn't quite far enough for yours truly, because then I said, "When we were in ABT, we often made our own travel arrangements, and it was never an issue. I don't understand why our mode of travel is any of Ballet du Nord's business."

"I don't care what *A... B... T* did. *You* will do what *I* say, and that's the end of it."

And then Willy chimed in. "Who do you think you are, young man? You have no right to speak to Alfonso this way."

"But—" I started to say.

"Don't say another word, Michael," Alfonso interjected. "This conversation is over. You will travel with the company to Torino, and that's the end of it."

A few days later, I received a letter in my mailbox at the theater. It was from the executive director of the company, Bernard Allombert. I was informed that if I were not on the bus to the airport for the trip to Torino, I would be fired. And, furthermore, that if I ever disobeyed Alfonso or had any disagreements with him in the future, I would be fired.

A weekend was upon us, and Julie and I decided to drive to Amsterdam to see her parents. As my fury over this episode with Alfonso began to subside, the whole thing struck me as silly. Even so, I knew my days in Ballet du Nord were numbered. I simply could not work for a man who wanted to control my life outside the ballet studio, and, rightly or wrongly, that's what this car issue represented for me.

Despite my newfound disdain for Alfonso and the fact that I hardly said two words to him over the next three months in Torino, he continued to act as if nothing had happened. Our performances were a big success. The experience of dancing *Rubies* on a stage as grand as the one in Torino was well worth whatever private humiliation I had to endure by kowtowing to Alfonso. Despite this success, not long after our return to Roubaix, Julie and I began auditioning for other European companies.

We went to Nancy, Antwerp, Madrid, Frankfurt, and Basel. In some cases, we were wanted, but wanted in ways I wasn't entirely happy with. I was a leading dancer, by gum! I wasn't going back down to the corps de ballet.

And then, during the summer of 1987, we went back to New York on holiday and spent a few days back in the very building we'd come to know so well, 890 Broadway. Only now we were taking the elevator past the third floor where ABT was located and up to the eighth-floor home of the Feld Ballet.

We took class for a few days and spent hours learning bits of Eliot Feld's choreography. Despite all the horror stories about what a complete ass he could be, we found Eliot utterly charming. He seemed to enjoy working with us, and at the end of those few days, he offered both of us contracts.

Julie, who couldn't wait to get away from Alfonso, wanted to start immediately, so as soon as we got back to France, she packed her bags and returned to New York. I, on the other hand, had a great deal more to consider.

Later that fall, Ballet du Nord was embarking on a tour of the U.S. that would include New York City. After that tour was over, there were performances scheduled in Belfast and other major European cities. And it would go on, far into the future, these career carrots.

When I approached Alfonso in his office to discuss my future at Ballet du Nord, he gave me what I realized in retrospect was some very sage advice. "What you have here won't be easy to duplicate anywhere else, Michael. Now, maybe that's not what you're interested in anymore, given the fact that Julie is in New York, but I would think long and hard if I were you about leaving here."

During the months that followed Julie's departure I became at once incredibly lonely and incredibly excited by my solitary life in France. After seven years with Julie, it was a difficult and unfamiliar transition for me to make, but I managed to cobble together an existence that surprised me.

I went to Paris regularly, and, because the friends I had there could not speak English, I finally became fluent in French, and that fluency has never left me. Furthermore, I had some of my most daring performances as a dancer during that time. I threw caution to the wind, so to speak, an approach I'd been gravitating towards for a long time but had never fully embraced. Prior to a performance at a TV studio in Lille one evening, a thought occurred to me. What are you saving yourself for? What's the worst that could happen? So you fall on your face. So what?

I knew I'd reached a milestone as a dancer that night, because after the show, Alfonso said to me, "Michael, that was remarkable."

A few months after Julie's departure, Ballet du Nord traveled to England to perform. I didn't think much about this prior to leaving, but as soon as we got there, I began to miss her so much I almost couldn't bear it. This was where she'd been born, after all. And in spite of the fact that she'd grown up with everything England lacked—glorious weather, good food, and an American accent, it was still very much a part of who she was. By the time our performances in Folkestone were over I realized it was time to go home. I didn't want to live without her any longer.

1987. Repatriation.

THE NEW YORK REVIEWS for Ballet du Nord were polite. Anna Kisselgoff, writing in *The New York Times*, had this to say about Jean-Pierre Bonnefoux's ballet *Concerto*: "Unfortunately Mr. Bonnefoux found himself battling a bombastic, jazzy symphonic score by Keith Emerson that made his plotless ballet for three soloists, three main couples and an ensemble seem comparatively academic. As usual, Mr. Bonnefoux has an exquisite sense of composition; his male choreography in the third movement (led by Mr. Langlois, who also partnered Miss Naranjo) suggested how the blander sections could be revitalized."

Clive Barnes, writing in the New York Post, said of my performance in Rubies: "Michael Langlois, in the old Edward Villella role, caught the jagged and jazzy neo-classicism of the work to perfection; yet, and this is important, gave it with a slightly less impersonal nuance than one expects from City Ballet."

My mother had come up from North Carolina to see my big New York debut, and she confessed she was in tears as she sat out in the audience watching me dance *Rubies* and "revitalize" the blander sections of Jean-Pierre Bonnefoux's ballet. All the difficulties she had endured carting me from ballet class to ballet class had finally come to some sort of fruition, and she was justifiably proud. My father had nothing to be proud of, however.

"Why didn't he come?" I asked my mom.

"He didn't come because, for the first time since you started dancing, I didn't insist. I told him if he wanted to come, come, and if not, I didn't care. I wasn't going to force him anymore. So I guess there's your answer. He just didn't want to."

Wow. Why don't you just drive a metal spike through my heart? It would feel about the same and probably linger a lot less.

It was inconceivable to me that my father didn't understand how important those shows in New York were for me and, in particular, my relationship with him. Was it that hard to figure out? Did he think that all the piddly-shit dancing I had done at ABT was very meaningful for me?

After all those years of being buried somewhere in the back or off to the side or in amongst the hand-clapping, happy-go-lucky, clueless peasants, my performances in New York with Ballet du Nord were my vindication. They were proof that I'd made it. Proof to my father and Misha and all my real and imaginary demons that I had amounted to something. I had become a leading dancer, even if it wasn't with American Ballet Theatre and the venue wasn't the Metropolitan Opera House.

My father's absence stung all the more because I had spent so much of my life and my dance career trying to get his attention. I also knew this would probably be the first and last time he would have a chance to see me dance the lead in a ballet like *Rubies*. Once the Ballet du Nord tour was over and I joined Feld Ballet, it was unlikely I would be dancing those kinds of roles ever again.

After what happened in New York, I harbored a great deal of resentment towards my father, a resentment made even worse by my mother's confession that throughout all the years I'd been dancing, he had never wanted to come. Five years would go by before I came to the realization that, although my father had missed the boat as a father in many respects, it wasn't up to him to validate who I was or give me a sense of self-worth or affirm the choice I'd made to dance. It was up to me.

My father wasn't that interested in ballet—that wasn't his fault. The mistake I made was in looking to him to provide what I should have been providing for myself: a sense of pride in what I had accomplished, instead of a constant feeling of failure for rarely living up to expectations that were, most of the time, quite unrealistic and doomed to fail. If your expectation is to be perfect or to be the greatest dancer in the world, then you've got a big window of disappointment to look through most of the time.

50¢   NEW YORK POST WEEKEND FRIDAY, OCTOBER 23, 1987

Classic dance — with a difference.

By CLIVE BARNES

DANCE review

WHAT is a ballet company? A collection of ballets, a group of dancers, an instrument for a choreographer? Or is it, more properly if perhaps more philosophically, simply a way of looking at dance through all three: dances, dancers and choreographers?

Over the years, ballet in New York has been enormously enriched by the dance program at Whitman Hall of the Brooklyn Center for the Performing Arts. Company after company, both native and foreign, have been brought here to make their New York debuts.

The best of them have always had one thing in common — a dance viewpoint. They share a sense of direction that is not merely the haphazard agglomeration of ballets or the hopeful recruitment of dancers. There is a particular style.

This is something that was evidenced last weekend by the program's latest visitor, Alfonso Cata's Ballet du Nord, which hails from Roubaix, France.

Founded by the French government four years ago and strongly influenced by George Balanchine, this is essentially a French classic company with a difference.

Cata's belief in Balanchine is demonstrated by Ballet du Nord's permanent repertory, unique among European companies for its inclusion of more than a dozen Balanchine works.

It was natural, therefore, that the company on its American debut should present a token sample of its Balanchine. The choice fell on "Capriccio for Piano and Orchestra," a Stravinsky-based work better known in this country as "Rubies" — for it is, in fact, the central section of Balanchine's full-evening plotless work "Jewels."

The cast that I saw, led by Ena Naranjo and a particularly bouncy Michel Langlois in the old Edward Villella role, caught the jagged and jazzy neo-classicism of the work to perfection;

yet, and this is important, gave it with a slightly different, a less impersonal nuance, than one expects from City Ballet.

Of course Cata has taken much more from Balanchine than a bunch of his ballets and a manner of dancing them. He has also absorbed the Balanchine esthetic of pure dance above everything, with emphasis upon the ballerina.

Clearly Cata is not particularly bent on promoting his own ballets: of the three new works

> Cata has absorbed the Balanchine esthetic of pure dance above everything.

in the Brooklyn program only one, "La Mer," was his.

Jean-Pierre Bonnefoux's "Concerto," danced by a smooth ensemble with Susan Rowe and

Yves de Bouteiller, suffered from its music, the emptily echoing First Piano Concerto by Keith Emerson, of Emerson, Lake and Palmer pop fame.

In "La Mer," Cata used Debussy music with more theatrical sensibility. Instead of using the tone-poem for a movement study of the sea — which a number of choreographers have attempted — Cata suggested three beach-side encounters between a woman, at different periods of her life, and three men.

The woman, eloquently danced from youth to maturity by Margaret Torrini, Mireille Favarel and Sylvie Mondoulet, is partnered in three neatly contrasted, yet romantically sensuous duets. The whole ballet had a pungency and definition the other two new works missed.

While needing more overall variety, this is a French provincial dance troupe obviously pursuing its own path of neo-classical dance in the Balanchine image but not the Balanchine mold. It will be fascinating to see what happens to it.

"CONCERTO": Susan Rowe, Yves de Bouteiller.

A review from Clive Barnes. 1987. Ballet du Nord in New York.

It's hard for many dancers—or any young person, really—to see their technical and artistic evolution as something inextricably linked to their maturation process as a human being. Most young dancers are hungry, and they want results. They are all young Apollos eager to explore what it is they're capable of doing. They don't often appreciate their own unique qualities, because they're still struggling to figure out who they are as people. They look to others for validation or try to emulate other dancers. They might look to other people in their lives for some indication that what they're doing is worthwhile and, by implication, that *they* are worthwhile. And by "they," I mean me.

I suppose one could argue, and I did for a long time, that my father should have come to New York because it was his son who was dancing, and that should have been enough. I understand that. It should have been enough, and parents are expected to do those types of things for their kids, but there came a moment when I realized I had a choice to make: I could go on hating my father, or I could accept him for who he was and move on, making the most of the relationship we did have.

———————

While I was dancing with Ballet du Nord, there had been a slow peeling away of my performing fears. There were moments when I was onstage dancing with a sense of confidence in myself that reminded me of the young boy I once was, a boy who was daring and self-assured and thought he should be the best at everything, an attitude that carried through quite often to actually being the best at many things. Unfortunately, as I grew older, that began to change.

By the time I was twelve or thirteen, I was no longer the fastest runner in my class. At fifteen, I couldn't get the better of my older brother in a fight the way I once had. And there were still miles to go before I could call myself the kind of ballet dancer I thought I should be. By the time I got to New York and looked around at all the talented dancers at the School of American Ballet and, later on, the dancers at American Ballet Theatre, my ego had taken quite a beating, and I was having serious doubts about just how special I was.

Standing near me at the barre almost every day for six years was the greatest dancer in the world by almost anyone's standard. How was I going to measure up to that? No matter how much of my own magic elixir I swallowed, I wasn't ever going to be in Misha's league, or even close to it. I had to find something in myself that was worthwhile in spite of Misha and my own unattainable standards, but I wasn't mature enough to figure out how to do that. I was young. And when you're young, things are very black and white. You're good or you're shit—there's very little in between.

Throughout my time at ABT, I always had the thought in the back of my mind when I was on stage that, more than anything in the world, I didn't want Misha or Charles France to see me screwing up or not dancing up to the ABT standard. I always suspected they were out there in the audience, not enjoying the show, but critiquing those who weren't measuring up. How, I often wondered, could Misha get any pleasure out of watching us do things that were so far beneath him? It never occurred to me that he would enjoy watching someone like Patrick Bissell dance, but, apparently, he did. I never knew he enjoyed watching any of us dance, because, as was his habit, he never ever told us.

When I finally got my golden opportunity in Ballet du Nord, I can't say I grabbed the spotlight with any great zeal. It was something I felt I *should* do. Something I *needed* to do to prove to myself that I could do it, and that's why after only fifteen months, I was happy to leave it behind. My ego had been sufficiently stroked. What I didn't realize before I had a prolonged taste of it was that, in many respects, it is quite lonely being on stage by yourself.

I had imagined beforehand that I would feel everyone's eyes and attention on me once I was a leading dancer and that this attention would be satisfying in ways unlike anything I ever experienced in the corps de ballet. More often than not, however, I found it to be an experience that was strangely cold and impersonal. It was just myself and the music and a vast, empty blackness lurking behind the lights that bore down on me. I used to laugh when I'd hear dancers talk about connecting with an audience. Hell, half the time I couldn't even see the audience, and if I could see them, I sure as hell didn't *want* to see them. How was I supposed to connect with them?

Strangely enough, ballet dancers aren't supposed to question whether or not they should like performing. It is assumed. And while being onstage was the final step in my evolution as a dancer, it was never necessarily my objective. My goal was to be the best dancer in the world, believe it or not. I never stopped to consider if that would translate into being the best performer in the world, because I was never taught *how* to perform. I was given a costume and some steps, and the rest was up to me.

The most important realization I came to after rising to the top of the food chain in Ballet du Nord was that I was actually more comfortable dancing in the ensemble. I understood my purpose in that role. There was a relationship there, a sense of feeding off someone else's energy that I enjoyed. I wasn't the center of attention. I didn't feel as if the entire performance was riding on my shoulders, or that if I made a mistake it was going to ruin the ballet.

After I'd been in Roubaix a while and had grown more accustomed to my new status, I realized something else about rising out of the corps de ballet: Happiness and contentment do not get stamped on your forehead the day you leave the corps de ballet behind. In many respects, of course, I was happier because I felt as if my talent and hard work weren't being wasted, and I wasn't continually frustrated by how little I was getting to do, but I had a director I was at odds with and no real coaching or mentoring that would help me evolve as a dancer. Whatever I was learning, I was learning on my own.

———————————

What is very disorienting about being a professional ballet dancer is that the image you grow accustomed to seeing every day in the mirror vanishes once you are onstage, and without that feedback, you have no idea what you look like or how you're being perceived. In my case, I would grope about in the ether looking for various clues. Is my arm in the right place? I wonder how high my leg is. It feels high, so I guess it probably is. Gee, it seems like I'm jumping ten feet off the ground. I bet my legs look long and lean and wonderful. And all the while that I'm thinking these things and wondering how I'm doing, I might not even be listening to the music, because if it's Stravinsky, I'm actually counting the music in my head and dancing to numbers.

It always seemed to me that much of what went on in the theater, both in front of and behind the proscenium arch, was incredibly disingenuous. Dancers were furrowing their brows in deference to some idea they had of projecting artistic intensity, and if they were not doing that, they were plastering on fake smiles so everyone knew that being a peasant just naturally made you happy!

In the meantime, most people in the audience were applauding because other people in the audience were applauding, even if they didn't particularly like what they saw or had no idea whether what they saw was any good. People applauded for all sorts of reasons. Sometimes they applauded the efforts of the dancers to overcome the lame chore-ography. Sometimes they applauded a new ballet because it was a new ballet, even if it was shit. Sometimes they applauded because the music and the dancing reached a predictable climax and the applause light went off in their collective minds. Sometimes they applauded because they honestly felt something, but not all of them feel something. It's a mixed bag. I never took it that seriously, and I certainly didn't trust it, because when you've danced a ballet from the perspective of the corps de ballet and have done what you perceive to be very little, those kinds of accolades almost make you angry.

This is what anorexia looks like on stage.

Eliot

M Y RETURN TO NEW YORK TO DANCE with Julie at Feld Ballet brought my life as a ballet dancer full circle. I was back to working at 890 Broadway (albeit on a different floor); back to studying with the man I considered the finest teacher in the world, David Howard; and back to living with the girl I'd fallen madly in love with seven years earlier.

It was at David Howard's studio, in mid-December, that I ran into Patrick Bissell, the bad boy of American Ballet Theatre. Patrick, who'd been Gelsey Kirkland's coke partner in crime for many years, looked healthier and happier than I'd seen him in a long, long time, and grounded in a way I rarely recall him being when he was in the company and running around like a mad man. He'd just gotten out of rehab and had moved over to Hoboken with Amy Rose, his girlfriend in Ballet Theatre. They were planning to get married. I was happy for him, but at the same time I was worried. Patrick was just that type of person: good or bad, you always wondered when the other shoe was going to drop. In this case, the shoe dropped on December 29th. Patrick was found dead in his Hoboken apartment, the result of a drug relapse. He was thirty years old.

As if Patrick's untimely death were not enough of a reminder of the life I left behind at American Ballet Theatre, every day that I went to work, I found myself going up and down in the same elevator with many of my old friends. We'd smile and laugh about "the same old, same old" as they got off on the third floor. Meanwhile, I would continue up to my new world with new dancers and a director who spent more time working with me in a day than Misha did in a year.

———————————

Eliot Feld may have had many more moments of genius than the average choreographer, but I soon realized that working for him and around him day after day was like being a rare tropical disease in a Petri dish at NIH. There was no escape. Eliot pretty much lived at 890 Broadway. Why he bothered wasting money on an apartment elsewhere, I never knew. He was in the studio every hour of the day and often well into the night. He began his day sweating buckets in his plastic pants during company class as if he were preparing for a full day of rehearsals and a show of his own. After that, he was in virtually every rehearsal because all the ballets were his and he wanted to be certain they were being done the way he wanted them done. And the way he wanted them done was with every fiber of your being.

Despite all the horror stories, I found Eliot to be quite human—likeable, even. He never yelled at me. I never saw him act like the insane, petulant child he had a reputation for being. Nevertheless, nearly everyone in the company assured me that underneath the charming fellow I saw most days lurked Mr. Hyde and it was only a matter of time before he made an appearance. Eliot was incredibly neurotic, certainly, but how could you not be when you lived your entire life indoors in a world of your own creation?

Feld Ballet was a close-knit group. There were only about twenty dancers in the company, and we generally worked together the entire day under Eliot's watchful eye. One of the first indications that my rose-colored glasses were developing a severe crack was Julie's confession that she couldn't stand Eliot and was going to leave the company when her contract expired in six months. She admitted this to me when I got back to New York and had just signed my contract.

Whatever Julie's issues with Eliot were, I knew they were probably justified. His reputation preceded him. In truth, he was much harder on the women than he was on the men, and for months prior to my arrival, he'd put Julie through his own unique hazing process. I could see that. I could see how hard she was working and how much he continually demanded of her. No matter what she gave, though, it was never enough.

In spite of Julie's announcement, I soldiered on, telling myself every day that it wasn't that bad, that I'd get used to taking class with Eliot, rehearsing every hour with Eliot, traveling with Eliot, listening to Eliot expound on what we weren't doing exactly the way he wanted it done, and, finally, performing for Eliot.

I learned two ballets immediately, *The Consort* and *Skara Brae,* and a few months after I joined the company, we were flying off to Anchorage, Alaska and Honolulu, Hawaii to perform.

This tour of Eliot's was a strange sort of initiation for me. Alaska was, obviously, a perfect setting for him. Perpetually dark. Perpetually cold. There wasn't a damn thing to do but stay inside and rehearse or perform. Eliot was in heaven.

When we got to Hawaii, I thought to myself, what the hell is Eliot going to do here? He was not a tropical kind of guy. Judging by how pale he was, you'd have to conclude he rarely saw sunlight, much less a beach. And I was right. Eliot was like a fish out of water in Hawaii. You could see how unsettling the environment was for him. He seemed disconcerted by the perpetual sunshine, warm weather, and stunning tropical vistas. True to form, he spent much of his time in the theater, always doing his barre in his plastic pants and creating a huge puddle of sweat we called Lake Eliot. For the few hours of the day when he wasn't in the theater, I suspected he was holed up in his hotel room with the drapes closed, fleshing out ideas for a new ballet—but I may have been wrong.

The unsettling thing for me about being in Hawaii with Eliot was that over the previous seven years, Julie and I had made many visits to Honolulu to see her parents, and those visits had always been blissfully happy holidays. Hawaii was a place that had seen us grow up, from young lovers to established dancers in ABT, to two people who were approaching the end of a chapter in their lives.

Julie was not only planning to leave Feld Ballet once we returned to New York, she was planning to stop dancing entirely. This did not surprise me. She had always been a girl of extremes. Once she decided to do something, it was full-steam ahead, no looking back. I assumed I would finish out my six-month contract and continue on into the next year with Eliot, but shortly after we returned to New York, I found a letter from Feld Ballet sitting in our mailbox.

Dear Michael, it read in part, *we will not be renewing your contract once your current contract expires. You will receive your full pay as per our agreement, but you needn't return to rehearsals in the coming weeks.*

Sincerely, Cora Cahan, Executive Director, Feld Ballet.

I sat down at our dining room table in utter shock. I had never been fired from a ballet company in my life. Was this really happening? Desperate for an explanation, I arranged a meeting with Eliot. When we finally sat down, he was calm and genial. He had nothing particularly earth-shattering to say. Things weren't working out with me the way he had hoped, and he thought it best that I move on. That was it.

The real "it," however, was that I'd never really been happy there. Watching Eliot's ballets was one thing; working for Eliot and dancing in Eliot's ballets was something else, and for me that something else was not all that much fun. I was humiliated about being fired, but that was just my ego talking. I knew Eliot was right. His company wasn't the place for me. I thought I wanted to work with someone as creative as he was. I just didn't realize how much effort that would entail.

For weeks after receiving Eliot's letter, I moped around our apartment, not knowing where to turn or what to do. Julie, as was her style, immediately went to work selling insurance, of all things, and never looked back. She seemed to enjoy working in an office. Who I was I to argue?

At that point, there really weren't any people left in the dance world I wanted to work with or thought I had a realistic chance of working with, and I was uninterested in dancing just for the sake of dancing. There had to be a larger purpose, a person whose work I respected who was still creating something of value, but the only person I could think of who fit that description for me was Jiří Kylián, the director of Nederlands Dans Theater, the man who'd offered me a contract with his second company years earlier. I was still so shocked by Eliot's dismissal, I thought, fuck ballet, I've had enough of this shit. I'm tired of these nutbags. I'm tired of being unhappy. I want to do something else.

Lost

I DIDN'T QUIT DANCING PER SE, but I didn't actively seek out a job in another ballet company. I started experimenting with things I thought I might enjoy doing once I "officially" retired. I took acting and voice lessons. I auditioned for some Broadway shows, but quickly realized I had no respect for those in charge of the dancing aspects of that genre. I continued to go to ballet class and perform occasionally, but I was more interested in speaking to people in different fields that were of interest to me.

In the midst of my many ruminations about the future, I realized I needed more help figuring out how to be happy than could be provided by Stanislavski or some book on what color my parachute might be, so I sought professional guidance from one of the thousands of psychotherapists who help Manhattanites survive "The Greatest City on Earth."

Unaware of the fact that most ballet dancers enter ballet companies while they're still teenagers, my therapist, Stanley, was appalled that my parents hadn't insisted I go to college, and, not wanting to disappoint him because he was the object of my psychoanalytic *transference*, I decided to win his approval by doing just that.

Stanley, it turned out, disapproved of a great many things, and my parent's negligence where college was concerned was just the beginning. After listening to me talk about my relationship for a while, it became obvious that he disapproved of Julie as well, despite never having met her.

It wasn't surprising, then, that after eight years together, it took Stanley about eight months to convince me I would be better off without Julie in my life (he was gay, after all). No doubt I presented this separation to her as something akin to an experiment, a temporary measure so we both could "find" ourselves. That was how Stanley couched it anyway, as a suggestion—not that he was trying to push me or anything, just something to think about, and so on and so forth. He made it all sound so benign, but Julie didn't see it that way. As far as she was concerned, once I left, there was no turning back.

A week later, in the midst of moving my things out of our apartment one afternoon, I sat alone at our dining room table, the one we'd bought at the flea market in France, and wept. Why am I doing this? Am I doing it to please Stanley or because I genuinely think it's the right thing to do? I have no idea. I only know that I feel powerless to alter the course I'm on.

When Julie came home that evening, I asked if she would help me with the last bit of my stuff, all of which I had crammed into one of the same trunks we used for our move to France. She took one end and I the other, then down three flights of stairs and out onto the street in front of our building we went. As we carried the trunk toward 8th Avenue, she said, "Why are you doing this, Michael?"

I didn't know what to say. I thought everything had been decided. When I didn't answer, she started crying, and between her tears and my silence, she became increasingly distraught.

"I don't know," I finally said. "Because I'm tired of taking all the blame. I'm tired of apologizing. Everything that's wrong in our relationship can't be my fault."

We kept hobbling down the sidewalk with the trunk between us, Julie sobbing on one end and me coming apart at the seams on the other. It was true that over the years I'd done a lot of apologizing to Julie. I took the blame for our dysfunction as a couple because it was always easy for me to find fault with myself. After all, I'd been doing that in front of a mirror in the ballet studio since I was ten years old. But as my therapy progressed and my desire for a happier existence took root, I became less willing to find fault with myself. Our problems were no longer my problems, they were Julie's problems.

When at last we reached the corner, we dropped the trunk near the curb. The lights from the Korean market on the corner spilled into my eyes. Julie stood there looking at me, tears running down her face. I was thinking of Stanley then, and all that we had discussed about the problems Julie and I had as a couple. It all seemed so dire as Stanley presented it to me in his perfectly comfortable Mr. Rodgers outfit in his perfectly tidy office. The one thing Stanley didn't give much credence to, however, was just how much I loved Julie.

What I felt about her from the very beginning couldn't be explained in any psychoanalytic textbook, or tallied up in some pro/con columns on a piece of paper, or truly understood by Stanley or Sigmund Freud no matter how many degrees they might've had. Julie's idiosyncrasies and her emotions were who she was. She could be difficult to deal with, certainly, but when I was with her, I felt as if I were home. I was where I belonged. For someone who'd lived such a rootless existence, that was a rare feeling indeed.

Having decided to go back to college, as I knew Stanley wanted me to, I began looking around for a job to pay my way through school. About the only thing I was qualified to do that would pay me more than minimum wage was teach ballet, and I had done very little of that at that point.

After a great deal of soul-searching and talking to various people, I realized that becoming a massage therapist would work quite nicely. It was a year of schooling, but it paid well and would allow me to tailor a work schedule around a school schedule. In addition, it was a skill I knew I could fall back on should my high-paying career as a writer fall through.

In the midst of these many changes, I stayed in contact with Julie. Much to my surprise, after less than a year apart, she told me she was planning to marry. When we were talking on the phone one day, she said, "You know, Michael, I feel as if I should thank you in some way."

"For what?"

"For not pressuring me."

"Not pressuring you about..."

"My bulimia."

And, finally, there it was, the truth. What I'd long suspected was now out in the open, and in some sanctimonious, Hollywood way, I suddenly felt as if our whole relationship had been a lie. Of course I was forgetting all about my own lies, my starvation, my bathroom scale, my portion control, my self-hatred, my secret life of punishment and reward. Who was I kidding?

My relationship with Julie was exactly the relationship we both needed at that time in our lives, and in many respects we were perfect for one another. We were handicapped in similar ways.

"The fact that you trusted me and left me alone helped me to work through it," she added. "I think if you'd pestered me about it all the time, it just would have made it worse. And now, I'm finally coming to grips with it."

I didn't know what to say. I felt like telling her to go to hell.

"Thank you," I said. "I appreciate that."

I didn't know it then, but by the time 1990 rolled around and I was making plans to leave New York to attend college in Boston, the ballet boom that began with the rise of George Balanchine and kicked into high gear in 1977 with the premiere of *The Turning Point* was coming to an end. Balanchine was dead. Misha's knees were shot. He was no longer capable of amazing audiences with the kind of dancing he once did, and he had no interest in trying. In 1989, he quit the directorship of American Ballet Theatre and went off to dance more modern works with Mark Morris and the White Oak Dance Project.

After moving to Boston, I went to see Misha perform with White Oak, and he was just as riveting a modern dancer as he'd been a classical one. I sat out in the audience thinking a lot about our time together at Ballet Theatre and how much he meant to me. Working in his shadow every day certainly hadn't been easy, but it made me feel as if I were respected and admired and working at the very highest levels of my profession. It made me feel as if I were involved in something important, something that mattered.

To go from the kind of adulation and pampering I received as a result of working with Misha and being a dancer in American Ballet Theatre to waiting tables in an Italian restaurant in Soho was not something I ever thought would happen to me, but while I was attending massage school, I ended up doing just that. When several of my friends from New York City Ballet happened to sit at my table one night, I put on a game face and acted as if this was the most natural thing in the world, but, really, I wanted to bury my head in a plate of linguini and cry. Those are the moments in an American Ballet Theatre dancer's life that no one sees, that no one really warns you about or can really help you through. And they are hard moments, some of the hardest I've ever had to face.

And Found

A MERICAN BALLET THEATRE'S FORTUNES after Misha's departure were bleak. The company nearly collapsed. Charles France was fired in 1989 by Executive Director Jane Herman for reasons that had more to do with a clash of strong personalities than anything else. This act was something Misha simply could not tolerate, and it became the catalyst for his early departure. Charles would never work in the ballet world again. He died penniless in 2005 at the age of fifty-nine.

In 1992, Kevin McKenzie, a former principal dancer with the company, was appointed artistic director. In 2004, Rachel Moore, a former corps de ballet dancer in ABT, was named executive director. Under their guidance, ABT became the ABT of old, a company filled with an international roster of superstars. In addition, the company's financial foundation grew stronger and stronger. In 2016, Kara Medoff Barnett became executive director of the company.

Over the past twenty years, touring in the United States has become prohibitively expensive for large ballet companies, and as a result, the American Ballet Theatre tour as I lived it no longer exists and probably never will again. Most of the cities the company once visited have developed their own ballet companies, and those companies have risen in quality and prominence in spite of the economic climate and the morbid prognostications of certain dance writers.

As for some of the other people I've written about here:

Susan Jones is still working as a ballet mistress at American Ballet Theatre.

Gelsey Kirkland left Ballet Theatre in 1984. She danced with London's Royal Ballet until 1986, then retired. In 2010, she opened the Gelsey Kirkland Academy of Classical Ballet in New York City.

David Howard died in August, 2013, in New York.

Julie has two children and lives in Florida. She is a speech pathologist and ballet teacher.

Mikhail Baryshnikov continues to dance and act the world over. In 2005, he opened the Baryshnikov Arts Center on West 37th Street in New York City, an organization devoted to fostering creativity in the arts.

As for yours truly, I stopped dancing professionally in 1994 and in 1996 graduated from Brown University. At a loss for what to do with my life, I traveled around the world for nearly a year. When I returned home, I began exploring my voice as a writer. For many years now I have been a regular contributor to Ballet Review, a quarterly dance journal published in New York. I currently live in Miami with my girlfriend, Rebecca, and our Miele S4210 Carina Canister Vacuum Cleaner in Melon Yellow.

American Repertory Theater, Boston. The Cherry Orchard. 1994.
One of my last performances on stage.

Valediction

I WAS AN UNREMARKABLE DANCER with remarkable ambition. The result of this conflict is that I look back at my life as a dancer with a mixture of nostalgia and regret. Try as I might, I cannot help but wish so many things had been different. If only I had worked with a different teacher, been given different advice, or seen more clearly the dancer I was and what was required for me to become the dancer I thought I wanted to be.

My occasional regret over what happened would be less troubling if I could convince myself I did the best I could with the hand I was dealt, but I know that wasn't the case. It was all an uphill slog, and there were many moments when I was only too happy not to put in the extra effort I knew was necessary because the effort that was necessary, in my case, was a great deal of effort indeed. I wanted to live and enjoy the life I was living, not chain myself to a barre in a ballet studio. I was a hard worker, harder than most, but as hard as I worked, it wasn't enough.

Given this, what I find surprising is how much I miss that life and how easily I can forget how unhappy I was. When people ask if I miss dancing, I quickly and invariably say, no. I don't miss going to class, although there were many aspects of class that I loved. I don't miss the ever-present feeling that there was something I should be doing to get better. And I certainly don't miss staring at myself in the mirror every day and hating myself because some part of me or my technique was not what I wanted it to be. That sort of constant negative reinforcement seeped into my pores, and I can still feel its residue today, no matter how many therapy sessions I endure or how many years pass me by.

What I genuinely miss about dancing, what truly makes my heart ache from its absence, is the feeling of belonging to a community of intensely talented and driven people, all of whom implicitly understand one another in ways no one who is not a dancer ever can or ever will. In my life beyond ballet, this is a feeling I have been searching for but cannot find. What this leaves me with, unfortunately, is the subtle but ever-present sense that I will never entirely belong to the pedestrian world that surrounds me.

In this book, I wanted to describe what being a ballet dancer is like, but I'm not sure I've succeeded in that effort. The life of a ballet dancer is something one simply has to live to understand. You have to be in those classrooms day after day, year after year. You have to feel the anxiety that simmers continually beneath the surface. We are all afraid—afraid of failure, afraid of success, afraid of being looked at, afraid of being invisible, afraid of what is going to become of us when we stop dancing. My relationship with ballet was, and is, one of contradictions. Loving it, hating it, wanting to do it, wanting not to do it.

It seemed at times, when I observed the atmosphere of apprehension that hung over the entire endeavor, that becoming a ballet dancer was a gigantic hurdle I placed in front of myself just to see if I could jump over it. My joy came partly in the jumping itself, certainly, but it seemed to come more fully in the memory of the jumping and the relief I felt at having put each hurdle behind me, as if those hurdles were symbols of my self-worth.

For all of its travails, I cannot deny there is great joy in ballet. After years of study and struggle, one arrives at a moment when one can actually "do" things, and in the doing, one realizes how far one has come. There is satisfaction in that, deep satisfaction, but more than that, there is the thrill that comes with knowing your body is capable of hurling itself into the air and doing all of these remarkable things that finally, at long last, look as deceptively easy as they are meant to look.

There were moments on stage or in the ballet studio when I was as happy as I have ever been in my life. My body was capable of feats rare for any human being, and that knowledge, that sensation, gave me a sense of euphoria. I was momentarily a god, and my body was my domain.

In the final analysis, what makes ballet so intensely satisfying and beautiful to me is that it is so spare. There are no props. There are no instruments that have to be manipulated. It is just the dancer at that moment, and whoever they are and whatever they are capable of doing exists then and only then. The fact that ballet dancers have to climb a veritable Everest of difficulty and suffering in order to arrive at something so fundamentally revealing is, I believe, what gives ballet integrity and makes it the remarkable art form it is.

Misha and I after his show at the Gusman Theater in Miami, 2004

Acknowledgments

I would like to thank the following people in no particular order of importance:

1. To my mother, Mandy, for her audacity.
2. To my father, Howard, for having the good sense to stay out of her way.
3. To Mikhail Baryshnikov, for inviting me to join American Ballet Theatre and for showing me what it means to be a dancer.
4. To everyone at American Ballet Theatre, for sharing their talent, their passion, and their lives with me.
5. To Rebecca, a woman who had no idea what she was getting into when she decided to get involved with a ballet dancer and is probably still wondering if that was a wise decision.
6. To David Howard, for teaching me what ballet is, and what it is not.
7. To my editors, Rebecca Heyman and Stephanie Fouts. Your faith in this book and your inexplicable passion for grammar and punctuation is both bizarre and touching.
8. To my agents, Jennifer Lyons and Sam Fleishman. Amidst myriad rejections you said, yes.
9. To Francis Mason and Marvin Hoshino at Ballet Review, for giving me the opportunity to write about this art form that I love. It means more to me than you know.

10. To Bob Gottlieb, for taking the time to read this book and for offering his words of praise.

11. To Clement Crisp, Joan Acocella, and Arlene Croce, for showing me what dance criticism could be.

12. To Toby, my grandfather, for introducing me to the beauty of the English language and for showing me what the body could do.

About the Author

Like most dancers in America, I started my ballet training in a small local studio run by a tireless soul who worked long hours and made little to no money. That soul was Paul Wallace and without people like him there would be no Baryshnikov's or Kirkland's or dancers in the corps de ballet at American Ballet Theatre. And again, like many ballet dancers, before finishing high school I was leaving home and moving to New York City to train at The School of American Ballet. My professional career began a couple of years later. When I was eighteen I was offered the role of Tadzio in San Francisco Opera's production of *Death in Venice*. Subsequently, I joined ATER Balleto, in Reggio Emila, Italy, and in 1980 was offered a job at American Ballet Theatre by Mikhail Baryshnikov, the company's new director. After six years in the corps de ballet at ABT I left to dance more important roles with Ballet du Nord in France. Once those satisfactions were behind me, I returned to New York to dance with Feld Ballet then worked at a succession of dance jobs in New York, Boston, and abroad. At age thirty-four, after sixteen years as a professional, I said goodbye to the performing life to devote attention to my studies at Brown University. Since 2004 I have been a regular contributor to Ballet Review, a quarterly dance publication in New York. I currently live in Miami where I make my living as a massage therapist.

CPSIA information can be obtained
at www.ICGtesting.com
Printed in the USA
LVHW111541130219
607425LV00003B/676/P